Corporate Decision-Making
in the Church of
the New Testament

Corporate Decision-Making in the Church of the New Testament

JEFF BROWN

PICKWICK *Publications* · Eugene, Oregon

CORPORATE DECISION-MAKING IN THE CHURCH
OF THE NEW TESTAMENT

Pickwick Publications
An Imprint of Wipf and Stock Publishers
199 W. 8th Ave., Suite 3
Eugene, OR 97401

www.wipfandstock.com

ISBN 13: 978-1-4982-6351-1

Cataloging-in-Publication data:

Brown, Jeff.

Corporate decision-making in the church of the New Testament / Jeff Brown.

xviii + 222 pp. ; 23 cm—Includes bibliographical references and index.

ISBN 13: 978-1-4982-6351-1

1. Group decision making in the Bible. 2. Group decision making—Religious aspects—Christianity. I. Title.

BV652.2 B67 2013

Manufactured in the USA

PERMISSIONS

To Joyce Brown, who introduced me to Jesus Christ
and to the spreading of His Gospel,

and to Linda Brown, whose desire to serve Christ in His Church,
since her youth, has been unquenchable and contagious.

"One can only know what the church should be now if one also knows what the church was originally."

—Hans Küng

Contents

Foreword

CHURCHES MUST BE ORGANIZED in order to exist as churches. They are not simply random aggregations of people. One does not form a church whenever one selects ten names promiscuously from the phone book. For a church to exist, it must have some boundary that distinguishes those who are in the church from those who are not. It must also have some way of designating who is in charge and who is accountable to whom. However rudimentary its form, without organization no church exists.

While all churches recognize the need for organization, they are far from agreed about the form that the organization should take. More fundamentally, they do not even agree about the way of deciding. Some believe that a church is free to adopt whatever order seems most useful, while others believe that a particular form of order is divinely ordained. Those who believe that church order is a matter of revelation disagree further about the locus of that revelation. Among those who restrict revelation to the written Scriptures, further disagreements occur over the actual form of order that is revealed.

Debates over church organization involve a complex of questions. What role do members play in the government of the church? What are the offices of the church, and what authority do they exercise? What does leadership look like? How are decisions made and enforced?

The last question is sure to provoke disagreement among Christians. For example, some American evangelical leaders have publicly stated that group decision-making on the part of the whole church is unbiblical. The pastor of one evangelical megachurch even blogged that congregational decision-making is "from Satan," charging that it neither honors Scripture nor advances the gospel.

Jeff Brown has written this book in order to move beyond opinion and to discover what the New Testament actually depicts in terms of congregational decision-making. He examines in detail the personal and organizational processes that the apostolic churches employed in reaching corporate decisions. He is interested to identify the agents in decision making, the parameters under which decisions were made, the sorts of circumstances that led to these decisions, and the resulting outcomes. Furthermore, he sets these processes against the backdrop of the social world of the New Testament, looking for both similarities and differences that will shed light on corporate decision-making in first-century churches.

This volume is not the final word on all questions of church order and polity. Rather, it focuses upon only one, rather narrow issue. It is an issue that affects several other questions, however, and needs to be taken into account in many debates about church organization.

The book that you hold in your hand is a patient, careful examination of the evidence concerning corporate decision-making in the New Testament. It is charitable in tone, but definite in its conclusions. I know of no other work that treats this topic in such detail, and I believe that Jeff Brown's book will be of significant help to any church leader or anyone who wants to be a church leader.

Kevin Bauder, Plymouth, Minnesota

Acknowledgments

BOOKS LIKE THIS ARE never the product of one person's effort. I would therefore like to say thanks to those who gave significant help to the completion of this one. First, I want to express appreciation to Kathy Todd, the original editor of the manuscript. She spent many hours reading, correcting, instructing, explaining word processing, and in numerous other ways helping me finish the project correctly for my doctoral committee. All the while she was also busy rearing three small children and launching into her own doctoral program. Next, I would like to thank Dr. Kevin Bauder, Dr. Jeff Straub, and Dr. Jon Pratt, who not only recommended changes in the text, but also directed me to interact with several other theologians, whose works significantly increased my breadth of understanding about church order and New Testament themes.

I would also like to say thanks to the library staffs at the University of Notre Dame, Central Baptist Theological Seminary, Dallas Theological Seminary, Southwestern Baptist Theological Seminary, the Bodleian Library at Oxford, and the theological and classical libraries at the Universities of Erlangen and Bamberg, Germany. I spent significant amounts of time researching in these libraries, and their people were always courteous and helpful.

Publishers always take on a certain amount of risk in producing works of authors new to them. I very much appreciate Pickwick's interest in working together with me to publish this book. I have enjoyed working with their editorial staff, because it is obvious that they take care to come up with a good product.

Dr. Lee Levine's seminal work, *The Ancient Synagogue*, has been a significant aid to many people (including myself) for studying and writing about that subject. I will always appreciate that, though he did not know me at all, he took time to correspond and answer questions, as I researched for my study.

Acknowledgments

This volume contains a chart, created by Phil Siefkes, after he read the manuscript. His purpose was to prepare something as a guideline for his own church leaders. He correctly added 1 Thessalonians 3:1–3, which the book does not discuss, but nevertheless belongs to one of the topics. I want to thanks Phil for letting me include his chart as an appendix.

Finally, I would like to say thanks to my brother, Tom. Few people have so encouraged me in my literary efforts as he. We all need encouragement for large tasks. And he has never failed to offer it when I have needed it.

Abbreviations

AB	*Anchor Bible*
ABRL	*Anchor Bible Reference Library*
ANF	*Ante Nicene Fathers*
ANRW	*Aufstieg und Niedergang der römischen Welt.* Edited by H. Temporini and W. Haase. Berlin, 1972.
AsTJ	*Asbury Theological Journal*
AThR	*Anglican Theological Review*
ATR	*Australasian Theological Review*
BBS	*Bulletin for Biblical Research*
BDAG	Bauer, W., F. W. Danker, W. F. Arndt, and F. W. Gingrich. *A Greek-English Lexicon of the New Testament and Other Early Christian Literature.* 3rd ed. 2000.
BDB	Brown, F., S. R. Driver, and C. A. Briggs. *A Hebrew and English Lexicon of the Old Testament.* Oxford, 1907.
BHS	*Biblia Hebraica Stuttgartensia.* Edited by K. Elliger and W. Rudolph. Stuttgart, 1983.
Bib	*Biblica*
BJRL	*Bulletin of the John Rylands University Library of Manchester*
BK	*Bibel und Kirche*
Bsac	*Bibliotheca sacra*
CAH	*Cambridge Ancient History*
CBQ	*Catholic Bible Quarterly*
CH	*Church History*
Chm	*Churchman*
CIG	*Corpus Inscriptionum graecarum.* Edited by A. Boeckh. 4 vols. Berlin, 1828–1877.
Comm	*Communio*
CTQ	*Concordia Theological Quarterly*

DJG	*Dictionary of Jesus and the Gospels.* Edited by J. B. Green and S. McKnight. Downers Grove,1992.
DLNT	*Dictionary of the Later New Testament and Its Developments.* Edited by R. P. Martin and P. H. Davids. Downers Grove, 1997.
DPL	*Dictionary of Paul and His Letters.* Edited by G. F. Hawthorne and R. P. Martin. Downers Grove, 1993.
EBC	*Expositors Bible Commentary*
EECh	*Encyclopedia of Early Christianity.* Edited by E. Ferguson, 2nd ed. New York, 1990.
EncJud	*Encyclopedia Judaica.* 16 vols. Jerusalem, 1972.
ESV	*English Standard Version*
ExpTim	*Expository Times*
HDR	*Harvard Dissertations in Religion*
HKNT	*Handkommentar zum Neuen Testament*
HTR	*Harvard Theological Review*
HTS	*Harvard Theological Studies*
ICC	*International Critical Commentary*
JBL	*Journal of Biblical Literature*
JECS	*Journal of Early Christian Studies*
JEH	*Journal of Ecclesiastical History*
JETS	*Journal of the Evangelical Theological Society*
JNES	*Journal of Near Eastern Studies*
JSNT	*Journal for the Study of the New Testament*
JSNTSup	*Journal for the Study of the New Testament: Supplement Series*
JTS	*Journal of Theological Studies*
JTSA	*Journal of Theology for Southern Africa*
KEK	*Kritisch-exegetischer Kommentar über das Neue Testament (Meyer-Kommentar)*
KJV	*King James Version*
LSJ	Liddell, H. G., R. Scott, H. S. Jones. *A Greek-English Lexicon.* 9th ed. With a supplement. Oxford, 1968.
LTK	*Lexikon für Theologie und Kirche*
Luth	*Luther translation of the Bible (rev. 1984)*
LXX	*The Septuagint. Alfred Rahlfs, ed.*
MM	Moulton, J. H., and G. Milligan. *The Vocabulary of the Greek Testament.* London, 1930. Reprint, Grand Rapids, 1976.

MS(S)	*Manuscript (s) (Greek)*
NBD	*New Bible Dictionary.* Edited by J. D. Douglas and N. Hillyer. 2nd ed. Downers Grove, 1982.
NAB	*New American Bible*
NAC	*New American Commentary*
NASB	*New American Standard Bible*
NCB	*New Century Bible*
NEB	*New English Bible*
NICNT	*New International Commentary on the New Testament*
NIDNTT	*New International Dictionary of New Testament Theology.* Edited by C. Brown. 4 vols. Grand Rapids, 1975–1985.
NIDOTTE	*New International Dictionary of Old Testament Theology and Exegesis.* Edited by W. A. VanGemeren. 5 vols. Grand Rapids, 1997.
NIGTC	*New International Greek Testament Commentary*
NIV	*New International Version*
NKJV	*New King James Version*
NovTSup	*Novum Testamentum Supplements*
NPNF1	*Nicene and Post-Nicene Fathers*, Series 1
NRSV	*New Revised Standard Version*
NTS	*New Testament Studies*
OCD	*Oxford Classical Dictionary.* Edited by S. Hornblower and A. Spawforth. Oxford, 1996.
ODCC	*Oxford Dictionary of the Christian Church.* Edited by F. L. Cross and E. A. Livingstone. 2nd ed. Oxford, 1983.
OGIS	*Orientis graeci inscriptions selectae.* Edited by W. Dittenberger. 2 vols. Leipzig. 1903–1905.
PGL	*Patristic Greek Lexicon.* Edited by G. W. H. Lampe. Oxford, 1968.
PW	*Pauly, A. F. Paulys Realencyclopädie der classischen Altertumswissenschaft.* W. Wissowa. 49 vols. Munich, 1980.
RAC	*Reallexikon für Antike und Christentum.* Edited by T. Kluser et al. Stuttgart, 1950-.
RE	*Realencyklopädie für protestantische Theologie und Kirche*
ResQ	*Restoration Quarterly*

RevExp	*Review and Expositor*
RGG	*Religion in Geschichte und Gegenwart.* Edited by K. Galling. 7 vols. 3rd ed. Tübingen, 1957–1965.
RNT	*Regensburger neues Testament*
SecCent	*Second Century*
SBLDS	*Society of Biblical Literature Dissertation Series*
SBLMS	*Society of Biblical Literature Monograph Series*
SBS	*Stuttgarter Bibelstudien*
SJT	*Scottish Journal of Theology*
SNT	*Studien zum Neuen Testament*
Str-B	Strack, H. L., and P. Billerbeck. *Kommentar zum Neuen Testament aus Talmud und Midrasch.* 6 vols. Munich, 1922–1961.
SUNT	*Studien zur Umwelt des Neuen Testaments*
TDNT	*Theological Dictionary of the New Testament.* Edited by G. Kittel and G. Friedrich. Translated by G. W. Bromiley. 10 vols. Grand Rapids, 1964–76.
THKNT	*Theologischer Handkommentar zum Neuen Testament*
ThTo	*Theology Today*
TJ	*Trinity Journal*
TRE	*Theologische Realenzyklopädie.* Edited by Gerhard Krause and Gerhard Müller. 34 vols. Berlin, 1980.
TRu	*Theologische Rundschau*
TynBul	*Tyndale Bulletin*
WUNT	*Wissenschaftliche Untersuchungen zum Neuen Testament*
ZTK	*Zeitschrift für Theologie und Kirche*

Introduction

FOR CENTURIES, CHURCH ORDER has been a recurrent topic of discussion and debate among Christian theologians. About the time of John the apostle's death, Clement of Rome wrote a letter to the church in Corinth, in which he devoted significant space to the subject of polity. A generation later, church government was a persistent topic in the letters of Ignatius of Antioch. Voicing differences about church order never really stopped throughout church history. At times, writing about and acting out one's views could be costly. Henry Barrow, a devout and orthodox Christian in the sixteenth century, ended his days in an English dungeon for this very reason. But the debate about church order has itself been a factor in the emergence of religious freedom, so widely enjoyed in many parts of the world.

Despite the increased activity and affirmation of ecumenical efforts, the church order debate shows no signs of diminishing. From the Protestant side, books such as C. K. Barrett's *Church, Ministry, and Sacraments in the New Testament*, Kevin Giles's *Patterns of Ministry among the First Christians*, Alastair Campbell's *The Elders: Seniority within Earliest Christianity*, and Andrew Clarke's *Serve the Community of the Church* are fresh approaches to an investigation of church order as it appears in the New Testament. From the Roman Catholic perspective, the subject of church order has been variously debated by Hans Küng in *Die Kirche* and Edward Schillebeeckx in *Church: The Human Story of God*, as well as by James Tunstead Burtchaell in *From Synagogue to Church*, Avery Dulles in *Models of the Church*, and Joseph Ratzinger and Hans Maier in *Demokratie in der Kirche*. Among Evangelicals, there is no lack of interest in the subject, evidenced by the publications of *Biblical Eldership* by Alexander Strauch, *Who Rules the Church?* by Gerald P. Cowen, *Elders and Leaders* by Gene Getz, *Perspectives on Church Government* by Chad Owen Brand and R. Stanton Norman, and *Who Runs the Church?* by Paul Engle and Steven Cowan. Most of these studies are not restatements of a particular theological position on church order; rather, they are investigations with the Bible in hand and can be read without the impression that one has heard it all before.[1]

Why then another book on church order? For this reason: recent discussions of the subject have dealt primarily with defining the role of church leaders. In addition to the works mentioned above, note the following dissertations: Leonard Hillstrom's "The New Testament Teaching on the Office, Qualifications, Appointment, and Work of the Elders," John Andrewartha's "The New Testament Teaching of Church Elders," Ronald Minton's "Biblical Perspectives on Elders," Alastair Campbell's *The Elders: Seniority within Earliest Christianity*, David A. Mappes' "Expositional Problems Related to the Eldership in 1 Timothy 5:17–25," and Benjamin L. Merkle's *The Elder and Overseer: One Office in the Early Church*.[2] An exploration of the American Theological Library Association's search engine yields at least two hundred journal or magazine articles or M.A. theses written on the subject of elders during the last half-century.[3] Although the topic of church order is a popular one, an investigation of the specific interaction between congregations and their leaders is rarely done. A new investigation of the New Testament passages that relate strictly to group decision-making is overdue.[4]

PURPOSE

This study will deal with one aspect of church order: namely, how the church of the New Testament practiced corporate decision-making. Many

---

1. Complete information about the books listed here, including dates, are found in the Bibliography. In each section of the text, they are listed in in their chronological order.

2. Complete information about these dissertations is found in the Bibliography.

3. One should not conclude that the subject has been over-researched. Journals which address church order represent various theological viewpoints and confessions, all of which have a stake in what the investigation of various Bible passages on the subject yields.

4. One dissertation deals extensively with passages portraying congregational decision-making: Vernon Doerksen's Th.D. dissertation, "An Inductive Study of the Development of Church Organization in the New Testament." The work, however, examines the entire concept of church order, and does not focus on the specific issue of group decision-making. Furthermore, it does not deal significantly with the social world of the New Testament, including concepts of the house church, voluntary associations in the Hellenistic world, the relation of the order of the synagogue to church order, or the understanding of group decision-making in the Jewish culture during the first century CE.

instances of group decisions in the New Testament exist, particularly in the book of Acts. The aim of the study will be to demonstrate the phenomenon of corporate decision-making exegetically, helped by the examination of common practices of decision-making in the culture of those times, commonly referred to as "the social world of the New Testament." The investigation will also attempt to understand how corporate decisions were made and the parameters they set, as well as the types of things church groups decided upon and those they did not. This study will also interact with the viewpoints of most major confessions of modern western Christianity on the subject of church order.

LIMITATIONS

As decision-making by church groups as found in the New Testament is examined, of necessity, the study will need to include the scriptural identity of apostles, elders, deacons and other church leaders, since the subject of group decision-making intersects with the activity and authority of church leaders. The work will, however, only give enough attention to these identifications so that analysis and discussion of the specific passages is understandable. In other words, although some discussion of authority of leaders is also necessary in order to understand how groups and leaders in the early church interacted, there will be no sections arguing for a particular view of what constitutes an apostle, an elder, or a deacon. In addition, confessional viewpoints about hierarchy, synodal structure, councils, and so forth will be brought into the discussion, since this is unavoidable in the historical argument; however, the book will not argue extensively about which of these confessional structures is biblical. Instead, it will seek to define from the New Testament itself the church's decision-making structures and discover how they functioned.

METHOD

After a survey of the history of the church order debate, the book will deal with the historical and cultural background for the writing of the New Testament passages that portray corporate decision-making. In particular, it will examine political, economic, and religious institutions that formed the background for the phenomenon of corporate decision-making. New

Testament churches used practices similar or identical to surrounding societies to arrive at their decisions. But their church order was also highly influenced by the statements of their Lord Jesus and the teachings of his apostles. The entire exercise of studying group decision-making in the early church is of necessity embedded in the theology of the New Testament. With this background, the book will examine the New Testament passages. Finally, the exegetical conclusions will be evaluated in light of how Christian writers in the first centuries after the apostles viewed church decision-making.

In the church order debate, many writers have called into question the historical accuracy of the book of Acts. Likewise the pastoral epistles have been ascribed to someone other than Paul, who supposedly wrote after the time of Paul's death. Furthermore, Christianity is portrayed by some writers as a conglomerate of multiple Christianities (for example, Matthean, Johannine, Pauline). The effect this has on the church order debate is to make many things indeterminate, since the New Testament statements bearing on them are taken to be inaccurate, non-historical, or non-authoritative. The weaknesses in these arguments are not hard to identify and will be mentioned in chapters 3 and 4. This study will take the approach of the composite picture of church order in the New Testament (that is, all that the New Testament has to say about the chosen portion of church order). This comprehensive approach will give the most accurate picture of what the New Testament has to say regarding corporate decision-making.

This book has been written as a theological work, not as a work of social history. Thus, theological terminology will appear frequently. The reader will notice that the longest chapter of this work is the exegetical examination of passages related to group decision-making. Any freshman theology student knows that good theology is based on good exegesis. That has been the aim of this treatise: theology based on serious examination of the relevant texts.

POSITIONS OF THE WRITER

The author does not aim to restate or to defend any particular theory of church order. Rather, the work will be limited to determining what the New Testament establishes about corporate decision-making.

Current views on church order can be narrowed down to three. The first view holds that there is no clear definition of church order in the New

Testament; it was developed at a later date and is subject to change. The second asserts that there is a basic and incomplete church order in the New Testament, resulting in the later development of the authoritative Christian church order. The third maintains that the full concept of church order from Christ and his apostles is contained in the New Testament. This view holds that, although other organization is allowed, it may never eliminate, restrict, or redefine the original New Testament church order. The final view is assumed throughout this study.

1

Historical Background

HISTORIANS HAVE DEBATED THE original order of the church for centuries, but none question that it developed significantly during its first six hundred years. By the time of the division of Christendom into East and West, church order was well established, including a separate class of clergy (priests), various orders of ministry, regional bishops, councils, and (at least in the West) a pope.[1] During the Middle Ages, church order became more complex and sophisticated.[2] The Pseudo-Dionysian writings exercised a profound influence upon the development of church hierarchy.[3] These writings claimed to be the ideas of Paul the apostle, given to Dionysius of Athens (Acts 17), who wrote them. Pseudo-Dionysius taught that all spiritual beings belong to an order of hierarchy. Earthly beings reflect the order of the heavenly (which includes nine orders). The heavenly order mediates from God to man. Thus various levels of ministry are delineated in the church on the basis of the

---

1. By 300 CE bishops had become regional, spiritual rulers whose authority was unquestioned. By 400 CE the clergy had become a separate, isolated class in society. Hatch, *Organization of Early Christian Churches*, 82–163.

2. "The early Middle Ages in the West produced novel shifts in the emphasis and practice, among which we may notice the development of diocesan episcopacy as we know it today, involving the separation from the sacrament of initiation of the rite of confirmation as the sole prerogative of the bishop; the extension of authority and importance to archpresbyters or deans, to presbyter-abbots, and not least to archdeacons." Shepherd, "The Development of Early Ministry," 136.

3. *ODCC*, s.v. "Dionysius, the Pseudo-Areopagite," 406–7. Historically, these writings were first cited by Severus, Patriarch of Antioch (513 CE). Some Roman Catholic scholars began to question their authenticity at the time of the Reformation. That they were actually written ca. 500 CE has been well established since 1900.

heavenly hierarchy. In fact, the word *hierarchy* entered the language of the West through Dionysius.[4]

CHALLENGES TO THE CATHOLIC POSITION ON CHURCH ORDER

During the late Middle Ages, men such as Arnaldo de Brescia, Jean de Paris, Marsiglio de Padua and John Wyclif raised their voices against the existing (Roman Catholic) church hierarchy.[5] Marsiglio de Padua argued that the authority to discipline heretics lies in the hands of the people and that bishops, in the New Testament sense, are local presbyters.[6] He likewise argued that the pope was neither the successor of Peter nor rightly had authority over any other bishop.[7] Independent of Marsiglio, Wyclif found only two offices for the church in the New Testament: presbyters and deacons.[8] He

---

4. *Hierarchy* is, in fact, "an authentically Dionisian term" (Luscombe, "Wyclif and Hierarchy," 234).

5. "What [Wyclif] set in motion was the abiding suspicion that the order of God's doings was not identical with the order of the church's doings." Burtchaell, *From Synagogue to Church*, 10.

6. Marsilius of Padua, *Defensor Pacis*, 140–51, 233–41. Marsiglio based his arguments about bishops and elders, in part, on the writings of Jerome on the same subject.

7. Ibid., 241–53. For a summary of his writings, see Schaff, *History of the Christian Church*, 6:72–77.

8. Since Marsiglio de Padua's *Defensor Pacis* appeared in 1326 and Wyclif's *De Officio Regis* in 1379. There has been much debate about whether Wyclif was indebted to de Padua. After extensive research, no connection can be established. Lahey, *Philosophy and Politics of Wyclif*, 66–67, says, "On the face of it, Marsilius and Wyclif appear remarkably similar. But these similarities are illusory. As has been mentioned, Marsilius advocated rule in accord with the will of the people, arguing that God used human wills as the medium through which He establishes government. The idea that God would make use of any sort of mediate cause to effect His will is foreign to Wyclif's philosophy. . . . Both hold that Scripture alone is the true authority in ecclesiastical disputes, and use this position to argue against the papal monarchy. But Marsilius believes that correct scriptural interpretation is only possible when made by priests and educated laity in council, contributing to a conciliarist theory that was to be influential in the coming centuries. Wyclif, on the other hand, was to argue that Grace alone is needed to ensure true interpretation of Scriptures; Wycliffite *Sola Scriptura* theology was the first ideology to be condemned when the conciliarists began their work at Constance."

concluded that the papacy and gradations of bishops were unscriptural.[9] Wyclif also asserted that the clergy should be elected by congregations.[10]

With the outbreak of the Reformation, the debate about polity became widespread and intense. The Reformers claimed that they were returning to the New Testament church order. Calvin, for instance, in his *Institutes,* draws conclusions about church order very similar to those of Wyclif.[11] However, as the Reformers were forced to make agreements with the local or regional governments to retain authority, Reformed church order took on a form which harmonized with the demands of local or regional government.[12] Burtchaell summarizes the development in this manner:

> The ideal scheme of congregational sovereignty and of a single, unranked ministry did not long endure. Supervisory needs prompted the creation of various hierarchies which, however differently from traditional episcopacy they were explained, in form and function resembled nothing so much as a reformed order of bishops. Congregational say-so often subsided to a perfunctory endorsement of the judgments of the clerical professionals. The aspiration to be free of prelates who acted like lay lords was not furthered when the new movement had recourse to the lay lords themselves as patrons, and when these patrons established themselves as dominant in the synods and consistories, and occasionally as the recognized authorities of last resort over the churches.[13]

The radical Reformers, principally the Anabaptists, rejected the union of church and state, and thus were an exception to this phenomenon of constriction as they developed their own views of church government.[14]

---

9. "If they had been necessary to the church, Christ and his apostles would not have held their peace about them." Vaughan, ed., *Tracts and Treatises,* 45.

10. Lechler, ed. *Johannes de Wiclif Tractatus de Officio Pastorali,* 39–40.

11. Calvin, *Institutes,* 4.3.4–12.

12. MacKinnon, *Calvin and the Reformation,* 81–82; Grimm, *The Reformation Era,* 183–84.

13. Burtchaell, *From Synagogue to Church,* 36.

14. See, for instance, Verduin, *The Reformers and their Stepchildren,* 23–62; Lumpkin, "The Schleitheim Confession," 22–30. See also Lumpkin, "The Waterland Confession," 41–65. Lumpkin does not denote the Schleitheim or Waterland confessions as Baptist confessions but as forerunners of Baptist confessions. Mennonites consider the Waterland Confession the earliest of Mennonite confessions; see the Global Anabaptist Mennonite Encyclopedia Online, s.v. "Confession of Faith." Some theological writers persist, wrongly, in identifying all Anabaptists as enthusiasts, like Thomas Müntzer. See, for instance, Küng, *The Church,* 194–95.

During the English Reformation, the Independents asserted a form of government which they claimed was based on the New Testament. They rejected the appointment of clergy, both by the state and by regional bishops; in fact, they defined bishops as local pastors, to be elected by the congregation. They further viewed themselves as small, local, democratically functioning bodies.[15] But the development of non-Catholic church government was not yet complete. In the nineteenth century, the Plymouth Brethren movement developed still another form of polity, represented by John Nelson Darby and George Mueller, which rejected the democratic concept.[16]

THE PROTESTANT CONSENSUS

In the middle of the nineteenth century, the church order debate was taken up as an academic one across denominational lines. Using historical research, theologians argued that the original church order of the New Testament was simpler and more democratic than its later developments; bishops and presbyters were the same and purely local officers.[17] All these writers, with varying views of how the later forms of church order developed, agree that the primitive church was a democracy which later degenerated into a monarchy.

An additional concept was added by theologians like Karl von Weizsäcker, Adolf von Harnack, and Rudolf Sohm, who saw a change of order within the New Testament church itself from charismatic leaders (e.g., the gifts mentioned in 1 Cor 12) to local, established leaders (bishops, presbyters, deacons).[18] Weizsäcker stated that the Pauline churches were clearly

---

15. See the 1596 statement, "A Brief Summe," in Carlson, ed., *Writings of Henry Barrow*, 3:118–50. Barrow believed that there was a specific kind of church government laid down by Christ and that it was to be distinguished from the civil government. Note also "The Savoy Declaration," a confession written in 1658, in Schaff, ed., *Creeds of Christendom*, 3:707–29.

16. Kelly, a prominent writer for the early Brethren movement, offers a good explanation of the Brethren position on church order and its differences from other views in his book, *The Church of God*.

17. Rothe, *Der Anfänge der Kirche*; Neander, *Geschichte der Pflanzung und Leitung*; Ritschl, *Die Entstehung der altkatholischen Kirche*; Lightfoot, *Epistle to the Philippians*, 181–269; Hatch, *Organization of the Early Christian Churches*; Hort, *The Christian Ecclesia*.

18. Weizsäcker, *Das apostolische Zeitalter*; Harnack, *Die Lehre der Zwölf Apostel*; Sohm, *Kirchenrecht*.

each ruled by their own self-governance and that all the churches (not just Pauline) elected their own officers and representatives. He was convinced that the first converts in the early churches became their first leaders; an office of bishop or deacon did not become fixed until after the death of the apostles.[19] Sohm, in particular, saw a conflict between the concepts of charismatic leaders and established, designated leaders in the New Testament; the organization of churches with established leaders was a result of man's sinfulness and a return to the Law.[20] Harnack denoted the government of the churches outside of Judea as "pneumatic democracies"; the Judean churches, by contrast, were dominated by the leadership of James and thus had the beginnings of an episcopal system.[21] By the end of the nineteenth century, the academic debate had developed into a consensus that the original church order had been simple, democratic, and local (with a majority of scholars seeing leadership as charismatic rather than fixed).

CHALLENGES TO THE PROTESTANT CONSENSUS

This consensus was challenged by Heinrich Holtzmann, Henry B. Swete's symposium in 1918, Karl Götz, B. H. Streeter, and Olaf Linton.[22] They saw church order developments as arising from varying types of order already present, from deliberative councils already present, or from prophecy in the church of the New Testament. J. Scott Horrell is a recent theologian who follows the view of B. H. Streeter.[23]

Other challenges to the Protestant Consensus came from Anglican theologians, such as Charles Gore and the Kenneth Kirk symposium.[24] These asserted the Anglican model as the true biblical concept. More recently, another Anglican, Roger Beckwith, has also presented Anglican order as biblical. He bases his assertions on the idea that early church elders

---

19. Weizsäcker, *Das apostolische Zeitalter*, 622–23, 630–41.

20. Sohm, *Kirchenrecht*, 28.

21. Harnack, *Kirchenverfassung und Kirchenrecht*, 34–40.

22. Holtzmann, *Lehrbuch der neutestamentlichen Theologie*; Swete, ed., *Essays*; Goetz, *Petrus als Grunder und Oberhaupt*; Streeter, *The Primitive Church*; Linton, *Das Problem der Urkirche*.

23. Horrell, *From the Ground Up*, 54–55. Horrell gives scant historic evidence for his view, but uses it in presenting what he feels is the right way to approach church order.

24. Gore, *The Church and the Ministry*, which was originally written in 1886 but caught the attention of theologians in its 1936 edition; Kirk, ed., *The Apostolic Ministry*.

were a continuation of the Jewish teaching elder, who appointed his own disciples; later, at the end of the first century CE, elders agreed on elevating one elder to the single bishop position.[25] Peter Toon is another theologian who presents the Anglican order as the right Christian order, but does not base his arguments on the New Testament.[26]

The Protestant Consensus Reasserted

Beginning in the middle of the twentieth century, the "Protestant Consensus" was reasserted by Edward Schweizer, Rudolf Bultmann, and Hans von Campenhausen.[27] Schweizer regarded the pastoral epistles as non-Pauline and undoing what Paul had achieved. He saw no structures in the Pauline churches. Bultmann argued that Sohm was incorrect to describe organization and charisma in the early church as being at odds with each other. He said that Paul organized each church as something of a "congregational democracy" ("Gemeinde-Demokratie").

Campenhausen challenged the idea that the settled officers and charismatics were two competing groups. At the same time, he recognized the three major modern church polities as beginning their development in the New Testament. Schweizer and Campenhausen, according to Burtchaell, have become established as the last best statements of Protestant theology's consensus.[28]

Modern Roman Catholic Debate

Roman Catholic theologians Hans Küng and Edward Schillebeeckx argue that the hierarchical form of church leadership, as presently found in the

25. Beckwith, *Elders in Every City*. Beckwith cogently argues, "It is therefore reasonable to ask whether the basic assumption underlying the liberal reconstruction of primitive Christianity, namely, that the free exercise of spiritual gifts and formal structures cannot co-exist but are mutually exclusive, is not a simplistic mistake? May it not rather be the case that the exercise of varieties of gifts by Christians in general, what is often called 'every-member ministry,' *demands* formal structures to be fruitful?" 17.

26. Toon, "Episcopalianism," 19–48.

27. Schweizer, *Gemeinde und Gemeindeordnung*; Bultmann, *Theologie des Neuen Testaments*; Campenhausen, *Kirchliches Amt*.

28. Burtchaell, *From Synagogue to Church*, 137.

Catholic Church, does not square with the New Testament where there is no division between clergy and laity.[29] Küng notes,

> The word λαός in the New Testament, as also in the Old Testament, indicates no distinction *within* the community as between priests ("clerics") and people ("laity"). It indicates rather the fellowship of all in a single community. The distinction it implies is one *outside* the community, between the whole people of God and the "non-people," the world, "the heathens." Not until the third century do we find any distinction between "clerics" and "laymen."[30]

Küng also feels that the Catholic Church has set too much weight on the pastoral epistles for its view of church order.[31] Schillebeeckx argues that the assertion of a divinely-willed hierarchical structure in the Catholic Church is an historical misunderstanding and "one of the most painful points of dispute between Catholic faithful and their leaders in our democratic age."[32] Schillebeeckx states that the Church's hierarchical structure was inspired by Neoplatonism and "no longer has anything to do with the nature of the church."[33] As a Feminist scholar within the Catholic Church, Elisabeth Schüssler Fiorenza asserts that the one ideal model for the Church is Jesus and his egalitarian community.[34]

Joseph Ratzinger (Pope Benedict XVI) argues for the opposing position. While allowing for democratic activity on a local level, he states that democracy has no place in the higher leadership of the church. He bases his assertion on the following concepts: the ordination of priests (completely exempt from democratic decisions); the separation of charisma from

29. Küng, *Die Kirche*; Schillebeeckx, *Church*.

30. Küng, *The Church*, 125–26. In this second aspect, he follows the ideas of the Protestant Consensus. One must be careful not to conclude that Küng believes that the writings of the NT establish the final model for the organization of the church. He states, "The New Testament Church is not a model which we can follow slavishly without any regard to the lapse of time and our constantly changing situation. . . . If the Church wants to remain true to its nature, it cannot simply preserve its past. As an historical Church it must be prepared to change in order to fulfill its essential mission in a world which is constantly changing, which always lives in the present, not in the past," ibid., 24.

31. Ibid., 179–81.

32. Schillebeeckx, *Church*, 188.

33. Ibid., 217.

34. Fiorenza, *In Memory of Her*.

democracy; and the historical precedent of decision-making by apostolic councils (rather than the people).[35]

Social Analysis

Social analysis has been added to the church order discussion through the works of Gerd Theissen, Bengt Holmberg, Wayne Meeks, Andrew Clarke, and others.[36] They assert that Paul's statements do not prescribe a church order but rather advise how to correct errors in church order. In addition, Max Weber's *Wirtschaft und Gesellschaft* has significantly influenced the social analysis of the early church.[37]

Other Recent Developments

More recent developments in the church order debate have, to some extent, reasserted old themes. James Tunstead Burtchaell asserts that the Church took its order directly from the synagogue.[38] Alexander Strauch and Gene Getz—whose books, while not written for an academic audience, are nevertheless exegetical—have emphasized the New Testament pattern of local church elders (essentially the brethren concept).[39] R. Alastair Campbell sees bishops as leaders chosen from the ranks of natural leaders (in his view, elders are not an office) within the setting of the house church. As house churches multiplied in cities, the bishop became the main leader over all the house churches in a city.[40] Benjamin Merkle, while paying careful attention to the context of the social world of the New Testament, concludes that elders and bishops are the same and normally function in plurality in a local church.[41]

From the works of the pre-Reformation voices, like Marsiglio de Padua and Wyclif to this latest treatise by Merkle, the circle of research on

35. Ratzinger and Maier, *Demokratie in der Kirche*, 23–34.

36. Theissen, *Soziologie des Urchristentums*; Holmberg, *Paul and Power*; Meeks, *The First Urban Christians*; Clarke, *Serve the Community.*

37. Weber, *Wirtschaft und Gesellschaft*; see esp. 379–490.

38. Burtchaell, *From Synagogue to Church.*

39. Strauch, *Biblical Eldership*; Getz, *Elders and Leaders.*

40. Campbell, *The Elders.*

41. Merkle, *Elder and Overseer.*

church order is nearly complete. The arguments throughout the centuries point towards a self-governing church order on the local level, limited to only two officers (with a variety of scenarios and interpretations offered in the process). What is lacking in the scholarly discussion is a renewed look at corporate decision-making in the church of the New Testament, a gap this study intends to fill.

2

The First-Century CE Cultural Background for the Concept of Corporate Decision-Making

As in other aspects of the life of the early church, the socio-political environment of the Roman Empire played a role in church decision-making. Despite an enormous amount of historical and archaeological information that has accumulated during the past 150 years, most details from the life of each church in the first century CE remain obscure. Therefore, a reconstruction of how church life functioned remains somewhat speculative. Nevertheless, if an overall pattern of one part of this socio-political life can be demonstrated, it will clearly influence the conclusions one would draw about scriptural passages; such is the aim of this chapter.

The Polis Concept in Ancient Greece

During the writing of the New Testament, one of the most widespread political concepts in the Roman Empire was the *polis* of ancient Greece, in which the decision-making body of a political state was the entirety of the citizenry (at least in theory). Citizens governed themselves—setting laws, electing leaders, and passing judgments. The *polis* began as a political unit in the Mycenaean age, and through the centuries developed into a city government.[1] Ian Morris states that from the eighth to the sixth centuries BCE society and government in Greece underwent significant changes. What

1. Drews, *Basileus*, 111.

resulted he terms, "The Strong Principle of Equality" (as opposed to the rule of elite persons or families).[2]

It is this principle of equality that developed into democracy.[3] The primary example of a city applying the *polis* concept is Athens.[4] Both Solon (594 BCE) and, following him, Cleisthenes (508 BCE) have been credited with defining the truly democratic Athens, although scholars continue to debate which of the two was responsible for making Athens democratic.[5] Many ancient writers discussed the *polis*, most notably Aristotle in his *Politics*. He states that democracy developed naturally from the household to the village to the state, the last of which was originally ruled by monarchs (Aristotle, *Politics* 1252a24–1252b37). However, centuries before Athens, other nations also held deliberative assemblies; this phenomenon has been well-documented and will be taken up later in the chapter.

In Athenian democracy there were no political parties or judges. There was no bureaucracy. Government was direct from the people.[6] Hanson says, "The fundamental democratic ideal was liberty (*eleutheria*), which had two aspects: political liberty to participate in the democratic institutions, and private liberty to live as one pleased (*zen hos bouletai tis*)."[7]

Oswyn Murray analyzes Athens as a conservative democracy. This phenomenon led to "ever innovative action in a rich flowering of new associations."[8] Still, the individual was very much subjected to the will of the community. As Murray points out, "The modern concept of individual freedom was completely unknown to the ancient world."[9] The *polis* govern-

2. Morris, "The Strong Principle of Equality," 10–20. Ibid., 20: "The Strong Principle of Equality is not synonymous with democracy as an institutional order. But when enough people hold views of this kind, it becomes possible—and perhaps logical—to respond to the collapse of an oligarchy . . . by developing new conceptions of majority rule, instead of simply finding a different group of guardians."

3. Ibid.

4. "The sovereign body of the Athenian democracy was the popular Assembly or *ekklesia*. This was open to all males who had reached the age of eighteen and who, at least after Pericles' citizenship law of 451, could claim to have both an Athenian father and an Athenian mother" (Staveley, *Greek and Roman Voting*, 78).

5. Cornell and Rhodes, "Cleisthenes," *OCD*, 344; "Solon," *OCD*, 1421–22. Aristotle credits Solon with establishing democracy in Athens, *Politics* 1273b35–45.

6. Murray, "Liberty and the Ancient Greeks," 35.

7. Hanson, "Democracy, Athenian," *OCD*, 451–53. Hanson cites Aristotle's *Politics* 1317a40–b17 and Thucydides' *The Peloponnesian War* 7.69.2.

8. Osborne, "The Demos and its Divisions in Classical Athens," 285–86.

9. Murray, "Liberty," 40. The Apostle Paul's concept of liberty would be an exception to Murray's statement, and will be taken up in chapter 3.

ment was not universally accepted in Greece, in the days before Alexander the Great but was instead a hotly-contested idea.[10] Nevertheless, it was a success, and was sure to be imitated. It possessed spontaneity, and its influence spread throughout the Greek-speaking peoples and beyond.[11]

> For a thousand years educated men persisted in thinking of the republic as the standard form of political organization. In meaning the term inevitably adapted itself to the changing ideas of new generations, and even new peoples, such as the Romans; but the classical notion was sufficiently tenacious for the process of definition to lag far behind the changing methods of government itself.[12]

The Spread of the Polis through Alexander the Great

Alexander the Great, undoubtedly influenced by his tutor Aristotle, adopted the idea of the *polis* as the best method for city government. He spread its influence throughout the Near East, including those areas traditionally Jewish, by establishing Greek cities that functioned on the basis of Greek democracy. Hayes and Mandell explain, "Hellenization was widely pervasive. It was resisted or possibly simply ignored only by certain classes or groups of people, particularly the urban masses along with the serfs or peasants in various outlying areas and backwater regions."[13] The Jewish nation essentially became Hellenized. The city was, in fact, Alexander's main tool for spreading Hellenistic ideas throughout the world.

> When Alexander freed the Greek cities of Asia he everywhere deposed the tyrants and oligarchies which had been ruling them in the Persian interest and established democracies. From this time on democracy and freedom became closely allied concepts. The old ideal of autonomy, that every city should keep its own or its ancestral constitution, was not formally abandoned, it is true; but it was tacitly assumed, often without much historical justification,

---

10. Hanson, "Democracy," 451. Plato regarded democratic *eleutheria* as a mistaken idea that led to a deplorable pluralism (*Republic* 565a); Alcibiades called it "absolute insanity" (Thucydides, *The Peloponnesian War* 6.89.6).

11. Judge, "The Social Pattern of Christian Groups," 12

12. Ibid.

13. Hayes and Mandell, *The Jewish People*, 13.

that democracy was the normal constitution of every city. . . . Democracy was then in the Hellenistic age universally recognized as the proper constitution of a Greek city, and as the institutions of the Greek city spread over barbarian lands it was the democratic type of constitution which was accepted as the norm.[14]

After the death of Alexander, the spread of Greek culture and democratic ideas continued apace through the founding of *polis* cities. Alexander's successors established 350 Greek cities in all.[15] Some cities, such as Tyre, Sidon, Arados, and Byblos, were completely converted into Greek *poleis*.[16] The cities of Lycia became thoroughly Hellenized under the Ptolemies. Even the remote parts of Phrygia adopted Greek constitutions.[17] Although the Greek world after Alexander was dominated by powerful kings, Greek cities were viewed as free institutions.

Theoretically the Greek cities were regarded as "allies" of the king; their relation to them was not that of subjects to their lord, but that of one of two political powers possessing equal rights. The defense of city rights, of their "freedom" and "autonomy," was a matter of honor in the eyes of the kings and an attribute of civilized political behavior. Hence the kings accorded license to the ancient cities (such as those of Asia Minor or the Aegean Islands) "to live according to their ancestral laws," that is, they confirmed the traditional constitutions of the cities; but they also permitted new ones to conduct their internal affairs freely, to elect a council and officials, to strike coins, to hold athletic contests, and so on. Each city possessed laws of its own, according to which its officials conducted its public life. . . . Even the cities most completely subject to the kings remained nominally free and did not miss any opportunity to convert theory into fact.[18]

Alexander's successors had to negotiate power with the Greek autonomous cities throughout the empire. This coexistence of competing powers required that the cities not provoke the kings' hostility; likewise, the kings disdained the freedom of the autonomous cities at their own peril.[19]

---

14. Jones, *The Greek City*, 157. Alexander wanted to eliminate the distinction between Greek and barbarian, and did so through Hellenization, 4.

15. Tcherikover, *Hellenistic Civilization and the Jews*, 22.

16. Ibid., 32. The cities of Lycia became democratic under the Ptolemies, 45.

17. Jones, *The Greek City*, 45.

18. Ibid., 24. This is not to say that all Greek cities were uniformly democratic.

19. Shipley, *The Greek World after Alexander*, 59.

In time, throughout the Greek world the *polis* ideal came to include equal political rights for all citizens.[20]

While it is true that eighty to ninety percent of the population of the Roman Empire lived in rural areas and villages,[21] it is also true that the cities dominated the areas surrounding them. The villages of Asia Minor largely adopted the political ideas of Hellenism as Hellenistic cities were established nearby.[22] Likewise, the villages in the mountain-belt of Syria were occupied by tribal communities, which "mostly possessed rudimentary forms of government in councils of elders and mass assemblies."[23] The magistrates of the villages of Batranaea, Trachonitis, and Auranitis (the area of Philip the Tetrarch's rule) were all chosen by popular election.[24] Perhaps this demonstrates the standard pattern of political development in the Graeco-Roman world. Certainly, the *polis* concept was widespread, well established, and well protected by the time the Roman Empire included the areas of Asia Minor, Egypt, Syria, Galilee, Samaria, and Judea. Thus, the church was born into a region where the idea of equal group participation in important decisions was well understood.

City Government under Augustus and His Successors

Discussions of the government of the Roman Empire tend to focus on its emperors, the Roman Senate, and regional governing structures. But the government of the Roman Empire was largely a collection of cities: "The city was where things happened, where the opportunities were. The civilization of the Roman Empire was an urban civilization to a greater extent than any time in the west up to the modern age."[25] The government of the Roman Republic included voting of all its citizens for public offices, making of laws, declarations of war, and (until the institution of courts) the trials

20. Jones, *The Greek City*, 159.

21. Schnabel, *Early Christian Mission*, 1:559.

22. Schuler, *Ländliche Siedlungen und Gemeinden*.

23. Jones, *The Greek City*, 39.

24. Jones, *Cities of the Eastern Roman Empire*, 282–85. "Owing to the enormous wealth of inscriptions which have been preserved in this area, we are able to form a remarkably detailed picture of its social and political structure under Roman rule." 283.

25. Ferguson, *Backgrounds of Early Christianity*, 39.

of citizens for serious crimes.[26] The choice of magistrates passed eventually into the hands of the senate.[27] Still, even in the times of the Roman emperors, there were numerous elections for municipal magistrates and municipal laws in Roman cities and colonies throughout the empire. The voting followed a standard procedure and participants included not only Roman citizens but also many non-citizen inhabitants.[28] Likewise, the Romans were much more willing to grant citizenship to people than were the Greek rulers.[29]

Though the rule of the Roman Caesars could at times assume tyrannical proportions,[30] the cities of the Roman Empire retained the same privileges that they held under the Greek kings.[31] The status of these cities varied: most privileged were the *coloniae civium romanorum* (colonies of Roman citizens), including Philippi, Corinth, Pisidian Antioch, Iconium, Lystra, and Troas. Lesser privileged were the "Latin" cities, which considered themselves free, including Ephesus, Smyrna, Tarsus, and Syrian Antioch; in these cities, their own laws governed their internal affairs.[32] In fact, the Roman government allowed cities to retain their governments and traditions "to a surprising degree."[33] Before Augustus, as the empire expanded, in many cases the Roman government promoted the free status of cities at the expense of territorial rulers. This encouragement of the establishment of city-states within the empire appealed to the Romans not only because it decentralized power but also because it was in harmony with their republican ideals.[34] At the same time, Rome reminded the new free cities that it was Roman rule which guaranteed their freedom.[35] Hayes and Mandel

26. March, "Elections and Voting," *OCD*, 516.

27. Marquardt, *Römische Staatsverwaltung*, 1:141.

28. Ibid., 142–45. Marquardt lists Paul's place of origin, Tarsus, as one of the cities in which city-wide elections were held, from which records are extant. See also, Jones, *The Greek City*, 174–77.

29. Botermann, "Paulus und das Urchristentum," 298.

30. See the accounts in Suetonius, *The Twelve Caesars*.

31. Ferguson, *Backgrounds of Early Christianity*, 40. "The Empire relied chiefly on senators to run it, and so no Emperor could be really secure unless his rule was founded on their consent and acquiescence. The Senate never lost its *esprit de corps*, and there was hostility to Emperors who were thought to abuse their great powers," Stockton, "The Founding of the Empire," 160.

32. Ferguson, *Backgrounds of Early Christianity*, 40.

33. Bernhardt, *Polis und römische Herrschaft*, 163.

34. Ibid.

35. Ibid., 164.

explain the free city/overlord relationship in the following way: "In Graeco-Roman antiquity 'free' does not mean what we today would construe it to mean. Rather, it denoted a status of nominal freedom, a status granted by a state's overlord. It does not however even hint that the state in question was no longer subordinate to that same overlord."[36] The assembly was still in theory the sovereign body, but the Roman rulers had a method of control, which was "quite frankly, to place the power in the hands of the well-to-do."[37] Because the average citizen was not wealthy enough to take on this financial burden, magistrates often paid the cost of civic rule from their own purse.[38]

In addition to the municipal assemblies these cities held, many provinces also had regional elected assemblies, including Asia, Bythinia, and Lycia.[39] These regional assemblies had the right to accuse Roman proconsuls for misdeeds and request their removal by the emperor.[40] Cities close to Rome adopted the Roman form of municipal government. From Greece west, they adopted more varied forms of city government. Again, like the Greek kings, the Roman emperor was master, but he was only successful in ruling by cooperating with the Roman senate and respecting the freedom of the various cities and their πόλις governments (Suetonius, *The Twelve Caesars Augustus*, 47). Some cities, like Alexandria, divided administrative sectors into πολίτευμα, giving each sector of its non-Roman citizens a measure of self-government.[41]

This survey of the historical relationship of the Roman emperors to the cities of the empire should not be interpreted as meaning there was universal approval of democracy throughout the Roman world. Not all writers of the Roman Empire were proponents of democratic political processes. Plutarch and Dio, for instance, believed that monarchy was the best form of government.[42] More, however, were in agreement with Polybius, the Greek

36. Hayes and Mandell, *The Jewish People*, 16.

37. Jones, *The Greek City*, 170, 177.

38. Ibid., 168–71, 179–80.

39. Magie, *Roman Rule in Asia Minor*, 1:446–47.

40. Ibid., 451–52. The proconsuls of Bithynia, C. Cadius Rufus, AD 49, and M. Tarquitius Priscus, AD 62, were accused by the assembly of Asia and convicted (Tacitus, *Annals* 12.22.4 and 14.46.1).

41. Tcherikover, *Hellenistic Civilization and the Jews*, 196.

42. "The rule of many is not good; let there be one lord, one king." (Dio, *Orations* 3.45). Plutarch, in *An seni* 11.790, calls monarchy "the most perfect and the greatest of all political offices."

historian of Rome, who viewed Rome as a government combining the best elements of monarchy, aristocracy, and democracy (Polybius, *Histories* 6.3–18).[43] Stegemann and Stegemann see the Greek *polis* as the most important pattern for the development of the structure of the Christian ἐκκλησία in the Diaspora. They note similarity in routine of prayers, praise to God, instructions, exhortations, and principles of order.[44] As the following material in this study will show, the *polis* was one of several concepts that influenced the organization of the church, albeit a very important one. As Judge notes, "Apart from the Jerusalem group . . . the early Christians known from the New Testament were practically all drawn from communities living under civil institutions of the republican kind."[45]

The Widespread Phenomenon of Voluntary Associations in the Roman Empire

In his work, *The Organization of the Early Christian Churches*, Edwin Hatch states,

> Among the many parallels which can be drawn between the first centuries of the Christian era and our own times, there is probably none more striking than that of their common tendency towards the formation of associations. There were then, as now, associations for almost innumerable purposes in almost all parts of the Empire.[46]

Hatch was one of the earliest scholars to suggest that voluntary associations of the Roman Empire gave the pattern of organization for the early Christian church.[47] Voluntary associations began to grow in importance during the Hellenistic period, "and by the time of the Roman empire they are attested in almost every city and town, despite official attempts to suppress them."[48] Their memberships consisted mostly of urban poor, slaves, and freedmen. Kloppenborg explains the rationale for their rise:

43. See also Aelius Aristides, who makes the same evaluation in 143 CE in, *Roman Oration* 26, as does Cicero, *Republic* 1.29.

44. Stegemann and Stegemann, *The Jesus Movement*, 275–76.

45. Judge, "Social Pattern of Christian Groups," 7.

46. Hatch, *Organization of the Early Christian Churches*, 26.

47. Ibid., 26–32.

48. Ascough, *What Are They Saying?*, 75–76.

> The reasons for the growth of such associations are not especially difficult to grasp. The ties that bound a citizen to the polis were weakened by the relative ease of travel and by the diminished influence that local inhabitants had over their own affairs. Significant dislocation of persons . . . created the need for social arrangements that would replace the older structures of the family, the deme, the tribe, and the polis. It might be said that voluntary associations compensated for the demise of the importance of the polis by imitating civic structures.[49]

As the voluntary associations replaced the function of the *polis* in people's lives, they were normally governed according to democratic principles. In fact, they were run as miniature cities (*poleis*); this provided the membership of a sense of power and control that they normally could not experience in the real world.[50] Records of voluntary associations in the Greco-Roman world are confirmed as early as the sixth century BCE with the formation of the school of Pythagoras in Croton in southern Italy.[51] The school of Epicurus (d. 271 BCE) established many centers throughout the Mediterranean world, becoming as much a "sect" as a philosophical school.[52] During the days of the apostles, mystery cults were another form of voluntary association, widespread throughout the Roman Empire, and were sometimes forbidden by the government.[53] There were also professional associations for craftsmen, businessmen, carpenters, bakers, silversmiths, etc. These are "widely attested in both Greek and Latin,"[54] and their functions normally included religious aspects.[55] Both Jewish synagogues and Christian assemblies were considered to be voluntary associations by outsiders in the Roman Empire.[56]

Arriving at a solid definition of what constitutes a voluntary association in the ancient world is somewhat problematic; attempts to make generalizations about them inevitably create misconceptions.[57] However, some gen-

49. Kloppenborg, "Collegia and *Thiasoi*," 17–18.

50. Cohen, *From the Maccabees to the Mishnah*, 116.

51. Ascough, "Greco-Roman Associations," 5.

52. Ibid., 7.

53. Ibid., 9–12.

54. Kloppenborg, "Collegia and *Thiasoi*," 23.

55. Wilson, "Voluntary Associations," 7.

56. Richardson, "Building," 54; Richardson, "Early Synagogues," 93; Poland, *Geschichte des griechischen Vereinswesens*, 158–63.

57. Richardson, "Building," 7–9. This difficulty is observable in the title and outline of

eralizations can correctly be made. First, "Voluntary associations—*collegia* in Latin, *thiasoi, koina, orgeones, eranoi*, and a variety of other terms in Greek—are essentially phenomena of the Hellenistic period, of the urban centres and of the urban poor."[58] Second, voluntary associations were formally organized.[59] Third, the size of associations was typically small: between twenty and two hundred members.[60] Fourth, associations in the ancient world usually had patrons, who were their benefactors.[61] Fifth, the same terms used for officers in the church of the New Testament are sometimes found to denote officers in the associations.[62] Sixth, voluntary associations in the Greco-Roman world tended to be democratic. They were attractive to slaves, freedmen, and poorer people who had little chance of upward mobility in the economy of the Roman Empire. Within a voluntary association, even the poor could exercise influence, and members of the associations normally developed a close bond with one another.[63]

Like Hatch, Mommsen, Renan, and Wilkin before him, Ascough favors the theory that the organization of the New Testament church was patterned after voluntary associations in the Roman Empire, though he believes not enough research is available to be conclusive.[64] His view follows that of his mentor, John Kloppenborg, who advocates an analogous pattern to the church, rather than a direct connection.[65] In at least one instance, Ascough concludes that a church planted by Paul functioned both externally and internally as a voluntary association, namely that in Thessalonica.[66] Wayne Meeks, however, has criticized this view. First, he says, "Christian groups were exclusive and totalistic in a way that no club nor even any pagan cultic association was." Second, "Christian groups were much more inclusive in terms of social stratification and other social categories

---

Ascough's "Greco-Roman Philosophic, Religious, and Voluntary Associations." Roberts, Skeat, and Nock, "The Guild of Zeus Hypsistos," define a voluntary association as "a group which a man [or woman] joins of his own free will, and which accepts him of its free will, and this mutual acceptance creates certain obligations on both parties," 75.

58. Kloppenborg, "Collegia and *Thiasoi*," 17.

59. Wilson, "Voluntary Associations," 9–10.

60. Ibid., 13.

61. Ascough, *What Are They Saying?*, 77.

62. Hatch, *Organization of the Early Christian Churches*, 36–39.

63. McCready, "*Ekklesia* and Voluntary Associations," 62. Ascough, "Greco-Roman Associations," 14–16.

64. Ascough, *What Are They Saying?*, 79–94.

65. Kloppenborg, "Edwin Hatch, Churches, and Collegia," 212–38.

66. Ascough, "The Thessalonian Christian Community," 328.

than were the voluntary associations." Third, there is an "almost complete absence of common terminology for the groups themselves or for their leaders" (exceptions would be the terms ἐπίσκοπος and διάκονος). Fourth, voluntary associations cannot explain the linkages of Christian assemblies beyond their locale.[67] Among others, Harland counters Meeks criticisms. First, "Meeks oversimplifies issues concerning the social composition of associations in antiquity. The evidence for the makeup of associations . . . is in fact varied." Second, "congregations and synagogues had in common with associations many organizational characteristics" (including more leadership terms than Meeks admits). Third, "Meeks exaggerates the extralocal character of Christian assemblies and underestimates the possibilities for these linkages among associations."[68]

It seems that there are too many similarities between voluntary associations and the Christian churches to deny the likeness of their organization. McCready likewise affirms that the structures of associations and that of the churches were similar: "Early churches shared significant common features with voluntary associations, with the consequence that they were viewed as such, certainly by outsiders and to a degree by insiders."[69] Rather than to conclude or speculate that voluntary associations gave their organizational pattern to the early church, it would be better to accept that in that day, there were common ideas among most people in the Roman Empire about group organization and function and that both voluntary associations and the early church shared these ideas.

THE HOUSEHOLD IN THE ROMAN EMPIRE

In ancient Greece, the household (οἶκος) was the fundamental social, political, and economic unit of society (Aristotle, *Politics* 1.2). Eventually the term οἶκος came to include all that pertained to the owner of the house. Likewise in Roman society, the household (*familia*) was regarded as the foundation of society (Cicero, *De Officiis* 1.54). For economic and protective purposes, a household could include not only the nuclear family of father-mother-children but also grandparents, slaves, freedmen, lodgers,

---

67. Meeks, *The First Urban Christians*, 78–80. Meeks was taking issue with Hatch, *Organization of the Early Christian Churches*, and Wilken, "Collegia, Philosophical Schools, and Theology," 268–91.

68. Harland, *Associations, Synagogues, and Congregations*, 180–82.

69. McCready, "*Ekklesia* and Voluntary Associations," 69.

and trade apprentices.[70] Likewise in the Jewish context, many households contained members beyond the nuclear family. It was customary for married sons to dwell with their parents. In fact, a household could have as many as forty to fifty people living in it.[71] The importance of the household in the Roman Empire is described by Malherbe in the following way:

> In New Testament times the household was regarded as a basic political unit. . . . The household member's loyalty to the interests of the household was so strong that it could rival loyalty to the republic. The closeness of the household unit offered the security and sense of belonging not provided by larger political and social structures.[72]

In 1939 Floyd Filson proposed that too little attention had been paid to the social structure of the household in the Greco-Roman world, which must have had a major influence on early church polity. He claims, "The Christian movement [was] really rooted in these homes"[73] and argues that studying house-churches in the apostolic times helps to understand the church itself in the following ways:

1. The house-church enabled churches to conduct distinctively Christian worship.

2. It explains the great attention paid to family life in the New Testament.

3. The existence of several churches in one area helps a great deal to explain party strife.

4. The house-church situation throws light on the social status of early Christians.

5. It is impossible to understand the development of church polity without understanding the structure of house-churches.[74]

70. Dixon, *The Roman Family*, 2. Klauck also cites numerous examples of this use of οἶκος in Greek literature in *Hausgemeinde und Hauskirche*, 15–17.

71. Warren, "House," 2:433.

72. Malherbe, *Social Aspects of Early Christianity*, 69.

73. Filson, "The Significance of the Early House Churches," 109.

74. Ibid., 109–12. With reference to point three, Filson goes so far as to say that the probable roots of the strife in Corinth have to do with the existence of four house-churches.

Corporate Decision-Making in the Church of the New Testament

Following the publication of Hans-Josef Klauck's *Hausgemeinde und Hauskirche im frühen Christentum*,[75] New Testament scholars and social historians have accepted Filson's advice. To a large extent, subsequent studies about house-churches and the New Testament have been an expansion of Filson's five points.

Klauck asserts that "the house, as the place where religious life goes on and becomes concrete, has a long, unbroken tradition in antiquity."[76] Note the statement of Cicero:

> What is more sacred, what more inviolably hedged about by every kind of sanctity, than the home of an individual citizen? Within its circle are his altars, his hearths, his household gods, his religion, his observances, his ritual; it is a sanctuary so holy in the eyes of all, that it were sacrilege to tear an owner therefrom. (*De domo sua* 109)

Going beyond the phenomenon of family religion in the οἶκος, Klauck cites the practices of private cults, mystery cults, voluntary associations, and even synagogue worship that took place in private houses.[77] L. Michael White adds, "many of the smaller 'foreign' religious groups that moved into the Roman world . . . tended to adapt existing buildings, especially homes and other nonpublic architecture, for their religious usage."[78] For the Christians to do the same, adapting private houses for their meetings, would have presented nothing out of the ordinary, either to the Christians themselves or to those living around them.[79]

There is no archaeological or documentary evidence for church buildings until the last half of the second century. At that time, Christians began converting houses to church buildings.[80] Large church buildings became common about the time of Diocletian's reign, 284-305 (Eusebius, *Ecclesiastical History* 8.1). Thus, it appears that in most cases the New Testa-

75. Klauck, *Hausgemeinde und Hauskirche.*

76. Ibid., 99. Translation by the author.

77. Ibid., 83–97.

78. White, "Synagogue and Society," 33–34.

79. "During the formative period of the house church (c. 50–150), the believers met in houses which belonged to benefactors in the Christian community. These home owners afforded the Christians with a venue which was immediately available, ensured a degree of inconspicuousness, and provided the necessary features, e.g., culinary appurtenances." Blue, "Acts and the House Church," 189.

80. Blue, "Acts and the House Church," 124–25.

ment congregations met at οἶκοι opened up to them by the more wealthy Christians.

There is significant biblical evidence for the existence of the house-church. The house-church is directly cited in four New Testament passages: Rom 16:3–5, "Greet Prisca and Aquila, my fellow workers in Christ Jesus. . . . Greet also the church in their house"; 1 Cor 16:19, "The churches of Asia send you greetings. Aquila and Prisca, together with the church in their house, send you hearty greetings in the Lord"; Col 4:15, "Give my greetings to the brothers at Laodicea, and to Nympha and the church in her house"; Phlm 2, "To Philemon our beloved fellow worker and Apphia our sister and Archippus our fellow soldier, and the church in your house." Likewise, there are greetings to and from "households" (οἶκος) in Paul's writings (1 Cor 1:16; 16:15–16; Phil 4:22; 2 Tim 1:16; 4:19). Luke applies the term "household" (οἶκος) seven times when describing believing groups (Acts 10:1–7; 11:13–14; 16:14–15, 31–34; 18:18). In addition, Paul uses the household concept in describing the Church of Christ (Gal 6:10; Eph 2:19–20; 1 Tim 3:15). It should be noted, however, that the New Testament use of the word οἶκος does not always refer to a house-church. For instance, no scholar has seriously put forth the conclusion that a house-church was started in Nero's domicile (Phil 4:22). Klauck points out that one meaning of "the household of Caesar" was an almost technical expression for the slaves and freedmen of Caesar, whether in Rome or throughout the empire.[81] Likewise, to assert that "greet the household of . . ." necessarily refers to a house-church would mean that Paul could never refer to a group of people or family in his letters who were not a house-church.

The study of the house-church phenomenon has led to a variety of conclusions, some of which are difficult to prove. One is that Paul's primary plan for the spread of the gospel was the conversion of households and the consequent formation of house-churches.[82] The book of Acts presents Paul as a preacher who used a variety of methods of evangelism, most frequently by preaching in synagogues, but also through addressing public assemblies (Acts 14:8–18; 17:16–31), speaking to a gathering of the Jewish women (Acts 16:11–15), addressing a gathering of disciples of John the Baptist (Acts 19:1–7), preaching at a rented hall (Acts 19:9–10), and speaking with political leaders in their places of authority (Acts 13:6–12; 24:24–27; 28:7–10). That some of his converts were owners of households

81. Klauck, *Hausgemeinde und Hauskirche*, 29.
82. Branick, *The House Church*, 18.

who offered their homes as places for the believers to gather seems rather a natural outworking of Paul's evangelism.

A second conclusion regarding house-churches which is difficult to substantiate is that the owners of the households automatically became the leaders of the newly-planted churches. Campbell asserts that "the patriarchal structure of the family determined to a large extent the leadership structures of the congregation."[83] Giles voices agreement, saying, "The owners of such homes in most cases would have continued to exert some leadership because of their social status and because they were the 'head' of the extended family that formed the nucleus of this little community."[84] This conclusion creates room for others; for instance, Klauck says that in Paul's missionary work, owners of households were not only motivated to adopt the Christian faith because of the Christian message, but also for the opportunity to become leaders in the new movement.[85] Another conclusion is that conversion was not necessarily individual, or at least not sincerely individual, but rather made in solidarity with the leadership of the household. Branick writes, "We can probably suppose some social pressure on individuals within a household to convert with the conversion of the head of that house. To the degree such pressure existed, the conversion of a household to Christianity would entail a diversity of personal conviction and engagement."[86]

Still another conclusion arising from the view that the owners of households became the leaders of the churches is that of Theissen, who asserts that there was necessarily a significant social stratification in the house-churches. This stratification was the cause, for instance, of the numerous conflicts in the Corinthian church.[87] He calls the leadership which was present in the house-church a "loving-patriarchy" (liebespatriarchalismus).[88] Finally, Campbell asserts that the New Testament ἐπίσκοπος was an elected leader from the natural leaders, known as πρεσβύτεροι, who were leading every house-church.[89]

---

83. Campbell, The Elders, 105. "The church in the house came with its leadership so to speak 'built in.' The church that met in someone's house met under that person's presidency." 126.

84. Giles, What on Earth Is the Church?, 121.

85. Klauck, Hausgemeinde und Hauskirche, 32.

86. Branick, The House Church, 18.

87. Theissen, Studien zur Soziologie, 231–71.

88. Ibid., 271.

89. Campbell, The Elders, 196–207.

Obviously, if the Roman household determined the church order of the New Testament, church order was preprogrammed to undergo significant changes after the death of the apostles. The arrangement could only function as long as churches met in the homes of wealthy converts. Once wealthy patrons were no longer needed to house churches, their leadership would quickly dwindle and church leadership would be based on different principles than in the first century CE.[90]

But there is reason to doubt that the Roman household was so determinative for early church structure. In the first place, though the majority of the churches in New Testament times were probably house-churches, the Roman household was not the exclusive meeting place for a church. In Acts 1:13–26, 120 disciples met in an upper room of a building, and the eleven formed the leadership of the group.[91] In Acts 4, the church of Jerusalem is described as meeting in Solomon's porch in the temple. In Acts 19:9 Luke tells us that Paul withdrew the disciples from the synagogue and spoke daily in the school of Tyrannus. In his letter to Trajan (110 CE), Pliny the Younger related the report from two Christian women διάκονοι that their church met in the open (Pliny, *Epistles* 10.96.7). An argument from archaeological findings rather than statements of classical writers is offered by Robert Jewett. He suggests that, because many of the Roman Christians in New Testament times were likely slaves, not all churches in Rome could be house-churches. Some churches would have met in a shop area of the *insulae* (multi-story apartment buildings). Thus there would have been no patron for the church.[92]

The idea that the local church would have been under the paternalistic leadership of the master of the household is strongly criticized by Wayne Meeks:

---

90. Branick, *The House Church*, 117–25, in fact, states that the shift from the house-church to other forms of church had begun to take place already in the days of Paul.

91. Klauck, *Hausgemeinde und Hauskirche*, 48, says that the number given by Luke in Acts 1 is anything but historical. But for anyone who has visited the traditional spot of "the upper room" in Jerusalem, it is obvious that 120 persons could fit comfortably in the room. Even if the traditional site is not the actual site, clearly private persons in Jerusalem in the time of the New Testament had rooms large enough to hold groups of one hundred or more.

92. Jewett, "Tenement Churches and Communal Meals," 23–43. This proposal of Jewett, represented in his commentary on Romans, has been criticized by Luke Timothy Johnson, "Reading Romans," 36.

> Important as the household was for Pauline Christianity, it leaves a number of aspects of the groups' life unexplained. It is not merely that the peculiar ritual processes, the central symbols and beliefs, of the Christians have scarcely any point of contact with the domestic cult of a Roman or Greek house; that is hardly surprising. Also, in purely social terms there are elements that are strange to the household structure. That hierarchy offers no clue to the source of the kinds of power and leadership that rival and prevail over the position of the householder, either in the persons of the itinerant apostle and his fellow workers or in the charismatic figures in the local group. It leaves unexplained not only the occasional expression of antihierarchial sentiments but also the sense of unity among Christians in the whole city, the region of province, and even beyond. Apparently there were other models and social ideas at work.[93]

Lane points out that Heb 13:7 contradicts the idea that leadership in the New Testament house-church came as a part of patronage:

> According to Hebrews 13:7, the function of the "leaders" consisted in preaching the word of God. From this fact they may be characterized as charismatically endowed leaders whose authority derived exclusively from the word they proclaimed and whose precedence was promoted by preaching alone. No other grounding and safeguarding of the position of the leaders is provided than the authority that results from the word proclaimed. . . . The reference to these former leaders is intriguing precisely because it implies an authority structure based on charisma rather than patronage.[94]

First Timothy 3:1–7 and Titus 1:5–9 also seem to contradict the idea that the ruler of the household was also made leader of the house-church. Like Heb 13:7, these passages define the preeminent skill of the elder/overseer (not to be confused with character traits) to be his ability to teach the Scriptures. No mention is made in the Timothy and Titus passages of being a manager of a household, only the leader of a family.[95] Marshall, arguing from the 1 Timothy and Titus passages, states,

93. Meeks, *The First Urban Christians*, 77.

94. Lane, "Social Perspectives on Roman Christianity," 220.

95. Branick, *The House Church*, 21, who says that the elder was to be one who demonstrated his ability as *paterfamilias*. Klauck, *Hausgemeinde und Hauskirche*, 56–57, says that the mention of the father of children relates to all married couples in the church, including slaves.

In the context of the patriarchal society of that day, it is significant that believers at Ephesus and Crete were appointed leaders in their respective congregations not simply because of their social position, age, or wealth but because of their appropriate qualities. Although the tendency of the time was to appoint people of social status, age, and wealth the examples of Timothy and (probably) Titus demonstrate the existence of leaders with none of these predispositions.[96]

The usual reply to this contradiction is that 1 Timothy and Titus were written after the death of Paul, when changes in church structure had already taken place.[97] But there are good reasons to accept the Pastoral Epistles as Pauline:

1. The letters ascribe their authorship to Paul. To deny Paul's authorship would force the conclusion that the writer used a pseudonym. Among the Jews and Christians of the period, "there is a rarity of pseudepigraphic *letters*."[98]

2. The early church fathers uniformly accepted Paul's authorship of the Pastoral Epistles.[99]

3. The argument that the Pastoral Epistles present a church order too advanced for the time of Paul's ministry (the most important consideration for this study) is based on circular reasoning and requires several passages in Acts to be unhistorical.

4. The argument that basic Pauline concepts are missing from the Pastoral Epistles has little hard evidence for the claim.[100]

5. The consideration that Paul at times used secretaries would explain differences in style between the Pastoral Epistles and other Pauline letters.[101]

---

96. Marshall, "Congregation and Ministry," in *Community Formation*, ed. Longenecker, 121–22.

97. Campbell, *Elders*, 176–79; Klauck, *Hausgemeinde und Hauskirche*, 62–77.

98. Carson, Moo, and Morris, *Introduction to the New Testament*, 367. Prior, *Paul the Letter-Writer*, 22, says, "There is, therefore, little support to be found in Christian sources that pseudepigraphical letters were common, and the examples we have are not at all like the Pastorals."

99. Knight III, *Pastoral Epistles*, 13–14.

100. Ibid., 32–33.

101. Prior, *Paul the Letter-Writer*, 168–69.

Still another who takes issue with the view that the household structure determined the leadership of the church is Johannes van der Ven, who summarizes the governance of the house-church in the following way:

> The hierarchical structure surrounding the *paterfamilias,* which was characteristic of the *oikos,* was broken through to form a different social formation of that time: the *collegium.* A *collegium* can be regarded as a free society, an association of equals, who held meetings in the house of one of its members. It had a free and democratic order.[102]

Branick's contention that the motivations to convert to Christ had as much to do with relationships in the Roman household as with genuine belief is based on the assumption that the household structure determined house-church order (which has been shown to be somewhat tenuous). The case of Onesimus in the book of Philemon shows that not all slaves automatically accepted or were forced to accept their owner's new faith.[103] Believing slaves are admonished to obey their unbelieving masters (Eph 6:5; Col 3:22; 1 Pet 2:18–19). In the case of unbelieving spouses, Paul makes it nearly axiomatic that the conversion of an unbelieving wife (which might have been the master's wife, the master's daughter-in-law, the slave's wife, etc.) is not a given (1 Cor 7:16). Branick's idea also contradicts repeated statements in the New Testament, both from Jesus and his apostles, that conversion was based on an inward, genuine, personal decision to accept Jesus as Messiah. The acceptance of Jesus could just as easily lead to household division as to household conversion (Matt 10:21–23; 11:28–30; Mark 13:12–13; Luke 8:15; John 7:38–39; 9:35–38; Acts 2:41; Rom 10:5–10; Heb 10:21–22). It is unquestionable that from the time of the apostles of Christ until now, whole families, including multiple generations, have been converted to belief in Jesus within a short time in nearly every culture. Nevertheless, the idea that whole households were converted by the first Christian missionaries, without respect to genuine belief, would have flatly contradicted their primary message.

Theissen's work on social gradations and social interaction within the church in Corinth has been highly commended. Indeed, his scholarship is impressive. Judge, however, criticizes both Theissen's conclusions about

---

102. Van der Ven, *Ecclesiology in Context,* 304.

103. Meeks, *The First Urban Christians,* 76. Branick also points this out in *The House Church,* 22.

stratification as well as the work of others, viewing them as theories which are untested:

> The basic question remains unasked: what are the social facts of life characteristic of the world to which the New Testament belongs? Until the painstaking field work is better done, the importation of social models that have been defined in terms of other cultures is methodologically no improvement on the "idealistic fallacy." We may fairly call it the "sociological fallacy."[104]

Finally, Campbell's assertion that bishops were elected from among the existing house-church leaders, who were the owners of the households, has been seriously challenged. Campbell's thesis is based on the view that the term πρεσβύτερος did not have reference to an appointed or elected position. It was rather "an imprecise, inclusive, term of respect for leaders of the community at many levels," and this designation included heads of Graeco-Roman households.[105] Merkle, interacting with Campbell, demonstrates from the Old Testament, the Mishna, Josephus, and numerous Graeco-Roman sources, that both the Hebrew, זָקֵן and the Greek πρεσβύτερος, though meaning aged, also frequently refer to designated officers of the nation, of cities or tribes.[106]

Investigations into the phenomenon of the house-church in the first century continue to yield fruitful insights into the life and structure of the early church. However, many conclusions put forth by writers need to be viewed with a certain amount of skepticism, particularly when they are unproven assumptions contradicting biblical writings. Even some statements not contradictory to the biblical account need to be questioned, such as the oft-cited conclusion of Murphy O'Connor that the maximum size of house-churches was forty to fifty persons.[107] But large private houses could have accommodated from one hundred to two hundred persons inside. Witherington, having examined villa excavations in Corinth, concludes

---

104. Judge, "The Social Identity of the First Christians," 128. Judge wrote the essay in 1980. He was making specific reference to Holmberg's arguments about social interaction in the NT church (see chapter 3), but had already mentioned Theissen's ideas previous to his discussion of Holmberg's. The denotation "idealistic fallacy" refers to the deficient methodology of theologians, including Bultmann and Schweizer.

105. Campbell, *The Elders*, 96.

106. Merkle, *Elder and Overseer*, 23–43.

107. O'Connor, *St. Paul's Corinth*, 158.

that several hundred Christians could have assembled at one of them.[108] The difference in these estimates is that O'Connor restricts church meetings to individual rooms; Ellis perceives them to have taken place in the main room (*atrium*) or in a colonnaded garden in the rear of the house;[109] Witherington refers to the property size of the villas, not to the size of a room. Thus, statements about the size of house-churches have as much to do with the perspective of the writer as with actual archaeological findings.

THE STRUCTURE OF THE SYNAGOGUE

The idea that the early church took its structure from the synagogue, at the very least in having a college of elders, has had many adherents since Campegius Vitringa (d. 1722). Lightfoot argues the point in the following way:

> The Christian Church in its earliest stage was regarded by the body of the Jewish people as nothing more than a new sect springing up by the side of the old. . . . As soon as the expansion of the church rendered some organization necessary, it would form a "synagogue" of its own. The Christian congregations in Palestine long continued to be designated by this name, though the term "ecclesia" took its place from the very first in heathen countries. With the synagogue itself they would naturally, if not necessarily, adopt the normal government of a synagogue, and a body of elders or presbyters would be chosen to direct the religious worship and partly also to watch over the temporal well-being of the society.[110]

Recent affirmations of this assessment come from Günther Bornkamm, Massey Hamilton Shepherd, Jr., Hans von Campenhausen, Carl Volz, Simon Kistemaker, John M. Frame, and J. Scott Horrell.[111]

---

108. Witherington III, "Review of *Reimagining Church*." Witherington is responding to Viola's contention that the proper NT concept of the church demands a small size.

109. Ellis, "Pastoral Letters," in *DPL*, 662. The Pompejanum in Aschaffenburg, Germany is a recreation of a villa of Pompeii, constructed on the basis of excavated foundations. The reconstruction includes a T-shaped hallway, which could have easily accommodated two hundred persons for a group gathering without use of the *atrium*.

110. Lightfoot, *Philippians*, 192.

111. Bornkamm, "πρέσβυς," *TDNT*, 6:662–63; Shepherd, "The Development of Early Ministry," 144–46; Campenhausen, *Ecclesiastical Authority*, 662–64; Volz, "The Pastoral Office in the Early Church," 360; Kistemaker, *Exposition of Acts*, 426–27; Frame, "Dealing with Differences,"; Horrell, *From the Ground Up*, 53.

James Tunstead Burtchaell has given the most complete presentation for the view that the organization of the synagogue was the predecessor of church structure. He is convinced that the leadership of the synagogue was a three-tiered synagogue structure, with its ἀρχισυνάγωγος, πρεσβύτεροι, and ὑπηρέτης. This later became the three-tiered ἐπίσκοπος, πρεσβύτεροι, and διάκονοι of the church. He observes that the New Testament specifically notes several important facets of synagogue life which were altered for Christians:

> We know that Christian Jews discontinued the fulfillment of *kashrut,* or dietary regulations, of Sabbath observance, of submission to authority or the Sanhedrin, or the rule of non-intercourse with gentiles. The New Testament bears heavy witness to these radical and highly controverted departures from Jewish practice. It is reasonable to doubt that an abandonment of the traditional community organization would have taken place without leaving any trace of controversy in the record.[112]

He further argues, "It is impossible to understand primitive Christian worship unless in continuity with Jewish worship."[113]

As the Christian faith gained more Gentile than Jewish adherents, there was a transfer of primacy from the church in Jerusalem to the church in Rome.[114] Contrary to those who agree with the Protestant Consensus, Burtchaell is convinced that there was church organization from the earliest days of the Christian movement. In the sixth and seventh chapters of his book, Burtchaell presents the development of synagogue structure: the assembly, the council of elders, the ruler of the synagogue, the servant of the synagogue, and other officers (which he also describes). Burtchaell does not say that these officers were present in every synagogue; rather, he states, "What we do claim to have discerned is a pattern that is typical rather than uniform."[115] The church naturally adopted the structure of the synagogue for its organization and as the two groups became divergent in their beliefs, the Christian synagogues preferred the title ἐκκλησία. "They replicated much of the customary Jewish practice and, whether they had by then shirked the word or not, they were a network of *synagogai.*"[116] The

---

112. Burtchaell, *From Synagogue to Church,* 188–89.

113. Ibid., 190.

114. Ibid., 195.

115. Ibid., 270.

116. Ibid., 279.

"triad of officers," found in the second century CE, Burtchaell contends, are already present in the earliest Pauline writings.[117]

Burtchaell makes a rich presentation of scholarly work. Clarke, noting this fact, calls the book "an encyclopaedic study."[118] Burtchaell's research is helpful to anyone who studies the history of the synagogue. There is, however, reason to be cautious about accepting a number of things that Burtchaell says. Franklin, for instance, notes that Burtchaell makes many assumptions and assertions to arrive at his conclusions.[119] Glenn Hinson also questions Burtchaell's basic conclusion, saying, "One comes away sensing a strong Roman Catholic effort to justify ecclesiastical structures acceptable to that church."[120] There are a number of difficulties with Burtchaell's thesis. The first is that though there were so many various officers in the synagogue, the majority of them never appear in any discussion of church organization in the New Testament. If the church adopted the organization of the synagogue, these offices should likewise appear in the documents. Secondly, according to Levine's study, although the assembly was an active part of synagogue life in the first century CE, there is no real pattern of officers in the synagogue. Instead, the type of leaders present varied from region to region or from locale to locale.

> While some titles of officials appear quite often in certain geographical regions, in others they are negligible, if not almost entirely absent. . . . To further complicate matters, some individuals bear more than one title, often leaving us to wonder what, in fact, the areas of responsibility of each office were. . . . Finally, these titles are recorded in the extant literary and epigraphical material with no explanation of their significance or meaning, thus offering little, if any, indication of the nature of the roles and functions involved. Even when we have an idea of the function of a given official, it remains unclear to which communal framework this title refers.[121]

The terms for synagogue leadership "were patently borrowed from the surrounding culture and were appropriated and adapted by the Jews

---

117. Ibid., 334. Burtchaell, a Roman Catholic, is not trying to read Catholicism into the New Testament. "The 'Catholic' theory," he states, "projects backward a scenario of dominating clergy who are simply not to be found in the first documents." 349.

118. Clarke, *Serve the Community*, 166.

119. Franklin, "James Tunstead Burtchaell: *From Synagogue to Church*," 499–550.

120. Hinson, "Review Article: *From Synagogue to Church*," 336.

121. Levine, *The Ancient Synagogue*, 413.

for their own needs."[122] Levine further notes that the office of elder did not exist in every synagogue. In many areas few synagogues had elders, and "it is difficult to pinpoint precisely the function of this office."[123] The ἀρχισυνάγωγος however, was "the official most commonly associated with the synagogue and its operation."[124] Finally, Burtchaell can offer no evidence that the church adopted the office of the ἀρχισυνάγωγος of the synagogue, which became the ἐπίσκοπος of the church.

A fact commonly misunderstood by those who assert that the church took over the organization of the synagogue (Burtchaell is an exception) is that the synagogue was not simply a religious institution. Instead, its primary function was that of a communal institution.[125] Levine states, "It was the townspeople or their chosen representatives who had ultimate authority in synagogue matters," and that the synagogue officials "were only as strong as the power vested in them by the community."[126] That the synagogue leadership and worship patterns influenced the leadership structure and worship of churches in the apostolic times is obvious; the question is, to what extent?

With respect to the institution of elders, to state that the early church adopted the council of elders from the synagogue is not an historically precise statement. Jewish elders in the time of Jesus were community elders, not primarily spiritual leaders. They did not lead synagogue worship, nor did they always teach.[127] This pattern is observable from the earliest records of Israel. According to the Old Testament, their presence in the Jewish nation preceded Moses, who spoke with them as he explained his calling and mission to Israel for the first time (Exod 4:27–31). In this instance, they appear to have been leaders of family groupings, but during certain periods of Israel's history, they became leaders of the entire nation. Their position evidently came through inheritance. Thus, they represented leadership from the bottom up.[128] Reviv explains that after the Babylonian captivity, the elders of Israel again became a prominent authority. He then notes the similarity of the leadership of elders in Israel with other Mesopotamian

---

122. Ibid., 452.

123. Ibid., 432.

124. Ibid., 415.

125. Ibid., 169.

126. Ibid., 382.

127. Schürer, *History of the Jewish People*, 2:427–39.

128. Reviv, *Elders in Ancient Israel*, 187–91.

nations: "The elders constituted a leadership institution within societies in the Ancient Near East, in all the countries and during all periods."[129] In addition, non-Jewish cities in the Roman Empire elected local officials, whom they called πρεσβύτεροι.[130] Rather than placing the origin of New Testament church elders in the synagogue, or even in Israel alone, the more likely origin was a common influence for both from the surrounding culture.

JEWISH PRACTICES OF DECISION BY ASSEMBLY

With the spread of Hellenism through Alexander the Great, Hellenistic ideas, including political ideas, made major inroads into Jewish life. As Tcherikover explains, "Hellenization encompassed Palestine on every side."[131] According to Hayes and Mandell, "There was far more Hellenization in the Jewish Temple state than 1 or 2 Maccabees or even Josephus openly acknowledged."[132] Hengel also emphasizes the pervasiveness of Hellenization in Jewish culture: "From about the middle of the third century BC all *Judaism* must really be designated 'Hellenistic Judaism' in the strict sense."[133] Greek was spoken throughout Judea and Galilee. Greek learning was already begun anew in Israel before the days of Herod the Great. The forces of conservative Judaism adopted the Greek education system to teach their own doctrine to the Jewish populous.[134] Through the Greek system, the idea of individualism gained emphasis among the Jewish people.[135] Roman laws frequently stated the legal right of Jewish communities to hold their own general assemblies and select their own elders (Josephus, *Ant.* 14.234–235).[136]

---

129. Ibid., 187.

130. Merkle, *Elder and Overseer*, 39–43. Merkle cites numerous examples of this phenomenon.

131. Tcherikover, *Hellenistic Civilization and the Jews*, 90.

132. Hayes and Mandell, *The Jewish People*, 13.

133. Hengel, *Judaism and Hellenism*, 1:104.

134. Hengel, *Judentum und Hellenismus*, 141. In fact, the early church fathers borrowed heavily from the apologetic arsenal of Hellenistic Judaism, 143.

135. Ibid., 145.

136. "The community had its own organization with its constitution, general assembly, council of elders, leaders of the council, elders of the synagogue and office-bearers of various kinds in the synagogue itself." Rabello, "The Legal Condition," *ANRW* 2.13:722.

Alexander's successors established thirty Greek cities in Palestine alone,[137] including, for example, the Greek city Scythopolis, located next to Galilee and populated with Jews. The city's contact with the surrounding Jewish countryside was friendly in Jesus' day, and commerce was frequent, thereby introducing new Hellenistic ideas into the region.[138] Herod Antipas built the city of Tiberias in 18 to 22 CE, on the western shore of the Sea of Galilee. This Jewish city had its own council (βουλή) and assembly (ἐκκλησία). Sepphoris, a Jewish city, was thoroughly Hellenized as well. Rebuilt by Herod Antipas (4–39 CE), it became an important military, cultural, and political center. The procurator Felix (52–60 CE) made Sepphoris the capital of Galilee. In Caesarea, until the reign of Nero, "Gentiles and Jews possessed equal civic rights . . . and were thus equally qualified to vote and to stand for election to the city council."[139] Nor was Hellenization restricted to the cities. As mentioned earlier, the Greek cities dominated their surrounding villages, which were their dependents.[140]

It would be historically incorrect to say that democracy was a way of life among the Jewish people living in New Testament times. Both in Palestine and in the Diaspora, Jews were subjected to various types of government, and many, in fact, believed that monarchy was the best kind of government for their nation. This belief in kingly power can be classified into three categories. First, there were those who believed that there should be no king but God. Second, others believed that the right kind of kingly power was the Herodian family. Finally, still others favored direct rule by the Romans.[141]

At the same time, and as explained earlier, Rome existed as an empire in which cities and territories held a significant measure of democratic or representative government. This was certainly true of the Jewish people, both before and during the time of the Roman Empire. After surveying a number of Jewish sources, Safrai concludes, "During the Second Temple period, . . . authority, it was then held, belonged to the community and

---

137. Tcherikover, *Hellenistic Civilization and the Jews*, 90–116. Tcherikover lists Acco, Dor, Straton's Tower, Apollonia, Jaffa, Yavneh, Ashdod, Ascalon, Gaza, Teda, Raphia, Canatha, Raphana, Susita, Gadara, Abila, Pella, Dion, Philadelphia, Paneas, Seleuceia, Antiocheia in Huleh, Philoteria, Scythopolis, Samaria, Arethusa, Marissa, and Adora.

138. Freyne, *Galilee from Alexander to Hadrian*, 108–13.

139. Ibid., 113. The editors note that this arrangement led to all sorts of trouble.

140. Ibid., 108.

141. Grant, *Early Christianity and Society*, 17–18.

the assembly. Fundamentally, the ruling authority was the gatherings of the local citizens to deal with civic matters, and of all the Jews to deal with national matters."[142]

Both Philo and Josephus at times described Jewish political life as democratic. From the time of the Ptolemies, the Jewish people in Alexandria were allowed to govern their lives according to their own traditions.[143] Josephus tells how the Jewish senate of Alexandria called all of its citizens together for an assembly during a particularly dangerous time of Jewish σικάροι. The assembly declared the troublemakers guilty and had them punished (Josephus, *J.W.* 7.409–417). In this account there is no evidence of vote-taking on the part of the assembly, as there would have been in democratic Athens. The response was more likely one of acclaim. Nevertheless, the assembly was directed to make the decision by its leaders. In another instance recorded by Josephus, a popular assembly in Jerusalem formed around 200 BCE, revoked the political authority of the high priest, and selected a different representative (Josephus, *Ant.* 12.164).

Philo also offers several descriptions of Jewish democratic activity. In fact, he presents the Jewish nation as more democratic in its dealings than the Romans were. Arguing against the Greek practice of choosing leaders by lot, "which is a sort of blunder on the part of fortune," Philo says that leaders, whether of cities or nations, should be chosen by election. Philo bases his argument on the teaching of Moses, using Deut 17:15 to establish his point.[144] Burtchaell says that Philo exaggerated in presenting Israel as so thoroughly democratic.[145] But one must remember that Philo was quite involved with the Jewish politics of Alexandria and their interactions with Roman rule. Though he exaggerated the democratic method in current Jewish politics, it is unlikely that his viewpoint was far removed from that of his contemporaries. His writings demonstrate that a major

142. Safrai, "Jewish Self-Government," 1:378.

143. Tcherikover, *Hellenistic Civilization and the Jews*, 299–302. Ben-Sasson, "Community," *EncJud*, 5:810.

144. "The appointment is to be a voluntary choice, and an irreproachable selection of a ruler, whom the whole multitude with one accord shall choose" (Philo, *Spec.* 4.151–57).

145. Burtchaell, *From Synagogue to Church*, 260: "In his time Rome ruled Greece and the emperors ruled Rome, and they made none of their personnel assignments by lot. Among the Jews, leaders were chosen by merit, but who assessed those merits was a matter of some finesse. There had long been a strain between the ancient theory of populism and the social reality of aristocracy, and that strain was creating a tension in the community organization."

voice for Judaism in the time of Christ believed democracy to be the most enlightened form of government.

A final instance of Jewish democratic activity is exemplified by the Essenes (often identified with the Qumran Community), who conducted decisions in an assembly, allowing any member to speak (1QS 6). The Essenes also practiced voting and majority decision in their meetings. Note Josephus' description of this activity:

> But in the judgments they exercise they are most accurate and just, nor do they pass sentence by the votes of a court that is fewer than a hundred. And as to what is once determined by that number, it is unalterable. What they most of all honour, after God himself, is the name of their legislator [Moses]; whom, if anyone blaspheme, he is punished capitally. They also think it a good thing to obey their elders, and the majority. Accordingly, if ten of them are sitting together, no one of them will speak while the other nine are against it. (*J.W.* 2.145–46)

Though democratic ideas were widespread in Judaism during the first century CE, large portions of Palestinian Judaism were not democratic in their orientation. Jerusalem itself was not a *polis*.[146] Instead, it was led by the Sanhedrin, composed of the high priests, the Pharisees, and the elders of the people.[147] At times, the Sanhedrin shared in governing the people and at other times was eliminated as a partner in government (as during the reign of Herod the Great).[148] The Sanhedrin was not a democratic institution: "The members of this boule, the Sanhedrin, were not chosen in democratic elections or the like, as in a city with an administration like that of a Hellenistic polis. Despite the broad public base of the Sanhedrin, no national assemblies took place in Jerusalem at fixed times and places."[149]

The absence of national assemblies is, of course, a change from what took place in the time of Nehemiah and Ezra.[150] However, though the Sanhedrin was not chosen by popular election, it did not remain insulated from public opinion. At times it was forced to follow the dictates of the public.[151]

---

146. This would have involved, among other things, active participation of the Jewish youth in the gymnasium.

147. Ibid., 384–86.

148. Safrai, "Jewish Self-Government," 382.

149. Ibid., 390.

150. Nehemiah 8–10.

151. Safrai, "Jewish Self-Government," 386.

Judge states that there was probably limited republican influence in the villages of Galilee where Jesus did a great amount of his ministry.[152] He also concludes that the main political concept of the disciples was the monarchy. In the sayings of Jesus about social distinctions, international affairs, or governmental administration, the concepts are always monarchical.[153] One should be careful, however, not to conclude from this that Galilee was set off from the commerce and political thinking of the Roman world. Porter points out that the village of Nazareth overlooked the Via Maris, one of the busiest trade routes in Palestine.[154] Likewise Capernaum was "part of a region that may have been one of the most densely populated in the Roman world."[155] That Jesus and his disciples would have had interaction with cosmopolitan thought is clear from several facts: Matthew was first a Roman tax collector (Luke 5:27–29); Jesus traveled to all the cities of Galilee (Matt 9:35); early in his ministry Jesus had contact with significant numbers of people from non-Jewish cities: "And great crowds followed him from Galilee and the Decapolis, and from Jerusalem and Judea, and from beyond the Jordan" (Matt 4:25; this following arose from the spread of his fame "throughout all Syria," v. 24);[156] and Jesus ministered to four thousand while in the region of the Decapolis (Mark 7:31—8:9). Judge understands all of the aforementioned contacts of Jesus and his disciples with people of republican thinking. He counters, however, by saying, "though the non-republican area (of Palestine) was geographically very limited, emotionally the gulf between it and the civilized world was profound. The real division was of course cultural."[157]

Some ideas about government in the Jewish population, which one might identify as democratic, originated from within the Jewish nation itself, not necessarily from Hellenistic influence. Numerous Jewish sources speak of popular elections of various officers both prior to and during the lifetime of Jesus. Jewish legal concepts have included the idea of "majority rule" for many centuries, both in judicial and in scriptural interpretations.

152. Judge, "Social Pattern of Christian Groups," 5.

153. Ibid., 5–6.

154. Porter, "Did Jesus Teach in Greek?," 211.

155. Ibid.

156. "The term 'Syria' reflects the extent of the excitement aroused by Jesus' ministry; if the Roman use of the term is here presumed, it shows his effect on people far beyond the borders of Israel," Carson, "Matthew," in *EBC*, 8:121.

157. Judge, "Social Pattern of Christian Groups," 9.

There is debate, however, regarding when this concept became a regular pattern in Judaism.[158] At the same time, there is historical evidence for democratic activity among Jewish populations in the Diaspora. The Jewish community of Berenice (Cyrene), for instance, governed itself in a thoroughly democratic way. Inscriptions from the ancient community include the statement that the decisions were made by "the community" (συναγωγή), including the taking of votes.[159]

Antecedents to Democratic Thinking in Israel's History

The acceptance of democratic ideals among Jewish people during and prior to the Roman Empire has antecedents in Israel's history. Jewish writer Lisa Katz argues that democratic thinking came rather naturally to Israel:

> Democratic concepts were always a part of Jewish thinking and derived directly from the Torah. For instance, the belief that all men are created in the image of God logically leads to the idea of all men being equal. And the idea of the covenant between God and the Israelites, in which both parties accepted upon themselves duties and obligations, shows that power is established through the consent of both sides rather than through tyranny by the more powerful party. One can easily see how the biblical covenant could lead to ideas such as government by consent, constitutional law and no absolutism.[160]

Of course, one cannot define the political organization of the nation of ancient Israel as a democratic one. At least from the time of King Saul until the Babylonian captivity, it was a monarchy in the fullest sense of the word. Nevertheless, as Burtchaell points out,

---

158. Shilo, "Majority Rule," *EncJud* 11:804–6.

159. Levine, *The Ancient Synagogue*, 96–104.

160. Katz, "Israel: Democratic and Jewish?" One must be careful not to misunderstand Katz. She is not arguing that Israel existed as a democracy in its history prior to and during the time of the NT. Ideas for democratically-governing Jewish communities, she says, began being formulated in the Middle Ages. In this last assessment, she is certainly wrong. As this chapter makes plain, democratic ideas entered Jewish community life, at the very latest, in the time of Alexander the Great.

> In their own nomenclature, the Jews *were* an assembly. The cultic and political act of a solemn and formalized convention of the whole population—men, women and children—was felt to be so typical and representative that, by metonymy, it provided the popular designation whereby one referred to the Jews.[161]

The Old Testament presents repeated instances of corporate decision-making within Israel during its pre-exilic days. For instance, in Num 35:24–25, the congregation (קָהָל) is called into judicial assembly. In Lev 24:10–23, the entire assembly is required to carry out capital punishment for various crimes. In Judg 20:1–9, the "congregation" (קָהָל) is challenged to make a decision about action against the tribe of Benjamin. In 2 Sam 5:1–3 all the elders of Israel come to Hebron to make a league with David and anoint him king (the elders thus representing all the people).[162] In 1 Kgs 11:12 the people approve of the selection of Solomon as king (instead of the oldest descendant). In 1 Kgs 12:3 the "whole assembly" (כָל־קָהַל) petitions with Jeroboam for changes from Rehoboam if he is to reign over them. In the days of Hezekiah, the "whole assembly" decided of themselves to extend the Passover celebration (2 Chr 30:23). Burtchaell concludes, "The plenary assembly was the rightful venue for all major events in and of the community of Israel. Whether in fact or in symbol, it had been the ancient usage that the people had to be convened for certain acts too momentous to be left to rulers alone."[163]

In this argument about Israel as an assembly, there is no assertion that Israel took votes and practiced majority rule. However, there are various ways of making decisions which demand the participation of a whole group of people. Wolf states,

> Real democracy and representative democracy have passed through many trials and tribulations in the history of mankind and of its social institutions. But representative democracy is a descendant of a more general type of democracy. In Israel the documents, the incomplete political records, the indifference of our sources to

161. Burtchaell, *From Synagogue to Church*, 209.

162. In the parallel passage, 1 Chr 12:23–37, the military forces listed as coming to anoint David are 340,800. Payne translates the passage as "commanders of thousands," "commanders of hundreds." Thus the number he arrives at is 398. Payne, "1, 2 Chronicles," 4:378.

163. Burtchaell, *From Synagogue to Church*, 211.

nontheological matters, and other factors make it impossible to demonstrate conclusively the evolution of the organization.[164]

As Israel met in assembly, its leaders were not simply announcing their decisions or instructions. They were looking for agreement and consent.

Another factor can be added to the tradition of corporate decision-making in ancient Israel. The practice of assembly was common in the Near East in ancient times. Rulers acted more on consensus of the governed than general histories have led one to expect. Mesopotamian social formations apparently used corporate forms of government at an early date, and the practice of assembly government was evidently present during the Uruk period.[165] Mesopotamian society frequently had recourse to open trials, allowing dissent. Schemeil, who summarizes from various studies, points out,

> Historical documents [from Mesopotamia] describe assemblies of citizens deliberating for days, each session including new members. When Mesopotamian elders were unable to agree, they opened their assembly to junior aristocrats and commoners; if necessary, they also invited women and teenagers to have their say in the final decision. Assyrian traders in Anatolia dealt with dissenting opinions in a similar way—their assembly divided into three groups which deliberated and voted separately before holding a last plenary session where majority ballots were added up with great sophistication.[166]

Schemeil concludes that this is the early form of democracy, adding, "What is of most importance for democracy is not a final vote but a set of intelligible justifications for each decision."[167] Rulers in Egypt and Mesopotamia enacted laws after first holding many assemblies and councils.[168] In addition to decision by assembly,

> Even without periodic electoral contests, it was possible to discredit someone as a true representative of a category or corporate interest, ousting him immediately from a political position. That

164. Wolf, "Traces of Primitive Democracy," 107.

165. Blanton, "Beyond Centralization," 155. The Uruk period extended from 4500 to 3100 BCE.

166. Schemeil, "Democracy before Democracy?," 104.

167. Ibid., 105

168. Ibid., 113.

could occur in the street, or through strikes, protests, and demonstrations, all well documented in Egypt and Mesopotamia.[169]

Fleming, however, disagrees with those who describe political activity in Mesopotamia as democracy.

> For a variety of reasons, however, the term "democracy" is not well suited to any ancient Near Eastern practice. . . . I find the word "democracy," however broadly defined, a barrier to understanding the diverse Near Eastern tradition of group-oriented decision making that may somehow stand behind the remarkable development in Athens. Besides the essential anachronism, the idea of primitive "democracy" artificially dissociates the more inclusive meetings from other forms that allowed only more limited participation.[170]

Still, the phenomenon of corporate decision-making is quite evident in ancient Mesopotamian texts. Fleming's research focuses on the documents of Mari, in which he found numerous references to group decision-making in regions, towns, and tribal groups. Most collective decision-making was done by representatives of the citizens (which could number as many as two hundred). But in some cases, there was a full assembly of the population.[171] "Mari," he says, "preserves not the direct antecedents of Greek democracy but a cross-section of its ancestry in the larger region."[172] Perhaps Israel's phenomenon of being an assembly was highly influenced by its Mesopotamian surroundings. But even if not, its actions of group decision-making in Old Testament times would not have appeared unusual in a Near Eastern setting of that time.

Chapter Summary

The purpose of the information in this chapter is not to determine specifically where democracy functioned, whether inside or outside the church. It has rather been to demonstrate that, both inside and outside of Judaism and throughout the Roman Empire, the concept of corporate decision-making was widespread and appeared in many venues of society: in the cities and

169. Ibid., 108.
170. Fleming, *Democracy's Ancient Ancestors*, 17.
171. Ibid., 232–34.
172. Ibid., 234.

villages of the Graeco-Roman world, the various voluntary associations, the synagogue of Judaism, the various city governments of Palestinian and Diaspora Judaism, and in the general history of the nation of Israel. Corporate decision-making had, in fact, an ancient history by the time the church was born and would have been understood and approved of by both Jewish and non-Jewish elements of the early church.

3

Theological Concepts Entering into
Corporate Decision-Making

THE CHURCH OF THE New Testament claimed to be founded by Christ and directed by the Holy Spirit. Though the social world of the New Testament influenced the church's activities, the early church and its mission were primarily directed by theological truths. The disciples of Christ in the first century CE believed that they were fulfilling a divine command by advancing the gospel and participating in local church life:

> The unity of the scattered Christian communities depended on two things—on a common faith and on a common way of ordering their life and worship. They called each other "brother" or "sister." Whatever differences there might be of race, class or education, they felt bound together by their focus of loyalty to the person and teaching of Jesus.[1]

It is therefore imperative to look at several theological concepts, found in the New Testament, which were crucial for determining church order. Although many writers include post-New Testament developments in the church to help define what church order should be like, and this and later chapters will address those developments, this study will restrict its principles for church order to the teachings of the Bible itself. This is necessary in order to be able to evaluate the direction of post-New Testament developments of church order.

Restricting the study to the teachings of the Bible is, of course, the logical approach of anyone affirming the divine authority of the Scriptures

---

1. Chadwick, *The Early Church*, 32.

and the position espoused by the Reformers, including the Anabaptists. The value of this restriction is affirmed by a statement from Avery Dulles in 1986: "Christians cannot agree about the measure of progress or decline [of the Church] because they have radically different visions of the Church. They are not agreed about what the Church really is."[2] This statement was made before the American dominance of the Willow Creek model, or the rise of the house church movement, or the emerging churches. Disagreement about the nature of the church has only increased since Dulles wrote. Thus, there is sufficient basis for defining the church exclusively according to Scripture.

THE CONCEPT OF AUTHORITY IN THE CHURCH OF THE NEW TESTAMENT

To rightly understand church order, the discussion needs to begin with Jesus.[3] According to the New Testament, Christians are followers of Jesus, the Messiah; all questions of authority ultimately go back to his person, his teaching, and his work of salvation. He is called the head (κεφαλή) of the church, signifying his authority (Eph 4:15, 5:23; Col 1:18). More frequently, Jesus is called Lord (κύριος) by his followers, even from the earliest times of the Jesus movement (Matt 8:23; Luke 11:1; Acts 1:21; 5:14; 9:1; 15:11, 36; Rom 1:3; 15:5; 1 Cor 1:2; 15:57; 1 Thess 1:3).[4] His authority in the church is therefore regal, absolute, and unquestioned. This principle of Jesus' regal authority makes his orders binding and limits creativity in church order. However, this position of kingly authority is singular. Jesus himself explained that his followers have no hierarchy outside himself; he

---

2. Dulles, *Models of the Church*, 6. Dulles does not look primarily to the authority of the New Testament to define the church. Rather, he comments, "In my own view, theological verification depends upon a kind of corporate discernment of spirits," ibid., 18.

3. Patterson, "Single-elder Congregationalism," 134.

4. Viola, *Reimagining the Church*, 67–71, tries to differentiate between Christ's headship and his lordship in the following explanation: "The Bible draws a careful distinction between Christ's headship and His lordship. Throughout the New Testament, the *headship* of Christ virtually always has in view the Lord's relationship with His body. . . . The *lordship* of Christ virtually always has in view His relationship with His individual disciples." The New Testament, in fact, does not in any sense bear this out. See, for instance, John 21:7–14; Acts 1:21, 15:11; Rom 1:4, 15:5; 1 Cor 1:10, 5:4; 2 Cor 8:9; Gal 6:14; Eph 1:2, 15. These passages, as well as many others, have corporate expressions of Christianity in view when speaking of the lordship of Christ.

alone is their teacher, and all disciples are brothers and, therefore, equals (Matt 23:8–10).

Equality among Disciples

In the Matthew passage, when Jesus says, "You are all brothers," he is using a term which Jews used of one another. ἀδελφός (Heb. אָח) denoted a member of the religious community of Israel.[5] This term for "fellow Israelite" is frequently expressed in the Pentateuch. It is also expressed in the book of Acts by Christian spokespersons in their addresses to their fellow Jews (Acts 2:29, 37; 13:26). In Matthew 10, Jesus was applying ἀδελφός in a special way to his disciples.

Meyer notes that the prohibitions not to be called rabbi, teacher, or father "have reference to the *hierarchical* meaning and usage which were at that time associated with the titles in question."[6] It has no reference to the familial relationship, since Christ used the term *father* in a positive light on other occasions (e.g., Matt 15:4–6). Paul used the term *teacher* of himself in Titus 2:7. With reference to the term *rabbi*, Glasscock writes,

> A rabbi was viewed as one having authority beyond the material taught, and Jesus' disciples were forbidden to take this title. The reason was that there was only one teacher (*didaskalos*), Jesus Himself. The disciples were brothers (implying equals). The major point here was that no individual disciple would be superior, but all would be equal.[7]

Thus, the emphasis of Jesus' teachings is on equality among the disciples.

One church polity that takes exception to this explanation is that of the Roman Catholic Church. The teaching of the *Catechism of the Catholic Church* distinguishes between the clergy and laity as follows:

> The very differences which the Lord has willed to put between the members of his body serve its unity and mission. For in the Church there is diversity of ministry but unity of mission. To the apostles and their successors [the pope and the bishops, § 862] Christ has entrusted the office of teaching, sanctifying, and governing in his name and by his power. But the laity are made to

5. *Str-B*, 1:277. This concept is illustrated in the New Testament, for instance in Acts 2:29, 37.

6. Meyer, *The Gospel of Matthew*, 391.

7. Glasscock, *Matthew*, 447.

share in the priestly, prophetical, and kingly office of Christ; they have, therefore, in the Church and in the world, their own assignment in the mission of the whole People of God.[8]

This distinction between the clergy and laity is based on the teaching that the bishops, and through them the rest of the clergy, are especially empowered by the Holy Spirit. This special enabling is not granted to the people of the church at large. Note the explanation:

> No one can bestow grace on himself; it must be given and offered. This fact presupposes ministers of grace, authorized and empowered by Christ. From him, bishops and priests receive the mission and faculty ("the sacred power") to act *in persona Christi Capitis*; deacons receive the strength to serve the people of God in the *diaconia* of liturgy, word, and charity, in communion with the bishop and his presbyterate. . . . Indeed, the ministry of the Church is conferred by a special sacrament.[9]

Finally, this sacramental ministry is in communion with the bishop of Rome, the successor of Peter.[10]

Though the *Catechism* bases this formulation on Rom 10:14–15, the interpretation is certainly debatable. The passage does not imply any sort of sacramental action, unless every command from God to go and tell is an identical sacrament. This would then have to include, among others, the healed demoniac of Gadara (Luke 8:38–39), the man not yet ready to follow Jesus (Luke 9:59–60), and the women who had left Jesus' empty grave (Matt 28:10). It is unlikely that the Catholic Church would designate any of these as bishops or priests. Paul himself presents a contradiction to the teaching of the *Catechism*, for it was Ananias, not known to be ordained to the clergy, who urged him to call on the name of the Lord (Acts 22:16). However, the *Catechism* is correct in that an authoritative messenger needs authorization. What Rom 10:14–15 is stating, however, is far broader than the *Catechism* asserts. It is also unlikely that Paul's words in this passage could ever have referred to priests, since as Banks notes, "One of the most noticeable features of Paul's writings is the absence of the term *hiereis* [sic], priest."[11]

---

8. *Catechism of the Catholic Church* §873, 251.

9. Ibid., §875, 252–53.

10. Ibid., §876, 253.

11. Banks, *Paul's Idea of Community*, 128.

The sacramental ministry of the Roman Catholic Church and its hierarchy were an historical development, which took place over a few centuries. In his discussion of the development of a distinction between clergy and laity, Hatch states,

> In those early days—before the doors of admission were thrown wide open, before children were ordinarily baptized and men grew up from their earliest years as members of a Christian society . . . the mere membership of a Christian Church was in itself a strong presumption of the possession of high spiritual qualifications.[12]

Tertullian was the first to use the words *ordo* and *plebs* to distinguish between regular ministers of the church and members who were not ministers (Tertullian, *De Baptismo* 17; *De Exhort. Castit.* 6). Still, "The view which he took of the nature of the office in the Church was that it does not, as such, confer any powers upon its holders which are not possessed by the other members of the community."[13] By the time of Origen, however, the term *clerus* was a fixed designation of the officers of the church (Origen, *Fr. Jer.* 11.3).

From the time of Cyprian (250 CE), clergy began to be addressed as "abstractions," such as "your holiness, father," etc.[14] After Constantine, "the clergy were increasingly given a special social status and developed into a distinctive social class."[15] Later writers, including Chrysostom, elevated the clergy to an even higher status:

> For indeed what is it but all manner of heavenly authority which He has given them when He says, "Whose sins ye remit they are remitted, and whose sins ye retain they are retained?" (John xx.23). What authority could be greater than this? "The Father hath committed all judgment to the Son?" (John v.22). But I see it all put into the hands of these men by the Son. For they have been conducted to this dignity as if they were already translated to Heaven, and had transcended human nature, and were released from the passions to which we are liable.[16]

12. Hatch, *Organization of the Early Christian Churches*, 118–19.

13. Ibid., 121.

14. Chadwick, *The Early Church*, 164. Hanson says, "The doctrine of Christian ministry as a priesthood finds its strongest expression in the work of Cyprian. . . . his definition of this priesthood is specific and goes beyond any such doctrine before him." Hanson, *Studies in Christian Antiquity*, 131.

15. Küng, *Christianity*, 212.

16. Chrysostom, *On the Priesthood* 3.5 (*NPNF,*1 9:47).

About the same time, *The Apostolic Constitutions* declared the following:

> The bishop, he is the minister of the word, the keeper of knowledge, the mediator between God and you in the several parts of your divine worship. He is the teacher of piety; and, next after God, he is your father, who has begotten you again to the adoption of sons by water and the Spirit. His your ruler and governor; he is your king and potentate; he is, next after God, your earthly god, who has a right to be honoured by you."[17]

Hatch offers three reasons for this development. The first is the wide extension of church membership from the fourth century CE onward:

> But when infant baptism became general, and men grew up to be Christians as they grew up to be citizens, the maintenance of the earlier standard became impossible in the Church at large. Professing Christians adopted the current morality: they were content to be no worse than their neighbours. But the officers of all communities tend to be conservative, and conservatism was expected of them: that which had been the ideal standard of qualifications for baptism became the ideal standard of qualifications for ordination: and there grew up a distinction between clerical morality and lay morality which has never passed away.[18]

The other two factors he mentions are the influence of the civil order in the Roman Empire and the growth of the analogy between the Christian and Mosaic dispensations.[19]

That the hierarchical structure of the church was not present in New Testament times is freely admitted by many Roman Catholic scholars. Johannes van der Ven, for instance, describes hierarchy as a development that began in the second and third centuries CE.[20] Hans Küng adds that hierarchy is not in harmony with the Scripture:

> If the Church is the true people of God, it is impossible to differentiate between "Church" and "laity," as though the laity were not in a very real sense *laos*. This would be *clericalizing misconception* of the Church: the Church is directly or indirectly identified with regard to rights and privileges. It is striking that the word λαός with the meaning "people of God" is so often used for the Christian

---

17. *The Apostolic Constitutions* 2.25 (*ANF*, 7:409).

18. Hatch, *Organization of the Early Christian Churches*, 136.

19. Ibid., 136–38.

20. Van der Ven, *Ecclesiology in Context*, 306–7.

community, whereas the word λαικός, "layman," whether in the Gentile meaning of the "uneducated masses" or in the Jewish meaning of one who is neither priest nor Levite, simply does not occur in the New Testament.[21]

One more source which contributed to the concept of hierarchy in the Roman Catholic Church, as mentioned in chapter 1, was the writings of Pseudo-Dionysius the Areopagite. "The supposed apostolic authority of these writings, added to their intrinsic value, caused the 'Pseudo-Dionysius' to exercise a profound influence on medieval theology both in the East and in the West."[22]

The Roman Catholic scholar Edward Schillebeeckx criticizes the impact of the pseudo-Dionysian writings in the following way:

> This pseudo-Dionysian principle of substitution devalued the pluri-form specialized ministries in the church which came into being historically as a result of church needs, being thought pastorally necessary. This hierarchical development at the top of the church devalued the laity, 'at the base of the pyramid,' so that they became merely the object of episcopal and priestly care. And in this situation pastoral care could at the same time be misused as a means of control in questions of power.[23]

In short, then, the Roman Catholic view of church hierarchy developed after the completion of the New Testament, as is historically demonstrated not only by Protestant but also by numerous Catholic scholars. Indeed, some Catholic scholars view hierarchy as being problematic for, rather than helpful to the faith.

The hierarchy of the Roman Catholic Church stands in contrast to the original point of this chapter, that Jesus taught an equality among his disciples. Though affirming ecclesiastical office, Küng cites the un-hierarchical viewpoint of the New Testament. Noting that there are various Greek terms to express authority for officials, he asks,

> Why is it that the New Testament obviously avoids using these then current and seemingly obvious terms? Clearly because despite the varieties of area they cover, they have one common

21. Küng, *The Church*, 125.
22. *ODCC*, s.v. "Dionysius, the Pseudo-Areopagite," 406.
23. Schillebeeckx, *Church*, 217.

factor: all express a relationship of rulers and ruled. And it is precisely this which makes them unusable.[24]

There is not sufficient space in this study to compare all church polities with the original New Testament statements on the equality of Jesus' disciples. Since both the Anglican Church and the Eastern Orthodox Church accept the development of the clerical order through the third century CE as authoritative,[25] the comparison made covers the majority of Christendom. The same evaluation holds true for all; namely, hierarchy is a post-New Testament development and does not constitute a part of the New Testament teaching on the church.

Exclusion of Party Division

The single headship and lordship of the church in Jesus the Messiah not only eliminates hierarchy but also automatically excludes factions in the church body. Because Jesus' lordship is direct to every believer, it creates unity. Paul uses this truth to exhort the Corinthian believers to live out this unity in 1 Cor 1:10: "I appeal to you, brothers, by the name of our Lord Jesus Christ, that all of you agree and that there be no divisions among you, but that you be united in the same mind and the same judgment." Paul is addressing factions that had developed in the Corinthian church in which various teachers became rallying points, though there is no indication that the teachers themselves had anything to do with the divisions.[26] Paul then asks the rhetorical question, "Is Christ divided?" (v. 13), to bring the Corinthians to their senses. Barrett explains, "Paul is asking, "Do you suppose that there are fragments of Christ that can be distributed among different groups?"[27] Part of Paul's argument comes from the baptism of believers: "Or were you baptized in the name of Paul? I thank God that I baptized none of you except Crispus and Gaius, so that no one may say that you were baptized in my name" (vv.13–15). Paul argues in a similar way in Eph 4:3–6, to admonish believers to unity. In this case he pictures the church as a body (v.4). In verse 5 he emphasizes again "one Lord" and "one baptism." By their organic unity to Christ, by their adherence to his name, and by

24. Küng, *The Church*, 389.

25. Toon, "Episcopalianism," 23.

26. Fee, *First Corinthians*, 48.

27. Barrett, *First Epistle to the Corinthians*, 46.

their confession of Christ in baptism, believers are bound to one another and need only exercise this existing unity for it to be experienced in church life.

Another instance of Paul exhorting believers to unity on the basis of the lordship of Christ is given in his prayer that the Roman Christians will "be of the same mind with one another according to Christ Jesus; that with one accord you may with one voice glorify the God and Father of our Lord Jesus Christ" (Rom 15:5–6). Paul does not mean "to come to the same opinion," but rather, "despite their differences of opinion [to have] a common perspective and purpose."[28] The universal and direct lordship of Christ in every believer and in the church prohibits all party spirit in the church. Factions can only be formed in a church in direct contradiction of this truth.

The Authority of Scripture

In addition to the authority of Jesus the Messiah, the early church followed the Scriptures as authoritative (2 Tim 3:16–17). The words of Scripture are the voice of God, and obedience or disobedience to them has consequences (Heb 3:7–19). For the apostles, this scriptural authority extends beyond the Old Testament: Paul identifies Luke 10:7 as Scripture (see 1 Tim 5:18); Peter puts the writings of Paul on equal footing with the Old Testament Scriptures for the church (2 Pet 3:15–16); at times, Paul identifies his own gospel preaching as the Word of God (1 Thess 2:13); and the Apostle John asserts that those who truly belong to God are the same people as those who receive apostolic teaching (1 John 4:6; cf. John 8:47). Huther explains the 1 John passage in the following way: "That the πνεῦμα τῆς πλάνης prevails in the false prophets, may be known by this, that *the world* hears them; that in us, on the contrary, the πνεῦμα τῆς ἀληθείας dwells, may be perceived by this, that those who know God, i.e., *the children of God*, hear us."[29]

The writings of the apostles, including those of 1 and 2 Peter and Paul's pastoral letters (which will be argued as apostolic in the next chapter), would have been taken as authoritative in their statements about church order. The early church was not left to create its own church structure.

28. Moo, *Romans*, 871.
29. Huther, *James, Peter, John, and Jude*, 583.

The Authority of the Spirit

The church also looked to the Holy Spirit as an authority for its actions and decisions (Acts 13:2–4; 15:28; 16:6; 20:28). Before his betrayal and crucifixion, Jesus promised to give the Holy Spirit to the disciples (something promised, in fact, to all Christians, cf. John 7:38–39). The Holy Spirit would take the truth of Jesus and further teach the church (John 16:13–15; Eph 3:4–5). His leadership of the Christians was to be expected (Rom 8:14). Resisting his direction was a serious sin (Acts 5:3–4; 1 Cor 3:16–17; Gal 5:25; Eph 4:30; Heb 10:15). It is the Spirit of God who gives the church a basis of unity. To experience this unity, Christians must act according to the teachings of the Spirit (Eph 4:1–4).

To summarize the teaching of the New Testament on church authority to this point, authority for the church has three sources: Jesus the Messiah himself, who is Lord; the Holy Scriptures, including the teaching of the apostles; and the Holy Spirit. According to Jesus and the apostles, these three authorities function harmoniously. Though the statements of a group of Christians may be accepted as authoritative for given situations (e.g., the church in Jerusalem in Acts 15, or the whole church when it exercises the power of the keys, as described in Matt 18:15–18), there is no other continuing authority for the church beyond these three entities. All three address all believers on a common level. In the New Testament, there is no elevated access to the Son, the Scripture, or the Spirit for any Christian when compared to any other Christian.

LEADERSHIP AMONG EQUAL DISCIPLES

Although Jesus taught that there was equality among his disciples, it would be wrong to conclude that there was no designated human authority in the early church. The movement of the followers of Jesus, which ultimately became the church, needed organization. It is impossible to function in a community without structure.[30] For that reason, Jesus appointed disciples to be his closest companions and, after his ascension to heaven, to lead the church (Mark 3:14–15; Acts 1:15–21). Jesus also gave Peter special instructions about being a shepherd to God's people in John 21:15–19.[31] Peter thus became an example to all who afterward would hold the pastoral office.

---

30. Horrell, *From the Ground Up*, 69.

31. Bruce, *Training of the Twelve*, 520, points out the nature of Peter's commission as

Equality of the followers of Jesus and organization in the church are not mutually exclusive concepts. This is the recurring error of the so-called "Protestant Consensus." Hans von Campenhausen, one of the most recent proponents of the Protestant Consensus, charges, "Paul knows of no 'obedience' in the strict sense of the word toward those in authority within the congregation."[32] Instead, the Holy Spirit endows Christians directly with gifts and authority, which ends when the people pass from the scene.[33] Campenhausen asserts that "Paul's own characteristic concern [was] to refract and relativize all authority in order to ensure the freedom of the congregation and their direct contact with Christ."[34]

This view of the Protestant Consensus can only be maintained by asserting that Paul did not write the Pastoral Epistles and that the references to elders in the book of Acts are "Lukan fictions."[35] Harris notes, "The cornerstone of this new approach was found in the opposition between Pauline and Jewish Christianity."[36] In 1831, F. C. Baur was the first to present this scenario based on Hegelian dialectic thought, and more recently Steinhauser echoes Baur in his assessment of the development of church order:

> This development may be understood in the light of two tensions which existed within the early church. The first tension is the relationship between Jewish and Gentile Christianity and the second the relationship between charism and institution. The offices and functions which grew out of these tensions existed initially parallel to and indeed sometimes in conflict with one another until eventually after a period of transition they evolved into a definite synthesis.[37]

Steinhauser's statement above is, in essence, identical to the view of Baur, as described in chapter 1. (Namely, charismatic gifts strike a contrast with established offices. These two were ultimately synthesized into the later church order.)

---

being one of example: "Had that passionate man, in some senses the strongest character among the twelve, been in other senses the weakest, then who could better illustrate men's need of shepherding?"

32. Campenhausen, *Ecclesiastical Authority*, 69.

33. Ibid.

34. Ibid., 117.

35. Holmberg, *Paul and Power*, 106.

36. Harris, *The Tübingen School*, 181.

37. Steinhauser, "Authority in the Primitive Church," 89.

The view of the conflict between charismatic gifts and established offices also lacks historical proof. Hanson, after reviewing the statements of
Irenaeus, Tertullian, Clement of Alexandria, and Hippolytus, concludes,

> On the question of charismatic persons and gifts, the men of the
> second and third centuries took positions which were not as clear-
> cut and stereotyped as might be thought. We do not find here a
> simple taking of positions on the one side or the other "between
> Rome and Sohm," in E. Schweizer's epigrammatic phrase.[38]

The idea that fixed offices and charismatic gifts are in conflict with
one another is patently based on circular reasoning, namely, that Paul did
not establish a fixed church order because the writings which are truly his
have no fixed church order. Writings claiming to be from Paul which teach
church order cannot be from his hand, because he taught no church order.[39]
Burtchaell points out the ideology which has driven the Protestant Consensus for the past 150 years:

> As one looks back over the library that had been a-building on our
> topic since the 1850s, one must remark that despite the fact that
> the arts and sciences of biblical exegesis and historical research
> had matured over the years, and despite the increased sophisti-
> cation of critical method used in these studies, the influence of
> ideology has, if anything, increased.[40]

The idea that fixed offices and charismatic gifts must be in conflict
with one another neglects a very basic understanding of human activity;
namely, that groups which exist for any length of time require organization.
Even the democracy of Athens required the βουλή (council) in order to
function in a reasonable fashion. The βουλή set the agenda for all meetings
of the ἐκκλησία.[41] Beckwith's statement, mentioned in chapter 1, is worth
repeating here:

---

38. Hanson, *Studies in Christian Antiquity*, 120–41.

39. Burtchaell, *From Synagogue to Church*, 184.

40. Ibid., 148.

41. Jones, *The Greek City*, 164. "All Greek cities, however democratic, recognized
that the primary assembly was a dangerously irresponsible body, and therefore, while
leaving to it the ultimate decision on every point of importance, took care that no ill-
considered proposal could be suddenly sprung upon it and passed in a snap decision. One
precaution, which seems to have been universal, was that no measure might be brought
before the assembly which had not been considered and approved by the council."

> It is therefore reasonable to ask whether the basic assumption underlying the liberal reconstruction of primitive Christianity, namely, that the free exercise of spiritual gifts and formal structures cannot co-exist but are mutually exclusive, is not a simplistic mistake? May it not rather be the case that the exercise of varieties of gifts by Christians in general, what is often called "every member ministry," *demands* formal structures, if it is to be fruitful?[42]

Greg Ogden, who emphasizes the teaching of 1 Corinthians about the gifting of every church member and their participation in ministry, adds, "It will come as no surprise, therefore, that in the same passage where Paul defines the essential nature of the church as an organism, the body of Christ, he also affirms the necessity of institution or order."[43] The lack of order leads to chaos. Leaders and continuity are essential to any movement of any significant size.

One might be tempted to think that the church as conceived by the Protestant Consensus is altogether an academic exercise. It is hardly identifiable in history. But whether by intention or accident, Frank Viola's view and practice of church life is essentially the Protestant Consensus in existential form. He contends that the early house-church meeting, which is the pattern for today's church, included "the absence of any human officiation." The church patterned after the New Testament "is clergyless, liturgyless, programless, and ritualless." It will not have any full-time, paid ministers, and the superintending of elders has a mostly passive function. "The New Testament," he says, knows no officers and "downplays the role of elders."[44]

Fairly early in the history of the Christian movement, local leaders designated as elders and deacons were established in local churches (Acts 6:1–6; 11:30; 14:23). Sometimes leaders are not designated by these names; nevertheless, their leadership and teaching are commended (1 Thess 5:12–13; Heb 13:17). Elders in particular are exhorted to teach the Word of God (Acts 20:28) and lead by example (1 Pet 5:1–4), and other church members are exhorted to submit to their leadership and teaching. This is the pattern mentioned in several places in the New Testament, which undercuts both Viola's and the Protestant Consensus' view of church order. In the Acts 6 passage, both the numbers and the ministry of the first deacons were well-defined. Their work in the new church gives the appearance of a necessary

42. Beckwith, *Elders in Every City*, 17.
43. Ogden, *The New Reformation*, 46.
44. Viola, *Reimagining the Church*, 55, 63, 162–63, 170, 184.

permanence. In 1 Peter 5 elders are to pattern their ministry after that of Jesus. His superintending was and is anything but a passive function.

It will be helpful to examine three prominent leaders in the New Testament church—Peter, James, and Paul—to get a better idea of how leadership functioned among equal disciples. Joseph Ratzinger claims, "That the primacy of Peter is recognizable in all the major strands of the New Testament is incontestable."[45] Indeed, Peter appears almost autocratic in his interaction with Ananias and Sapphira in Acts 5. However, he is confronting a deceptive corruption entering the body. On closer examination it is evident that Peter's statements must be understood as prophetic: "How is it that you have agreed together to test the Spirit of the Lord? Behold, the feet of those who have buried your husband are at the door, and they will carry you out" (9). The same analysis must be applied to Peter's statement to Simon Magus in Acts 8:20–23. The prophetic gift, however, does not determine primacy in the church.

The New Testament, therefore, does not substantiate Ratzinger's statement, for Peter rarely asserts his authority. In fact, he accepts the leadership of James at the meeting of the Jerusalem Church in Acts 15 and the correction of Paul while in Antioch (Gal 2:11; in 2 Pet 3:15–16, it is evident that he accepts the correction). Peter even submits his actions to the judgment of the body of believers in Jerusalem (Acts 11:1–17). In Peter's epistles, he adopts a method of appeal. He certainly addresses his readers as a preacher would, but there is no note of *ex cathedra* dogma. The tone of his epistles strikes a vivid contrast with the writings of Cyprian, for example, who stresses the authority of the bishop. Although Peter is prominent in Acts 1–12, he only appears once after that (chapter 15). Indeed, if anyone besides Christ is pre-eminent in the New Testament, it is the apostle Paul.

The teaching of the Catholic Church further declares that Peter's authority is passed on to all successive bishops of Rome. Ratzinger states that "the Roman Primacy, or, rather, the acknowledgement of Rome as the criterion of the right apostolic faith, is older than the canon of the New Testament."[46] In fact, no Roman bishop claimed this authority for himself prior to the late second century CE (Stephen I). As previously mentioned, Jesus gave Peter the special task of shepherding the flock of God (John 21:15–17). However, this commission involved no anointing or laying on

45. Ratzinger, *Called to Communion*, 64.
46. Ibid., 70.

of hands. It would be a leadership on the basis of gifts and character with a dependence on the Spirit of Jesus.

The Lord was using Peter as an example. That this is the case is demonstrated by Peter's address to all the elders of the churches to whom he writes (1 Peter 5:1–4). He does not identify a successor, but rather passes on the commission to the elders of each local church. The first Roman bishop to use Matt 16:18 to assert Rome's superior authority was Damasus (366–384).[47] Even Schatz, who defends the papacy, admits that it does not have its origin in the New Testament:

> If one had asked a Christian in the year 100, 200 or even 300 whether the bishop of Rome was the head of all Christians, or whether there was a supreme bishop over all the other bishops and having the last word in questions affecting the whole Church, he or she would certainly have said no.[48]

Ratzinger's statements regarding Peter's (and with it Rome's) primacy are not historically accurate. In addition, his assertion does not follow any biblical precedent. When successors were necessary in biblical tradition, their designation was explicit (e.g., Moses and Joshua, David and Solomon, Elijah and Elisha). The actual primacy of Peter in the New Testament and the Roman Catholic interpretation of his primacy are contrasted by Calvin. His explanation is a fitting conclusion to the preceding discussion:

> If one man presided over twelve, will it follow that one ought to preside over a hundred thousand? That twelve had one among them to direct all is nothing strange. Nature admits, the human mind requires, that in every meeting, though all are equal in power, there should be one as a kind of moderator to whom the others should look up. There is not senate without a council, no bench of judges without a president or chancellor, no college without a provost, no company without a master. Thus there would be no absurdity were we to confess that the apostles had conferred such

47. Küng, *Christianity*, 313. Schatz points out that in 341 CE, Bishop Julius had already asserted Roman primacy for all of Christendom in matters of doctrinal controversy. Schatz, *Der Päpstliche Primat*, 38.

48. Schatz, *Der Päpstliche Primat*, 14. This quote follows the translation of Otto and Maloney, *Papal Primacy*, 3. Schatz goes on to say that this is the wrong question, and that primacy in those centuries was not thought of in the same terms that 19th and 20th century writers mean, 3. But this is surely a wrong assertion. The leading priest of Rome was called the *pontifex maximus*. This was a term whose use stretches back to the days of the Roman Republic. In the days of the Roman Empire, this title was taken over by the emperor himself. It later came to designate the Roman bishop.

a primacy on Peter. But an arrangement which is effectual among a few must not be forth-with transferred to the whole world, which no one man is able to govern.[49]

There is no question that James, the brother of Jesus, was a leader in directing and molding the early Christian movement. Though James was not one of the twelve apostles, he was an authority in Jerusalem and is named in a prominent way in the book of Acts (15:13, 21:18). Because Herod did not try to kill James the brother of Jesus at the same time he apprehended James the brother of John and Peter, it is likely that James did not become the prominent leader of the church in Jerusalem until after the events of Acts 12.[50] By the time of the Jerusalem meeting in Acts 15, James has obviously become the spokesman for the Jerusalem church; Paul calls James one of the "pillars" of the Jerusalem church (Gal 2:9).[51]

> In the ancient world, where the pillars which support a building were an essential feature of most substantial buildings, the pillar was a natural image of someone who stands firm in support of others or of an institution or ideal. It could also designate an important person or leader in a community. Such usage can be found not only in classical, but also in Jewish and early Christian literature.[52]

Outside of Scripture, both Ignatius and Papias refer to James as the bishop of the Jerusalem church (Ign., *Trall.* 7.7; Papias, *Fragments* 10). There is, however, no description of his authority beyond leadership in the Jerusalem church. His letter to other Jewish churches is authoritative. But again, there are no *ex cathedra* statements in its five chapters.

The Apostle Paul is the one human personality, after Jesus himself, mentioned most frequently in the New Testament history of the church. As one would expect, Paul's exercise of authority has been analysed more than any other New Testament figure outside of Christ. Duke lists five ways in which Paul exercises authority toward churches:

1. as a father (1 Cor 4:14–16; Phil 3:17)

2. entreaty (2 Cor 8:8; 2 Thess 2:1)

---

49. Calvin, *Institutes*, 4.6.8.

50. Bauckham, "James and the Jerusalem Church," 441.

51. Whether one interprets Gal 2:9 as referring to the meeting in Acts 15 or to an earlier meeting, the status of James would be the same.

52. Bauckham, "James and the Jerusalem Church," 444.

3. command (1 Cor 7:10; 11:17, 1 Thess 4:2)

4. apostolic *exousia* (2 Cor 10:8; 13:10)

5. humility (Rom 12:3; Phil 2:3)[53]

When Paul uses command, it is always with reference to apostolic tradition already taught.[54]

Paul understands himself to be one who speaks for God (1 Thess 2:1–4; 1 Tim 2:5–7); however, he only appeals to his position as apostle infrequently. Whenever Paul mentions his apostleship in salutations, "He adds a qualifying phrase to support the uniqueness of his apostleship and thus the legitimacy of his authority to direct the Gentile work."[55] When Paul particularly emphasizes his apostleship in Galatians, he does so because "he has to prove the independence of his apostolate and show that he is not subordinate to the church in Jerusalem or inferior to its foremost apostle, Cephas."[56] When Paul requests an action of Philemon, he does not apply his authority from Christ as an apostle, but rather appeals to him on the basis of Christian love (Phlm 8–9). He does not command (ἐπιτάσσειν), he appeals (παρακαλῶ).

Paul's view of his authority is demonstrated in his interactions with his co-workers. Paul names over one hundred assistants in his mission work,[57] and his comments about them demonstrate a concept of shared authority (Phil 2:29; 1 Tim 4:12; Titus 1:5). Pillette points out that, though Paul directs the movements of his assistants, he relies on earned authority to obtain their compliance.[58] Various terms Paul uses show that he holds his co-workers to be on a common plane with himself, such as *fellow worker* (συνεργός–thirteen times), *fellow traveller* (συνέκδημος–once), *fellow soldier* (συστρατιώτης–twice), *yoke fellow* (σύζυγος–once), *partner* (κοινωνός– once), *fellow slave* (σύνδουλος–twice).[59]

---

53. Duke, "Apostolic Authority in the Primitive Church," 57–61. The last approach, humility, is not one that Paul depicts of himself, but urges others to practice (thus, assuming he does the same thing).

54. Ibid., 59.

55. Pillette, "Paul and His Fellow Workers," 29.

56. Holmberg, *Paul and Power*, 29.

57. Ellis, "Paul and His Co-workers," 437–38.

58. Pillette, "Paul and His Fellow Workers," 3.

59. Ibid., 92–136.

Eckhard Schnabel explains that exegetes are sometimes confused about Paul's authority because they neglect the context of his ministry. Paul functioned in widely different roles in his travels. His authority varied in accordance with his role:

> Paul was at different times in differing roles, sometimes simultaneously: cross-cultural missionary traveling from region to region, evangelist in a city, pastor of a local congregation, counselor, coordinator of the affairs of churches in an interregional framework (the bishop or superintendent of today), leader of a missionary team, teacher of co-workers, teacher of new converts, theologian, author of theological writings, author of hymns (perhaps), and leather worker who needed to earn money. A missionary who explores new territory without any existing models, who is ready to value co-workers more than self, who is prepared to carry the cross daily, is using every opportunity for preaching the good news of Jesus Christ, and striving to nurture new believers in any way necessary.[60]

Peter, Paul and James demonstrate their comprehension of Jesus' teachings on authority rather well, namely to be servants, not to be lords, and to regard all other Christians as brothers who are on the same spiritual plane as themselves. Although Holmberg is making a general evaluation, he summarizes their concept of authority in the following way:

> All authority is considered as ultimately flowing from the same source, viz. the Founder of the Church, and this is recognized as being the basis for the legitimacy of the exercise of authority in the Church. This is why all local churches stand in a relation to one another as parts of one and the same Church. All local leaders, itinerant missionaries and apostles stand in relation to others on the same or another level.[61]

THE MEANING OF EKKLESIA

The entity Jesus Christ established was the church. As the term translated *church*, ἐκκλησία, is used 115 times in the New Testament, its meaning helps define how the church functions. In classical usage, ἐκκλησία was the most inclusive word to describe an assembly. In its most basic definition,

60. Schnabel, *Early Christian Mission*, 1:428–29.

61. Holmberg, *Paul and Power*, 193.

it was "an assembly duly summoned."[62] The secular usage of ἐκκλησία normally meant the full assembly of all who possessed the rights of citizenship.[63] "The word belonged to language of the political sphere and was especially at home in democracy."[64] Though the ἐκκλησία had religious aspects in the Hellenistic world, it was never used for a religious group prior to Christianity. In fact, its secular usage has retained the idea of "assembly" throughout its history.[65] Campbell emphasizes this phenomenon, saying, "Even in New Testament times the specific sense, of an assembly of the citizens, continued to be the most common meaning of the word."[66]

Earl Radmacher notes that "when the Christian church annexed it for its purposes, *ekklesia* was already a word with a history, and a double history–both Jewish and Greek."[67] Part of this history was its use in the Septuagint (LXX), where it occurs eighty times. In the LXX, ἐκκλησία is used to translate the Hebrew word קָהָל. Though one might expect ἐκκλησία to acquire a specifically religious connotation, in fact this never happens.[68] Unlike the Greek πόλις, the assembly of Israel only met on special occasions. Like the Greek πόλις, one had to be present to be a part of the assembly.[69] The LXX does use ἐκκλησία in combination for the term, "the assembly of the LORD" (Deut 23:1–3). This assembly was determinative for all later assemblies (see Josh 8:35; 1 Kgs 8:14, 12:3; 1 Chr 13:2; the expression in these passages is "congregation of Israel"). For Philo, who used the LXX, ἐκκλησία retained the Hellenistic, even political, meaning for Israel (*Spec.* 2.3.44). But likewise, for him the ἐκκλησία of Israel is also the ἐκκλησία τοῦ θεοῦ.

In the New Testament, ἐκκλησία retains its meaning of assembly. Linton claims that the Hellenistic meaning of the word cannot be eliminated from the Christian meaning, since, for example, in both instances the ἐκκλησία was the assembly.[70] The Christian ἐκκλησία had various similari-

---

62. *LSJ*, 509.

63. *RAC*, 4:905.

64. *RAC*, 4:906.

65. Ward, "*Ekklesia*: A Word Study," 165.

66. Campbell, "Origin and Meaning of EKKLHSIA," 132.

67. Radmacher, *The Nature of the Church*, 115.

68. Johnston, *The Doctrine of the Church*, 35; Campbell, "Origin and Meaning of EKKLHSIA," 132–33.

69. Radmacher, *The Nature of the Church*, 131.

70. *RAC*, 4:906.

ties with the Hellenistic ἐκκλησία, including hymns and prayer (Eph 5:19), speaking, order (the problem of order, as in 1 Cor 14:40, was an issue in the Hellenistic assembly as well), formal agreements, sending of messengers (Acts 15:25), exclusion (1 Corinthians 5), and sending of letters about decisions (Acts 15:22).[71] Berger concludes, "In many details of concrete examples the Christian *ekklesia* is truly comparable to the Jewish-Hellenistic and the secular-Hellenistic *ekklesia*."[72]

For Paul, the word most commonly means the local church. However, in his letters Paul extends the meaning of Christ's ἐκκλησία beyond that of "assembly," in that he uses it to denote God's new people, whether assembled or not (1 Cor 10:32; Eph 1:22; 3:10; 5:23; Col 1:18). Ward notes, "This is not a development which can be detected prior to Christian history, and the change is probably to be explained strictly as a Christian phenomenon."[73] There are three primary theological conclusions to this phenomenon. The first is to interpret ἐκκλησία to mean both the local and universal church.[74] The second is to interpret Paul's use of ἐκκλησία as the beginning of the concept of the universal church, including regional churches.[75] The third is to interpret ἐκκλησία as the Christian assembly, whether assembled locally or participating in the eschatological, heavenly assembly.[76]

Kevin Giles sees the primary meaning of ἐκκλησία in a theological context as "the Christian community."[77] In so doing, he actually re-defines ἐκκλησία in the New Testament to mean "community" and not "assembly" at all. The reason that most have not understood this, Giles claims, is "because our cultural glasses, heavily tinted by Western individualism, hinder us from seeing what is in the text."[78] It should be noted that Giles is not alone in giving this meaning to ἐκκλησία; Ratzinger, for instance, says the same thing.[79] In a similar way, Getz broadens the definition of ἐκκλησία.

---

71. Berger, "Volksversammlung und Gemeinde Gottes," 178–82. Berger is not asserting that these activities are the exclusive domain of the Hellenistic ἐκκλησία. Worship, for instance, involved prayers and hymns, regardless of assembly.

72. Ibid., 184. Translation by the writer.

73. Ward, "*Ekklesia*: A Word Study," 168.

74. Calvin, *Institutes*, 4.1.3.

75. Giles, *What on Earth is the Church?*; Ratzinger, *Called to Communion*.

76. O'Brien, "The Church as a Heavenly Entity," 88–119.

77. Giles, *What on Earth is the Church?*, 15–19.

78. Ibid., 100.

79. Ratzinger, *Called to Communion*, 29–31.

Though he does not assign a particular English word, his definition is, essentially, "Christians, wherever they are." Note his explanation:

> In defining the "church," we tend to focus on the literal definition of the word *ekklesia*, which actually means an "assembly" or "congregation" of people. However, this definition is too narrow when we observe the way believers functioned in the New Testament world. Biblical writers used the word to describe Christians whether they were gathered for worship and practicing certain rituals or scattered throughout a particular community–in their homes, at work, shopping, visiting relatives, or recreating at the local spa. Furthermore, each believing family in a given community, ideally speaking, was to be the "church in miniature" and the father the primary spiritual leader (1 Timothy 3:4–5).

Because Giles presents the most comprehensive explanation for a new definition, the remainder of this discussion will interact primarily with his arguments. He explains his choice of the definition, "community," first by arguing that secular usage of ἐκκλησία in the time of the New Testament had little influence on its scriptural meaning.[80] Secondly, he asserts that in later Judaism (including the LXX), the ἐκκλησία τοῦ κυρίου (and thus also the Hebrew, קָהָל) came to mean "the covenant community of God."[81] In this he follows Schürer.[82] The church then replaced Israel as the "new community of God."[83] According to Giles, Nehemiah 13:1 actually "anticipates the New Testament title, 'the church of God.'"[84]

There are several problems with Giles' explanation. First, Schürer's four Talmud passages, used to prove the concept, do not hold up to closer scrutiny.[85] Second, the Hebrew words קָהָל and עֵדָה[86] "do not occur in any of the important passages which describe or imply the distinctive position of Israel as a peculiar people. Their use is mainly confined to historical parts

---

80. Giles, *What on Earth is the Church?*, 4–8, 23–25, 230–40.

81. Ibid., 230–40.

82. Schürer, *History of the Jewish People*, 2:429–30.

83. Giles, *What on Earth is the Church?*, 63, 108–18, 154–57. In 1 Peter, Israel "almost ceases to exist," 164.

84. Ibid., 235.

85. Hort, *The Christian Ecclesia*, 15.

86. עֵדָה likewise means "assembly" and is used to denote the nation of Israel in assembly. However, it is never translated as ἐκκλησία in the LXX.

of the historical book. They have no place in the greater prophecies having what we call a Messianic import."[87]

The absence of קָהָל and עֵדָה in any of these passages of the Old Testament, it would seem, is a serious problem for the interpretation of Schürer, Giles, and Ratzinger. Third, the evidence to demonstrate that ἐκκλησία meant "covenant community" in Jewish writings outside of the New Testament is completely lacking. Fourth, as Ward argues,

> If *ekklesia* had come to mean, People of God, or Israel of God, through the Hebrew *qahal*, it is difficult to understand why N.T. writers do not use it as evidence when trying to prove that Christians are the People of God; Paul does not use it in Rom. 1–15, nor does Peter in 1 Pet. 2:4–10.[88]

Finally, Giles gives little reason for rejecting the influence of ἐκκλησία from secular Greek. Berger contends, in quite the opposite direction, that ἐκκλησία, as it appears in historical passages in the LXX, is clearly influenced by the Hellenistic concept.[89] If Giles is to be convincing, he must more fully explain his rejection of the influence of secular Greek. Radmacher, who bases his summary on two exhaustive studies of the use of ἐκκλησία in the LXX, concludes, "All uses of the word never go beyond the simple meaning of assembly."[90]

David Peterson suggests that Giles has, in fact, lost the biblical sense of ἐκκλησία: "Despite his arguments to the contrary, Giles has let go of the congregational or assembly aspect of this terminology, replacing it with 'community' as the fundamental notion."[91] It appears that, in this instance, Giles commits the error which James Barr calls "reading the maximum possible theological content into a linguistic choice."[92]

Addressing the concept of the universal church, Ferguson states, "The idea of assembly is not lost even in the extension of the word to the

87. Hort, *The Christian Ecclesia*, 12.

88. Ward, *"Ekklesia: A Word Study,"* 167.

89. Berger, "Volksversammlung und Gemeinde Gottes," 185: "Man kann nicht glaubhaft machen, das frühe Christentum habe bei der Verwendung des Begriffes per se an das Bundesvolk des Dtn denken müssen. Dagegen kommt der Begriff in der überwiegende Anzahl der Belege in 1.2 Chr, in Sir und bei Philo vor, stellenweise deutlich hellenistisch beeinflusst und überall mit Gegenwartsbezug."

90. Radmacher, *The Nature of the Church*, 129. The exhaustive studies are those of Hort, *The Christian Ecclesia*, and Baker, "Development of the Study of Ecclesiology."

91. Peterson, "The 'Locus' of the Church."

92. Barr, *Semantics of Biblical Language*, 9.

universal people of God, for in the background is the eschatological assembly of all the saved . . . (2 Thess 2:1; Matt 24:3)."[93] The fact that ἐκκλησία retains its concept of "assembly" throughout the New Testament indicates that the people of the New Testament churches viewed themselves as an assembly, and thus, among other things, a decision-making body. The word itself does not prove this, but its very meaning makes it likely that the early churches practiced group decision-making.

THE PRIESTHOOD OF THE BELIEVER

The New Testament teaching of the priesthood of all believers (1 Pet 2:5–9) indicates that every believer in Christ is capable of spiritual worship and ministry. It also has a leveling effect in terms of each member's standing before God. Küng says, "Christians are not subjects, but rulers together with Christ, are not profane men confronting the sanctuary, but priests through Christ: 'Thou has made them a kingdom and priests to our God, and they shall reign on earth' (Rev 5:10)."[94] All Christians are already equipped and are expected to involve themselves in spiritual ministry. In Romans 12, Paul charges every Christian (v. 3), exhorting them, "Having gifts that differ according to the grace given to us, let us use them" (v. 6). Since the believer is a gifted priest, he should be able to make decisions about his ministry. In some cases, where decisions involve multiple ministries or multiple leaders, a collective decision among the priests is required.

This emphasis on the priesthood of the believer and his standing before God has in recent decades been criticized as "individualistic." Horton argues that this individualism in Evangelicalism stems from both pietism and the Enlightenment (which he blames, in part, on pietism).[95] According to Stanley Grenz and others, the highly individualistic character of evangelicalism is characterized by "private Bible reading," "private prayer," and "being saved as an individual."[96] Horton contends that this error can only be corrected by a return to interpretation of Scripture in the community, which means a return to tradition.[97] Roger Olson answers the critics

93. Ferguson, *The Church of Christ*, 132.

94. Küng, *The Church*, 373.

95. Horton, *Made in America*, 23–27, 108–9.

96. Grenz, *Revisioning Evangelical Theology*, 50. Chan, *Spiritual Theology*, 116. Bingham, "Evangelicals, Irenaeus, and the Bible," 34–38.

97. Horton, *Made in America*, 177.

of the individualism found in Evangelicalism, countering that "it would be good to remember, of course, that Protestantism itself appears hopelessly individualistic to adherents of the Eastern Orthodox and Roman Catholic traditions."[98] Likewise, the individualism of Free Churches and Evangelicals is not the individualism of the Enlightenment, "but the strong belief in the priesthood of believers that energized the Protestant Reformation and especially radical Protestantism of the sixteenth century."[99]

Indeed, Olson's argument is confirmed many times over by the writings of the Reformers and later Protestant writers. For example, Luther praises the position of the believer-priest: "Who could ever imagine the honor and exaltation of the Christian? . . . Through his priesthood, he is mighty before God, for God does what he asks and desires."[100] Likewise, Bunyan's story of the Christian in *The Pilgrim's Progress*, written ahead of the Enlightenment and widely read by Christians in many countries, presents the road to salvation as very individualistic, finally being transacted between the lonely pilgrim and Christ alone. The believer, acting as priest, has direct contact with God the Father through Christ. His ability to interact with God directly leads one to expect that each genuine believer can participate with a community of believers in decisions that communities undertake.

The Direct Ministry of the Holy Spirit in Every Believer

The Bible teaches the indwelling of the Holy Spirit in every believer (Rom 8:9; 1 Cor 6:19; Gal 4:6). In its very essence, the experience of receiving the Holy Spirit frees the sinner to choose the right way of living and thinking (Rom 8:2–4):

> The working of the Holy Spirit shows itself chiefly in the "testing" (*dokimazein*), that is, in the capacity of forming the correct Christian ethical judgment at each given moment, and specifically of forming it in connection with the knowledge of the redemptive

98. Olson, "Free Church Ecclesiology," 170.

99. Ibid.

100. Luther, "Von der Freiheit eines Christenmenschen," in *Luther Deutsch*, ed. Aland, 2:28. Translation by the writer.

process, in which, indeed, the Holy Spirit is a decisive figure. This "testing" is the key to all New Testament ethics.[101]

Banks summarizes Paul's view of Christian freedom in the following scheme of three components:

1. Independence (from sin, the law, death; for righteousness, conformity to Jesus, and suffering)

2. Dependence (upon Christ and upon the Spirit)

3. Interdependence (with others, since liberty leads to service; with the world, since the universe itself will be transformed)[102]

The Bible also teaches that each believer can expect that he or she will receive guidance from the Spirit of God. This truth, in fact, is stated in the Old Testament (Ps 143:10). On the night before his death, Jesus announces to his disciples that he will be departing from them. Up to this time, he has been their advisor, teacher, and guide. In John 14:16–18, Jesus tells his disciples that he will not leave them as orphans, but that the Holy Spirit will come in his place. This will create a new spiritual working between the Trinity and believers in Jesus. "Jesus had been a teacher and leader, but his influence was that of external word and example. The Spirit, however, is able to affect one more intensely because, dwelling within, he can get to the very center of one's thinking and emotions."[103]

In his epistles, as noted above, Paul instructs believers that this principle, given by Christ to the eleven, holds true for each of them as well. This ministry of the Spirit, which also includes guidance, is unmediated (Gal 5:16–18; Rom 8:14). Smeaton explains this phenomenon in the following way: "The expression, 'led by the Spirit' refers to an inward prompting, impulse, and inclination, which so rules and guides them that they cannot omit duty or neglect privilege."[104] Thus, each Christian in a community of believers can expect to be led by the Spirit.[105] The truth of the leading of the Spirit would logically anticipate that in decisions which affect an entire

101. Cullmann, *Christ and Time*, 228.

102. Banks, *Paul's Idea of Community*, 25.

103. Erickson, *Christian Theology*, 874.

104. Smeaton, *Doctrine of the Holy Spirit*, 81.

105. Moo, *Romans*, 498, says that this probably means "to have the direction of one's life as a whole determined by the Spirit." But if the Spirit is on the inside of the believer, helping him make correct ethical decisions, the guidance of the Spirit would be far more than just the direction of one's life as a whole.

church, the Holy Spirit could potentially lead every one of the people in the church to that decision.

The ministry of the Holy Spirit in the believer extends to the ability to understand Scripture and interpret it correctly (1 Cor 2:10–11; 1 John 2:20, 27). The teaching of the Bible is particularly the domain of teachers (Eph 4:11–13; Heb 13:7, 17); however, the understanding of the Bible is not their exclusive domain. In fact, the average believer should be at a level of competence that he can himself teach others (Col 3:16; Heb 5:12). For this reason, though obviously teachers should guide the church in decisions about doctrine, any believer should be qualified to participate.

Luther was one of the first in modern times to extend this discerning ability of Christians to their right to choose their teachers. He did so by combining the teaching of 1 John 2 with John 10:1ff and Matt 7:15. For Luther, the ability to understand the Scriptures and the ability to choose pastors went hand-in-hand. Thus, he says, it is the task of the people of a local church to choose their pastors.[106] Calvin agrees with Luther's assessment as well.[107] One hundred years later Turretin strongly affirmed these evaluations. One of his many arguments for the choice of the pastor by the church includes the same points made by Luther regarding the ability of the believer to understand Scripture and to recognize false teachers.[108]

Getz argues that the choosing of leaders for the church requires maturity, and therefore not every Christian is allowed to participate in the decision.[109] However, maturity is never presented in the Scriptures as a requirement for choosing a leader; maturity is only required to be chosen as a leader (1 Tim 3:6). Getz has thus incorrectly expanded the requirements for leaders to those who choose leaders.

Finally, the Holy Spirit gives each Christian the ability to perform ministry in the church (1 Corinthians 12; Rom 12:3–8; Eph 4:7–13). Divinely-empowered ministry implies divine authority for the task. These phenomena make all believers (potentially) capable of participating in corporate decision-making in the church. Diversity in Spirit gifts (1 Cor 12:4–6) would imply diversity in aspects of church order. The gifting of the

---

106. Luther, "Das eine christliche Versammlung oder Gemeinde Recht und Macht habe, alle Lehre zu beurteilen und Lehrer zu berufen, ein- und abzusetzen, Grund und Ursache aus der Schrift," in *Luther Deutsch*, ed. Aland, 6:47–55, §§ 409–14.

107. Calvin, *Institutes*, 4.3.15.

108. Turretin, *Institutes*, 3:228.

109. Getz, *Elders and Leaders*, 208.

members of the church extends to the organization, unity, and perfection of the whole body (Eph 4:7–15). "The truth that each member of the church is equipped for ministry by the Lord through the Spirit would point again to a certain diffusion of authority throughout the entire church."[110]

Beyond the priesthood of the believer and the direct ministry of the Holy Spirit, there are other New Testament concepts which affect the way churches practice corporate decision-making. For instance, freedom in Christ gives the believer the ability to decide what is right (Rom 6:18; 8:2. 10:4; Gal 5:1; 1 Cor 9:19). This freedom anticipates that individual Christians and Christians as groups will make choices that are honoring to the Gospel. Then there is the command of Christ to love one-another (John 15:12–17), repeated by the apostles. Adherence to this command would not only qualify the subject and method of discussion in group meetings but also eliminate power struggles. Still another important concept for group decision-making is the exhortation to unity found frequently in the epistles (2 Cor 13:11: Phil 2:2); unity would guide and limit what is done in the corporate gathering.

Metaphors for the Church

Giles asserts that the concept of Christ's church includes more than simply the meaning of the word ἐκκλησία, and he is right.[111] Metaphors which further define the ἐκκλησία include the household, the body, the family, the temple, and the people of God. In this argument, Giles was preceded by Millard Erickson, Robert Banks, Alfred Kuen, Earl Radmacher, and Paul Minear.[112] Images serve as tools of rhetoric, a mode for perceiving a given reality, and for the advancement of self-understanding.[113] Thus the metaphors help explain the entity which Christ created in a way that the word ἐκκλησία alone cannot. These biblical concepts also play a role in defining how the assembled body of God's people made corporate decisions and in determining behavior in the church. Scott Bartchy explains their impact in the days of the early church:

110. Saucy, "Authority in the Church," 228.

111. See Giles, *What on Earth is the Church?*, 5.

112. Erickson, *Christian Theology*; Banks, *Paul's Idea of Community*; Kuen, *Gemeinde nach Gottes Bauplan*; Radmacher, *The Nature of the Church*; Minear, *Images of the Church*. Of all these books, Paul Minear's has been the most influential.

113. Minear, *Images of the Church*, 22–24.

The absence of a clear connection between religious worship and the inter-personal behavior of the worshipers had far-reaching consequences. While religious concerns were enmeshed in every crevice of Greco-Roman life, the concept of "god" (Greek, *theos*; Latin, D*eus*) did not bring to Gentile minds the practice of "fellowship," "community," or "close personal relationship."[114]

The Body

The body is Paul's most frequently used metaphor for the church and is the only metaphor which he directly equates with the church: "And God placed all things under his feet and appointed him to be head over everything for the church, which is his body, the fullness of him who fills everything in every way" (Eph 1:22–23, NIV). Likewise Paul tells the Colossian believers, "And he is the head of the body, the church" (Col 1:18). In 1 Cor 12:27 Paul states emphatically that the believers in the Corinthian church "are the body of Christ." Radmacher notes, "A comparison to the human body becomes for Paul the most descriptive and most accurate way to picture this corporate body of believers."[115] Giles adds, "It is no 'mere metaphor,' but a metaphor (like all powerful metaphors) that conveys something of the reality indicated by the words."[116] Minear, however, cautions that

> In some passages the church is explicitly identified with Christ's body, but in other passages this identification becomes very tenuous indeed. This variety of usage should warn us against seeking to produce a single inclusive definition of the image, and against importing into each occurrence of the analogy the range of meanings which it bears in other passages.[117]

Nevertheless, in many passages the equating of "the body" with the church is easily distinguishable.

In 1 Cor 12:13 Paul says, "For by one Spirit we were all baptized into one body, whether Jews or Greeks, whether slaves or free" (NASB). This union of the believer with the body of Christ is pictured in water baptism, where believers are baptized unto Christ's death (Rom 6:3–4). Minear notes

---

114. Bartchy, "Divine Power in Acts," 90.

115. Radmacher, *The Nature of the Church*, 235.

116. Giles, *What on Earth is the Church?*, 104.

117. Minear, *Images of the Church*, 174.

that Christians "cannot understand themselves as church apart from understanding their death to the law, their new belongingness, and their new vocation."[118] Referring to 1 Cor 12:13, Banks draws the following conclusion: "This suggests that wherever Christians are in relationship there is the body of Christ in its entirety, for Christ is truly and wholly present there through his Spirit (12:13). This is a momentous truth. We find here further confirmation of the high estimate Paul had of the local Christian community."[119]

Paul actually images the members of the church in Corinth as various body parts. The members of the Christian body share their delights and pains with each other.

> He does not say that experiences of individuals within the community, both pleasurable and sorrowful, should be shared by all the others who belong to it. He says instead that they *are* shared, whether consciously experienced or not. The "body" has a common nerve. There is a common life within it in which each is identified with the other–all in one, as it were, and one in all (12:26). The interrelationship of the individuals who make up the community could scarcely be more strongly emphasized.[120]

In the midst of his discourse on spiritual gifts in 1 Cor 12:27, Paul tells the Corinthian believers that they are part of Christ's body. In the next sentence he lists various gifts, thus pointing out their diversity. "This means that individually they are members with a variety of 'assigned' parts."[121] Banks adds, "It is precisely in this difference of function that the wholeness and unity of the body resides."[122] This aspect of the body of Christ teaches a mutuality in the body in which "each member encourages and builds up the others."[123]

Paul's mention of the church as the body of Christ in Col 1:18 gives special emphasis to Christ's headship.[124] The same is true in Eph 5:23,

118. Ibid., 176.

119. Banks, *Paul's Idea of Community*, 59.

120. Ibid., 60.

121. Fee, *First Corinthians*, 618.

122. Banks, *Paul's Idea of Community*, 60.

123. Erickson, *Christian Theology*, 1037–38.

124. Dunn, *Colossians and Philemon*, 95, asserts that the words *the church* "have in fact, been added. . . . And thereby the thought of the hymn has been abruptly wrenched from a consistent and rounded theme by identification of "the body" not with τὰ πάντα but with ἡ ἐκκλησία." Dunn is convinced that the epistle is using the Platonic-Stoic thought

where Paul states, "Christ is the head of the church, his body, and is himself its Savior." This is a crucial aspect of understanding the church, showing that all wrong ecclesiology is rooted in wrong Christology.[125] In the Col 1:18 passage, Paul uses the metaphor to emphasize Christ's superiority and priority in the church. Minear observes that "the thought of Jesus Christ as head thus articulates the perception of a single sovereignty with multiple threads binding him to his community."[126]

Paul picks up the theme again in Col 2:19. Regarding Christ as the head, he says, "From whom the whole body, nourished and knit together through its joints and ligaments, grows with a growth that is from God." Regarding this verse, Lightfoot comments, "The source of all (ἐξ οὗ) is Christ Himself the Head; but the channels of communication (διὰ τῶν κ.τ.λ.) are the different members of His body, in their relation one to another."[127] In the Ephesians passage, Paul emphasizes Christ's leadership of the church and his role in maintaining it. It is expected that the church will submit to Christ. "Paul projects boldly the idea that Christ is supreme. He has lordship and dominion over His church, precisely as the head rules the body."[128] Metzger draws the following conclusion: "Insofar as the members of the body are in subjection to and respond to orders from the head, the body is healthful and efficient; when such harmony does not prevail, there is discord and anarchy."[129]

A further aspect of the church as the body of Christ is the union of Jew and Gentile in this one body in Eph 2:14–16:

> For he himself is our peace, who has made us both one and has broken down in his flesh the dividing wall of hostility by abolishing the law of commandments and ordinances, that he might create in himself one new man in place of the two, so making peace, and might reconcile us both to God in one body through the cross, thereby killing the hostility.

Minear notes that "in the assertion of Jesus' headship was the emancipation of his community from the ingrained division between Jews and Greeks."[130]

---

of τὸ τοῦ κόσμου σῶμα. There is no textual evidence for Dunn's assertion, however.

125. Minear, *Images of the Church*, 208.
126. Ibid.
127. Lightfoot, *Colossians and Philemon*, 200.
128. Radmacher, *The Nature of the Church*, 238.
129. Metzger, "Paul's Vision of the Church," 55.
130. Minear, *Images of the Church*, 211.

The union created by Christ, overcoming this cultural and religious barrier is, mildly put, remarkable. If the headship of Jesus can overcome this barrier, it can eliminate all factions. In summary of this point, the church is the body of Christ. Christians are united to him and to one another. Christ is the head of the body and provides it with leadership. He deserves first place in everything in the church. Though the church is diverse in its makeup, it has unity in its diversity. The church is nourished by Christ, but the nourishing process happens in part through the assistance which the members give to one another. When the church is submissive to Christ, there is harmony within.

The Household

According to Robert Banks, "To embrace the gospel . . . is to enter into community. A person cannot have one without the other."[131] Chapter 2 of this study explains that most Christian gatherings in the first decades of the church probably took place in the confines of a household (οἶκος). Paul borrows from this part of everyday life to paint images of church life. There has been an unfortunate tendency among some authors to use these images as citations of household churches. This misinterpretation has led to a poorer understanding of what the Christian church should be. On the other extreme, one writer denies that there is any reference in the New Testament to the church as "the House of God."[132] In Gal 6:10, Paul describes Christians as "those who are of the household of faith." In Eph 2:17 he states that Jews and Gentiles have been brought together into "the household of God." In 1 Tim 3:4–5, the apostle argues that overseers are to be able to manage the household of the church well, just as a good father manages his own children well. In 1 Tim 3:15, Paul points out that there is both acceptable and inacceptable behavior in the church, God's household. He also tells Timothy that there are things that need to be purged out of the life of God's workman in order for the house to function well (2 Tim 2:20–21). Peter likewise calls the body of Christians "a spiritual house" (οἶκος πνευματικὸς—1 Pet 2:5) and "the household of God," saying that it is about to be judged (1 Pet 4:17). This last figure is likely a Hebrew expression for the group he has just named ("house" means "you").[133]

131. Banks, *Paul's Idea of Community*, 27.

132. Horrell, *From the Ground Up*, 45.

133. *Str-B*, 3:767.

The above cited expressions lead to the conclusion, "The gospel is not a purely personal matter. It has a social dimension. It is a communal affair."[134] Christians in a local church have a sense of belonging because the gospel has the unique effect of binding believers to one another in a permanent way. Thus, believers have a unity created by the household and its leader: the household is the body of Christians and the leader of the household is Christ himself. The metaphor also determines how people of the church handle themselves. Citing 1 Tim 3:15, Marshall says, "The implication of this metaphor is that God is like a householder who exercises authority over his household, and so there should be appropriate behavior in the church."[135] At its core, the household of Christians known as the church is a spiritual entity. The community is to be well-ordered, rather than uncontrolled:

> Families in Antiquity were patriarchal and hierarchical, with the father ruling the household (though, if the father were deceased, at times the mother would become the head of the household). Slaves and servants often had managerial roles as well as menial tasks. Everyone performed his or her assigned duties for the welfare of the household. Thus when the Christian church was referred to as a "household" (whether "of faith" or "of God"), ideas of order, structure, and functional responsibility would inevitably have arisen in the minds of both those who used and those who heard such terminology.[136]

One aspect of household life as a picture of the church needs to be further explained. The household was, as mentioned, patriarchal. The church is likewise patriarchal, but only in a qualified sense. Apart from family relationships, only three persons are called a "father" of believers: God, Abraham (Rom 4:11–16; Jas 2:21), and Paul (1 Cor 4:14–15). No other persons are ever described in this light.

Before considering God as father, the fatherhood of the two other personalities needs to be explained. Regarding Abraham as father, it may well be argued that Paul has believing Jews in view in Rom 4:12.[137] However, Paul expands the fatherhood of Abraham to all believers in verse16: "who

134. Banks, *Paul's Idea of Community*, 26.

135. Marshall, "Congregation and Ministry," 113.

136. Longenecker, "Paul's Vision of the Church," 77. Following this explanation, note that the church leaders, according to 2 Tim 2:15–21, are not relegated to the position of head of the household, but as one of the servants in the household.

137. Moo, *Romans*, 270–71. As James was writing to Jewish believers in Jesus, "Abraham our father" could be interpreted in the same light.

is the father of us all." This fatherhood of Abraham to all believers is on the basis of possessing the same faith. Gentiles who believe in Jesus as Messiah are recipients of the ἐπαγγελίαν and become Abraham's σπέρμα through their faith. It is in this sense that they are "sons of Abraham."

Paul calls himself a "father" to the Corinthian believers in 1 Cor 4:15. This, however, is in a restricted sense:

> It was Paul's missionary work that made them Christians. According to *Sanhedrin* 19b, if a man teaches his neighbour's son Torah, Scripture counts it to him as if he had begotten him. . . . Here, as in 1:14ff., Paul is careful that this relationship shall not be taken too far. If he has begotten them (it is worth noting that Paul does not use the metaphor of regeneration; contrast e.g., John 3:3,5; Titus 3:5), it is not in his own right but *in Christ Jesus* and *through the Gospel*. Christ is the agent and the Gospel the means by which men are brought to new life. Paul does not use the title "father" for a Christian minister (cf. Matt 23:9), but keeps the metaphor for the special purpose of describing the relation between an evangelist and his converts.[138]

Thus, in the New Testament, there are two special senses in which two different people are called a "father" of other Christians. No ἐπίσκοπος is ever referred to as "father." In addition, Paul as an apostle is only denoted as a father in the sense that he evangelized the believers in Corinth. No other apostle is called "father" in the New Testament.

In contrast to other persons, God is frequently called "the father" of Christians (e.g., Rom 1:7; 8:15; 1 Cor 1:3; 8:6; 2 Cor 1:2; Gal 1:3–4; Eph 1:2; Phil 1:2; 1 Thess 3:13; Heb 12:7; 1 Pet 1:17; 1 John 3:1). These passages describe a tender, familial relationship between God and believers (see the following section, The Reality of the Family Relationship). Believers worship, love, pray to, depend on, obey their Father. Thus, in the concept of the church as a household, a paternalism exists. It is, however, a relationship exclusively between every believer in the household and God the Father.

138. Barrett, *First Corinthians*, 114–15. Orphans in Israel also called those who reared them "father." Still another aspect of the use of the word "father" in Jewish thinking was to designate one who had converted a proselyte to the Jewish faith: "It is as though he had created him [the proselyte]," *Str-B*, 3:340.

The Temple

In 1 Cor 3:16–17 Paul asks, "Do you not know that you are the temple of God and *that* the Spirit of God dwells in you? If anyone defiles the temple of God, God will destroy him. For the temple of God is holy, which *temple* you are." In this context he is clearly talking to the local church in Corinth. Paul brings up the subject again in Eph 2:21–22, stating, "In whom the whole building, being joined together, grows into a holy temple in the Lord, in whom you also are being built together for a dwelling place of God in the Spirit." Here the identification goes beyond the local church, since he has been talking about the phenomenon of Jews and Gentiles now being united in the faith into one body (Eph 2:14–19). This temple is indwelt by the Holy Spirit, who gives to it its life.

In the 1 Corinthians 3 passage, Paul says to the believers, "You are (ἐστε) the temple of God." Thus, all believers together in the one local church constitute God's temple.[139] The idea of God dwelling in a believing person was not totally alien to Jewish thought.[140] The statement that Christians are a part of God's temple would quite naturally create images of the Jewish tabernacle or of Solomon's or Herod's temple in the mind of Paul's readers. Order and worship for the tabernacle were given to Moses in detail and written in the books of Exodus, Leviticus, and Numbers. Both the commands given as well as the description of events surrounding worship (e.g. the death of Aaron's sons who offered strange fire) make it clear that Yahweh wanted his people to take his dwelling and worship performed there very seriously.

Paul offers a stern warning that those who destroy the church will also be destroyed by God (v.17). "Destroy" is one meaning for φθείρω, and is the choice here by Bauer,[141] and likewise followed by the ESV, NASB, and NIV. The idea that someone could destroy the church poses a theological problem, which is answered by C. K. Barrett:

> It is sometimes said that Paul's verb (φθείρειν) cannot be translated "destroy," because the church, God's temple, cannot be destroyed. In a sense this is true: even the gates of hell . . . cannot prevail

139. Calvin, *Commentary on Corinthians*, 1.142, translates "you are temples" (pl). Later in his commentary, Calvin says that the Christians in Corinth combined to form the temple of God.

140. *Str-B*, 3:335.

141. Bauer, *Wörterbuch zum Neuen Testament*, 1709. This dictionary is the basis for the English *BDAG*.

against the church (Matt 16:18). It must be remembered, however, that Paul is thinking of a local manifestation of God's temple, a local church: and it is a matter of fact that local churches have, under various pressures, including that of heresy, simply gone out of existence.[142]

In Paul's view, the local church is God's temple. Activity done in the church must respect his holiness. God has jealous concern over his local churches, to the point of recompensing those who deal with them unjustly.

THE REALITY OF THE FAMILY RELATIONSHIP

The subject of the family of God in the New Testament does not fall under the category of metaphor. It is an exact expression of that to which Christians belong. From its first chapter until its last, the book of Acts refers to Christians as brothers. Every letter in the New Testament canon either addresses Christians as brothers or speaks of Christians as brothers. The terms *brother, brothers,* or *brotherhood* are used 190 times in the epistles. *Adelphoi* "brethren," it appears, is by far Paul's favorite way of referring to members of the churches to whom he is writing.[143] The Christian life is not a lonely pilgrimage: "How could it be, when love is its motive power and chief glory? The love of Christ involves the love of Christians. Believers are sons, members of a family. They have brethren."[144]

The previous section on authority in the church mentions that Jewish people referred to one another as "brothers" from the time of the patriarchs. Eventually this term came to signify a member of the covenant nation. However, in the church the meaning of ἀδελφοὶ goes beyond national or covenantal signification. The basis of the family relationship among Christians is their spiritual birthing by God (John 3:3–8; 1 Pet 1:3, 23; 1 John 5:1). The basis for joining God's family is also adoption by God (Rom 8:15; Gal 4:5; Eph 1:5). An even more impressive family trait of Christians is that they are called brothers of Jesus (Matt 28:10; John 20:17; Rom 8:16–17). In Eph 5:1 Paul identifies the believers as "children of God." John does the same in 1 John 2:29.

---

142. Barrett, *First Corinthians*, 91.

143. Banks, *Paul's Idea of Community*, 51.

144. Johnston, *The Doctrine of the Church*, 75.

In harmony with the family identity, Paul frequently addresses Christians in loving expressions, such as 1 Cor 16:24: "My love be with you all in Christ Jesus"; 2 Cor 2:4: "For I wrote to you out of much affliction and anguish of heart and with many tears, not to cause you pain but to let you know the abundant love that I have for you"; 2 Cor 12:15: "I will most gladly spend and be spent for your souls. If I love you more, am I to be loved less?"; and Phil 4:1: "Therefore, my brothers, whom I love and long for." Likewise, Jesus and his apostles repeatedly urge the members of the family to love one another (John 15:12; 1 Cor 8:10–13; 16:14; 2 Cor 8:24; Gal 5:6; Heb 10:24; 1 Pet 1:22; 1 John 4:7). Just as family members love each other, so Christians should be loving towards each other. They are all part of the same spiritual family. As parents teach love to their children, so Jesus taught love to his disciples, and his disciples taught love to those they evangelized and instructed.

CHAPTER SUMMARY

The theological concepts discussed in this chapter have been those which play a prominent role in determining how group decision-making would take place in a church context. The first collection of these concepts—authority in the church, the meaning of the word ἐκκλησία, the priesthood of the believer, and the direct ministry of the Holy Spirit in the believer—substantially lay the groundwork for group decision-making in the local church setting. The second group of theological concepts—the metaphors of the church and the reality of the family relationship in the church—create added requisites for group decision-making.

All Christians are on the same spiritual plane. They all have equal access to God. They are all responsible to the teachings and commands of the Scriptures. They are all indwelt by the Holy Spirit, who gifts them for ministry. Even apostles viewed themselves as co-laborers with other Christians. Christ specially instructed them that all Christians are brothers and none should be called "father." Apostles held leadership in the church but had no special authority themselves which superceded the authority of a local church. Instead, all Christians and all churches are under the direct authority of Jesus Christ as their head. While this headship creates an equality for all, it also excludes party division.

Since all Christians are on an equal spiritual plane and all capable of ministry in the church, quite naturally they would be expected to participate in decisions which affect the entire church body. The New Testament does not relegate decisions about the church exclusively to the apostles or to elders in churches. In terms of direct teaching, all Christians are expected to be involved in ministry, in prayer, in instruction, in exhortation, and in decision-making. They can all expect the direction of the Holy Spirit; this is not the exclusive domain of the mature.

The church is the ἐκκλησία, "the assembly." The word always carries with it the concept of a group which meets to hear and to decide. Its members listen, speak, and act. Thus, the members of a church would be expected to participate in decision-making by the very nature of its name. The entire biblical concept of the church is not contained in the definition of ἐκκλησία. Instead, metaphors in the New Testament and the reality of the family relationship in the church further describe it. These metaphors denote a close unity with Christ as its head. The church is his body. It is a household, which includes servants and which necessarily must have order to function correctly. It is almost correct to say that the dominant images of the church are non-hierarchical. If the Kingdom were a major image used for the church, one would have to argue in the opposite direction, but this is not the case.[145] However, paternalism exists in the local church as well as in the universal body of Christ. This paternalism is identical in both: God is the Father of all Christians. There is also a special fatherhood for believers in Christ, in their relationship to Abraham. Otherwise, the New Testament knows no other kind of patriarchy in the church. The church is a temple, whose precincts are holy. God values this temple with a jealousy which will not tolerate its abuse. Self-assertiveness, divisiveness, quarreling, deceit, worldly-ambition, strange doctrine, or personal agendas have no place in the ministries of a church, including her times of group decision-making.

145. Hammett, *Biblical Foundations*, 147. Hammett is also very close to correct in saying that none of the dominant images for the church in the New Testament are hierarchical. But the image of Christ as the head of the church body, and God as the father of believers would be the exceptions. Fatherhood and headship have to be regarded as hierarchical.

4

Scripture Passages Directly Relating to Corporate Decision-Making

THIS STUDY ASSERTS THAT the New Testament church practiced corporate decision-making; this chapter will illustrate the fact from fifteen New Testament passages. It will also examine the purposes for which the church met together to make decisions. Some passages are unclear as to whether the entire body of believers made the decision or whether a select group did; other passages clearly demonstrate that a group made a decision affecting one ministry but not the entire church. The passages in question will not be completely exegeted word for word, but only insofar as the issue of corporate decision-making is clarified. The chapter will quote exegetes, theologians, and classicists who conclude that the early church functioned democratically—although this is not an assertion the chapter itself makes. It will restrict its findings to the proof and explanation of corporate decision-making. This is, in fact, the matter with which the study is concerned.

The New Testament presents corporate decision-making in four areas:

1. Choice of Officers or Representatives: There are ten New Testament passages which describe corporate decision-making in choosing church leaders or representatives: Acts 1:15–26, Acts 6:1–6, Acts 8:14–17, Acts 11:19–22, Acts 11:30, Acts 13:1–3, Acts 14:21–23, Acts 15:36–41, 1 Cor 16:3–4 and 2 Cor 8:18–19. Most classicists and exegetes come to the conclusion that these passages describe corporate decision-making (excepting perhaps the Acts 14 passage).

2. Church Discipline: There are two New Testament passages describing corporate decision-making for purposes of church discipline:

1 Corinthians 5:1–13 and 2 Cor 2:5–11. These examples are premised on the instructions of Jesus to his disciples in Matt 18:15–18.

3. Doctrine and Practice: Acts 15 describes group decision-making to determine doctrine and practice, specifically relating to the role the Law of Moses played in the life of Gentile Christians and how they were to handle themselves in four areas of ethical behavior.

4. Ministry Choices: One passage specifically describes decisions by a group regarding ministry apart from the direct authority of or interaction with the original local church: Acts 16:9–11.

The material for the presentation of corporate decision-making is primarily historical from the book of Acts. Since many theologians do not regard the book of Acts as historically accurate, it is important to summarize their judgments and explain why Acts should be taken as historical and thus authoritative.

The Historicity of the Book of Acts

Through 1800, the book of Acts was viewed by scholars and clergy as the history of the early church. This view remained essentially unchallenged until 1826, when Wilhelm de Wette published his *Introduction to the New Testament* in which he argued that the writer of Acts could not have been a companion of Paul and that the book was written after AD 70.[1] Since the time of his writing, many New Testament scholars have questioned or denied the historical validity of the book of Acts. Ferdinand Christian Baur held that early Christianity was divided between the Jewish (or Petrine) party and the Gentile (or Pauline) party and that this division resulted in significant controversy.[2] This method of studying the New Testament is called *Tendenzkritik* (tendency-criticism).[3] In 1838, Baur proposed that the book of Acts was written by a member of the Pauline party of Christianity who attempts to smooth over the differences of the two parties.[4] The first major response to Baur and his followers was made by H. A. W. Meyer,

1. Wette, *Lehrbuch der historisch-kritischen Einleitung*, 208.
2. Gasque, *History of the Interpretation of the Acts*, 27.
3. In *History of the Interpretation of Acts*, 27, Gasque explains *Tendenzkritik* in the following way: "[It is] the study of a New Testament writing in terms of its special theological point of view within the context of the history of primitive Christianity."
4. Baur, *Ursprung des Episcopats*, 142.

who, using critical methods, concluded that the author of Acts was a companion of Paul in his travels.[5] Around the same time, Henry Alford, who had studied German higher criticism in Germany, presented his conclusion that the book of Acts was written by a companion of Paul around 63 CE and is historically accurate.[6] Other English scholars of the latter half of the nineteenth century who argued for the historicity of Acts included James Lightfoot and Frederick Farrar.[7]

William Ramsay was originally a follower of the ideas of the Tübingen school (F. C. Baur). He later became convinced that the book of Acts was historically accurate, in contrast to the *Tendenzkritik* of Baur and his followers. Ramsay changed his mind about the accuracy of Acts through his archaeological studies in Asia Minor and wrote a series of books, all of which illuminate his point about Luke's accuracy, beginning in 1897.[8] Ramsay regarded Luke as the author of Acts and "among historians of the first rank."[9]

Half a century after Baur, Adolf von Harnack, though an adherent of the historical-critical theology, also emphasized at length Luke's authorship and his careful recording of history.[10] His conclusions are significant, because as Gasque points out, "No one could ever accuse him [Harnack] of any prejudice whatsoever in favor of either orthodox theology or traditional views in the realm of biblical criticism."[11] Harnack was convinced that the historical facts surrounding the question required the book of Acts to be viewed as historically accurate. Gasque also notes that Harnack's "study of the subject is probably the most exhaustive examination of [the features of the book] which has ever been made, and it remains as a thesaurus of

---

5. Meyer, *Handbuch über die Apostelgeschichte*.

6. Alford, *The Greek New Testament*, 2:1–31.

7. Lightfoot, *Galatians*, 87–132. Farrar, *Life and Work of St. Paul*, 1:7–12.

8. Ramsay, *St. Paul the Traveller*.

9. Ibid., 4.

10. Harnack, *Lukas der Arzt; Mission und Ausbreitung des Christentums*, 89–105. Writing about Luke's presentation of Paul as a true follower of the Law, Harnack states, "Und das ist ein weiterer Beweis, dass Lucas der ältesten Zeit persönlich sehr nahe gestanden hat; denn welcher Hellene hat solche zarte, uns fast unverständliche Rücksicht auf die jüdische Religion und die neben dem Christentum bestehende alttestamentliche Frömmigkeit genommen, wie er sie hier und auch sonst in seinem Werke bekundet hat?," ibid., 102.

11. Gasque, *History of the Interpretation of Acts*, 146.

information for the student of the Book of Acts."[12] Harnack placed the date of the writing of Acts at 62 CE.[13]

Two other works deserve mention in the debate about the historicity of Acts. In 1923, Eduard Meyer published the first edition of his *Ursprüng und Anfänge des Christentums,* in which he regarded Luke as reliable but not infallible. He demonstrated Luke's reliability from Greek and Roman history, ancient literature, and inscriptions. He devoted over five hundred pages to addressing the findings of those whom he called "hypercritics" (e.g., Baur and Wellhausen).[14] The authority of Meyer's conclusions is emphasized by Gasque, who highlights Meyer's scholarship, stating, "Meyer is recognized by all historians as one of the greatest masters of the whole range of ancient history which the world of scholarship has ever produced."[15] Lake and Cadbury's commentary on the Acts of the Apostles, a very complete critical commentary, was published in 1932, and also deserves note in the debate. Lake and Cadbury evaluated the author of Acts as confused about some things but generally historically reliable.[16] In Cadbury's own work, *The Making of Luke-Acts* (1927), he stated, "The admiration that Harnack expresses for the achievement involved in the composition of Acts we can share, even if we do not agree in all details."[17]

The first to introduce an analysis of the book of Acts according to the method of *Formgeschichte* (a style-critical study) was Martin Dibelius. He argued that Acts is distinguished from other New Testament books by its literary character and began his study by purposely avoiding the question of historicity.[18] Dibelius essentially did not interact with the evidence for the historicity of Acts presented by Ramsay, Meyer, and Harnack.[19] In analyzing different styles in Acts, Dibelius defined some as "myth," "legend," "novel," and "anecdote."[20] Thus, by avoiding questions of historicity

---

12. Ibid., 153.

13. Harnack, *Neue Untersuchung zur Apostgelgeschichte.*

14. Meyer, *Ursprüng und Anfänge des Christentums,* vol. 3.

15. Gasque, *History of the Interpretation of Acts,* 158.

16. Lake and Cadbury, *Beginnings of Christianity: Part I.*

17. Cadbury, *The Making of Luke-Acts.*

18. "Ich habe dabei absichtlich nicht gefragt," Dibelius, "Stilkritisches zur Apostelgeschichte," 28.

19. Gasque, *History of the Interpretation of Acts,* 207.

20. Dibelius, "Stilkritisches zur Apostelgeschichte," 28.

and classifying the writing types as non-historical, Dibelius gave the strong impression that Acts was not historical. Longenecker explains further,

> It is true that Bultmann, Martin Dibelius and Karl Schmidt, for example, as distinct from Barth in this regard, developed an historical methodology in support of their philosophical positions. But that methodology, which generally is labeled the "New Hermeneutic," as to its overall thrust, is built upon the revolutionary principle that documents tell us more about the people who wrote them than about the events they purport to relate. It asserts the antithetical relation of proclamation and historical events . . . and holds presuppositions hostile to the New Testament's own understanding of itself.[21]

Ernst Haenchen applied the method of Dibelius to the entire book of Acts in his massive commentary, *Die Apostelgeschichte*. For Haenchen, Luke was as creative as he was historical; some of the scenes in Acts, in fact, Luke made up from varying traditions.[22] He also claimed that Luke did not feel compelled to be strictly historical.[23] In 1971, Haenchen's commentary was translated into English. "The impact of Haenchen's work [in the English language] meant that historical questions largely were not raised for another fifteen or more years."[24]

Hans Conzelmann's commentary also followed the method of *Formgeschichte* in its exegesis of Acts, but it went beyond Haenchen's work in that it regarded Acts as unhistorical.[25] Jürgen Roloff, also applying *Formgeschichte*, argued in the introduction to his commentary that there are serious errors in details about Paul in Acts. He maintained that the author uses highly contradictory material and traditions, and most likely wrote two or three generations after the events.[26] The effect of *Formgeschichte* on historical questions in Acts is summarized by Helga Botermann, who wrote in 1991 that ancient historians of Germany had left the origin of Christianity completely in the hands of theologians for at least two generations.[27]

---

21. Longenecker, *Biblical Exegesis in the Apostolic Period*, 53.

22. Haenchen, *Die Apostelgeschichte*, 210.

23. Ibid., 217.

24. Walton, "Acts: Many Questions," 229.

25. Conzelmann, *Die Apostelgeschichte*, 7.

26. Roloff, *Die Apostelgeschichte*, 5, 1–16.

27. Botermann, "Paulus und das Urchristentum in der antiken Welt," 296.

Since the rise of *Formgeschichte*, numerous authors have responded, demonstrating the historical accuracy of Acts. Martin Hengel points out that "even the reconstruction of the so-called *Sitz im Leben* [of *Formgeschichte*] remains for the most part a highly questionable business."[28] With regard to the explanation that Luke edits tradition in order to maintain a theological direction in Acts, Hengel reminds the reader that for ancient writers, it was primarily the size of the writing scroll, rather than the editing of theological traditions, which determined what went into a work and what did not.[29] J. Dupont has demonstrated that finding the sources of Acts is essentially an impossible task.[30] Eckhard Plümacher's *Lukas als hellenistischer Schrifsteller* takes issue at length with the conclusions of *Formgeschichte* analysis of Acts, particularly those found in the commentaries of Haenchen and Conzelmann. He asserts that there is a close connection between the aim of Acts to present the facts and its use of Hellenistic literary forms.[31] F. F. Bruce presents many instances of the historical accuracy of Acts in his work and concludes by quoting A. N. Sherwin-White: "Yet Acts is, in simple terms and judged externally, no less of a propaganda narrative than the Gospels, liable to similar distortions. But any attempt to reject its historicity even in matters of detail must now appear absurd. Roman historians have long taken it for granted."[32]

Another voice that joined the defense of the historicity of Acts is that of W. C. van Unnik, who compares the Acts of the Apostles with the canons of writing given by historians who lived in the same general time period as Luke. Van Unnik lists ten such canons and compares them with the book of Acts; he views Luke as adhering to the canons.[33] C. J. Hemer added to the argument by devoting page after page of his book, *The Book of Acts and the Setting of Hellenistic History* (1989), to multiple confirmations of the historicity of Acts. He concludes that the evidence demonstrates the author had intimate knowledge of local circumstances in the events recorded. Hemer says that those who try to drive a wedge between history and theology in

28. Hengel, *Acts and the History of Earliest Christianity*, 23.

29. Ibid., 8. Schnabel, *Early Christian Mission*, 1:641, states, "The size of a book was limited by the capacity of the papyrus scroll: academic books generally had 1,100 to 4,500 lines of text, poetic books between 700 and 1,100 lines."

30. Dupont, *Sources of Acts*.

31. Plümacher, *Lukas als hellenistischer Schrifstelle*, 31.

32. Sherwin-White, *Roman Society and Roman Law*, 189.

33. Unnik, "Luke's Second Book," 37–60.

Acts create a false antithesis. He concludes that Luke was a companion of Paul, who wrote an historically accurate account.[34] Lee Levine, though writing as an expert in the area of the ancient synagogue, not Acts, makes the following pertinent observation:

> Much has been written about the historical reliability of Acts—from the more sceptical to the largely accepting. Theological agendas aside, one may assume that the specific events reported, especially those relating to the synagogue, are largely credible. The author was certainly familiar with the Jewish Diaspora and wrote for Christian Diaspora communities. It is hard to imagine that he would invent accounts for a population that knew a great deal about the synagogue, its workings and Paul's activities. At the very least, even were one to doubt the specific details included in Acts, one would have to admit that such events could well have taken place, even if not precisely in the manner recorded.[35]

One of the more recent studies of the genre of the book of Acts which questions its historicity was written by R. I. Pervo. Pervo says that the problem of the historicity of Acts can be overcome when one recognizes that it is an historical novel, not a history book.[36] Loveday Alexander counters that the book of Acts does not match historical novels of Luke's time. Unlike the novel, the book of Acts does not present exotic and desolate landscapes, does not attribute miracles to natural causes, does not provide final resolution for its hero's *pathe*.[37]

Philip Esler has applied the knowledge of modern social science and redaction criticism to the book of Acts and places the date of writing at the end of the first century CE. He also argues that Luke rewrites the history of the church to help the early Christians legitimatize themselves against Judaism.[38] In light of Hemer's numerous demonstrations of historical accuracy in Acts, plus Levine's comparison of Luke's statements with what is now known about the early synagogue, Esler's charge of rewriting history is hard to defend. Among other things, Walton points out that Esler underestimates how radical a shift took place when Jewish believers began

---

34. Hemer, *Acts in Hellenistic History*.

35. Levine, *The Ancient Synagogue*, 116.

36. Pervo, *Profit with Delight*.

37. Alexander, "Fact, Fiction and the Genre of Acts," 95–97.

38. Esler, *Community and Gospel in Luke-Acts*, 71–109.

to eat with non-Jewish believers. This change, of necessity, took time as is reflected in Acts.[39]

One argument that those who challenge the historicity of Acts have yet to address is the fact that Acts is necessary to make sense of the rest of New Testament history. Botermann notes, "As everyone knows, one cannot understand [the history of the early church], especially for the time before and after the Pauline letters, without the book of Acts."[40] In the same vein, Irina Levinskaya writes,

> On the whole the use of Acts as evidence for the first century is rather inconsistent. On the one hand, its narrative is widely used for locating Jewish communities in the first century: such places as, for instance, Iconium or Philippi appeared on the map of the first century Jewish Diaspora exclusively from the pages of Acts. On the other hand, the veracity of Acts' evidence for Jewish life and, in particular, for the relations with surrounding Gentiles, is often questioned.[41]

Cadbury highlights just how problematic an understanding of early church history becomes if the historicity of Acts is questioned:

> The book of Acts is . . . indispensable. No narratives parallel to it have survived. It is our sole record of the apostolic age. The other New Testament books only indirectly throw light on events in that most significant era. The Book of Acts, written independently of them, forms the background to their understanding, and it alone tells the story behind them. Even the extensive and self-revealing correspondence of Paul would leave his life and setting afloat for us in a sea of ignorance were it not for the succinct outline of his career sketched for us in Acts.[42]

Summary

The debate about the historicity of Acts, which has continued for over 150 years, shows no signs of diminishing. The discussion is now so detailed, it is impossible to argue reasons for or against historicity without composing

39. Walton, "Acts: Many Questions," 235.

40. Botermann, "Paulus und das Urchristentum," 301. Translation by author.

41. Levinskaya, *Acts in Its Diaspora Setting*, 2.

42. Cadbury, *The Making of Luke-Acts*, 2.

a book-sized treatise.[43] For that reason, a summary of the debate has been presented here. Many competent scholars argue their case on either side. Those who question or deny the historicity of Acts usually focus on internal inconsistencies, missing information, (sometimes supposed) writing style, theological traditions, and supposed sources; they also tend to place a division between history and theology in Acts. Those who assert the historicity of Acts typically compare the book with historical events, archaeology, inscriptions, and literature from the first century CE.

At this date, historical confirmations of the events and social settings in the book of Acts are very, very numerous. The burden of proof lies heavily on the side of those who criticize the historicity of Acts. Likewise, the writing style of Luke and his methods of recording history are not at all foreign to those of historical writers of his own day. For these reasons it is both scholarly and credible to adopt the position that the book of Acts is historical. If the book of Acts presents a true picture of the early church, then church order was certainly a reality from the earliest days of Christianity. The book of Acts is thus essential for a correct understanding of corporate decision-making in the church.

PASSAGES DESCRIBING THE CHOICE OF OFFICERS OR REPRESENTATIVES

Acts 1:15–26

The beginning of the book of Acts presents Jesus instructing his eleven disciples to be witnesses to his messiahship and salvation, first in Jerusalem and ultimately throughout the whole world (1:2 "after he had given commands through the Holy Spirit to the apostles whom he had chosen"). The quickness with which they acted to appoint a successor for Judas demonstrates how seriously they viewed their task and how soon they expected to receive power from heaven (Luke 24:49). As Gooding notes, "It was still not seven weeks since the Lord Jesus had been executed, and within a few days the apostles must go and stand publicly in the city to begin their witness

---

43. Green and McKeever, *Luke-Acts and New Testament Historiography*, list five hundred works in their annotated bibliography about the subject. They describe their bibliography as almost wholly comprised of English-language works and "incomplete."

to him."[44] Barrett adds, "The dating [in verse 15] is emphatic because Luke wishes to emphasize that the church was in a state of readiness for the gift of the Spirit."[45]

The usage of μάρτυς here means "a witness to the life, death and resurrection [of Jesus]."[46] The commission to be a witness would have been easily understood by the disciples, since the concept was well defined in their theology and life. As Chisholm notes, "The Mosaic Law carefully regulated legal testimony. A man could not be condemned by the testimony of only one witness (Num 35:30; Deut 17:6; 19:15)."[47] The עֵד functioned not only in court cases, but also at the transfer of property, betrothal, and in civil and social relations.[48] Particularly significant for the history of the Jesus movement is one of its several theological usages:

> In Isa 43:10 and 44:8 Yahweh commissioned Israel to serve as his witnesses. Before the nations, their gods, and their witnesses, Israel was to affirm that Yahweh is the incomparable God who decrees and acts, demonstrating his infinite superiority to the manmade deities of the pagan world. In establishing a new covenant with Israel, Yahweh promised to make the nation his witness to the Gentiles, a role he had earlier assigned to the Davidic kings (Isa 55:3–7).[49]

Jesus had specified that his disciples were to be μάρτυρες for him as Messiah: of his sufferings, resurrection, return, and his offer of salvation (Luke 24:33–48). However, the eleven were to fulfill this role in a special sense (Acts 1:1–8): they took the leadership role among the witnesses.[50] At his first sermon, only ten days after Jesus' commission, Peter emphasized to his hearers, "This Jesus God raised up, and of that we all are witnesses" (Acts 2:32). Peter later referred to himself as "a witness of the sufferings of Christ" (1 Pet 5:1).

44. Gooding, *True to the Faith*, 43.

45. Barrett, *Commentary on the Acts*, 1:95.

46. Bauer, *Wörterbuch zum Neuen Testament*, 1002, "von den Jüngern Jesu als den Zeugen seines Lebens, Sterbens und Auferstehens." Other passages that Bauer notes that have this meaning are Luke 24:48; Acts 1:22, 3:15, 5:32, 10:39, 26:16.

47. Chisholm, "עֵד," *NIDOTTE*, 3:337.

48. *BDB*, 729d.

49. Chisholm, *NIDOTTE*, 3:337.

50. The twelve disciples had already, to a certain extent, experienced what their ministry as witnesses would be like, in that they had been on preaching tour, proclaiming the kingdom of God and healing the sick (Luke 9:1–6).

Bock explains the effectiveness of the witnesses of Jesus the Messiah in the following way:

> A witness in this sense is someone who helps establish facts objectively through verifiable observation. As such, a witness is more than someone with merely subjective and personal impressions. This objectivity and fact-based quality of the witness are why the direct experience of Jesus's ministry and resurrection are required of Judas's replacement in Acts 1:21–22, a passage that shows what stands behind Luke's use of this term.[51]

Like Judas, the successor to Judas would also be an apostle (v. 26). Longenecker explains the importance of this office for the church:

> An apostle . . . was not an ecclesiastical functionary, nor just any recipient of the apostolic faith, nor even a bearer of the apostolic message; he was a guarantor of the gospel tradition because he had been a companion of the earthly Jesus and a witness to the reality of his resurrection because the risen Lord had encountered him.[52]

A second factor played a role in the selection of a replacement for Judas; namely, the disciples were awaiting the restoration of the kingdom (Acts 1:6; later emphasized by Peter in Acts 3:21). While on his final journey to Jerusalem, Jesus promised the following to the twelve disciples: "Truly, I say to you, in the new world, when the Son of Man will sit on his glorious throne, you who have followed me will also sit on twelve thrones judging the twelve tribes of Israel" (Matt 19:28). He repeated the promise on the night of his betrayal: "And I assign to you, as my Father assigned to me, a kingdom, that you may eat and drink at my table in my kingdom and sit on thrones judging the twelve tribes of Israel" (Luke 22:29–30).[53]

This statement of Christ was reminiscent of Dan 7:9 ("As I looked, thrones were placed, and the Ancient of days took his seat"). Jesus explained that he would return to reign as Messiah, and that the disciples would "share in the judicial functions of the Son of man."[54] For the apostles, after his death and resurrection, "Jesus is and remains the Messiah (cf. Acts

---

51. Bock, *Acts,* 64.

52. Longenecker, *Acts of the Apostles,* 265.

53. Marshall, *Commentary on Luke,* 818, says that Luke has probably deleted "twelve" before thrones since the promise is addressed to the eleven in this context.

54. Ibid., 818. *Str-B,* 4.2:1103–4, points out that several rabbinical interpretations of Dan 7:9 conclude that the elders of Israel would sit together with the Ancient of Days, judging the nations.

2:36), and as such, is and remains the promised king of Israel."[55] On the basis of this promise, in expectation of the restored kingdom, the disciples saw the need to replace the deceased Judas.[56]

The importance of choosing the successor of Judas can hardly be overemphasized. He was to be, at once, one of the primary spokesmen for Jesus the Messiah, one of the primary leaders in the new Jesus movement (v. 25—an apostle), and one of the primary judges of Israel in the Kingdom age. As the young Jesus movement did not yet have its own Scriptures, convincing proof of its beliefs lay with the witnesses. How the choice of the successor took place is not so difficult to discern in the passage of Acts under consideration. In summary, the decision involved the group of believers assembled, under the leadership of Peter, following the instruction of Scripture, and directed by God.

Luke identifies the assembled group as the eleven apostles (whom he names, v. 13), the women ("Mary Magdalene, Joanna, Susanna, and many others"),[57] Mary the mother of Jesus, and the brothers of Jesus (James, Joseph, Simon, and Judas—Matt 13:55). Those identified do not add up, however to the number of 120 that Luke specifies in verse 15. He uses the expression, ἦν τε ὄχλος ὀνομάτων, literally, "now the multitude of names was." Of all the explanations for this expression, the best seems to be that Luke applies an Hebraism to his writing at this point (see Num 1:18; 26:53).[58] The whole group is simply called "the brothers" (τῶν ἀδελφῶν). This is the religious idiom commonly used by Luke to identify believers in Jesus.[59]

Many writers have pointed out that 120 inhabitants is the number which is required in Jewish teaching to form a Sanhedrin in a village. Thus, they argue, Luke created this part of the story to make the early followers of Jesus qualify as a legitimate, believing Jewish group. Lake and Cadbury,

55. Rengstorf, "Die Zuwahl des Matthias," 60. Translation by the author.

56. Wikenhauser, *Die Apostelgeschichte*, 33, says that this factor was a greater motivation for the election of Judas' replacement than was the idea of having a twelfth "witness." Kruse, "Apostle, Apostleship," *DNLT*, 76, says, "The importance of completing again the full number of the Twelve is probably best understood in the light of Jesus' promise that the Twelve would sit on thrones judging the twelve tribes of Israel (Lk 22:30)." Campenhausen, *Ecclesiastical Authority*, 13–14, and Küng, *The Church*, 348–49, say the same, albeit more emphatically.

57. Kistemaker, *Acts*, 59. "We assume that the women Luke refers to are those . . . who accompanied Jesus during his ministry and supported him financially (Luke 8:2–3)."

58. Barrett, *Commentary on the Acts*, 1:96. BDAG, 714b, gives the definition of "persons" here. But note Barrett's arguments against this translation.

59. Longenecker, *Acts*, 262.

for instance, state, "It can scarcely be an accident that this number is that of the Twelve multiplied by 10. It is remarkable that the number of officers in a community shall be a tenth of the whole and that 120 is the smallest number which can hold a "small sanhedrin."[60]

Zwiep contends that one can accept the symbolism of 120 without questioning the historical reality of the account.[61] Barrett answers the symbolic view by saying, "The 120 of 1:14 included women, who would not have been counted in assessing the size of a Jewish community."[62] Likewise, a Sanhedrin of a town consisted of twenty-three persons, not twelve.[63] A second reason not to take the number as symbolic is that the verse does not make the number specific; instead, there were "about (ὡσεὶ) 120." On this basis one may safely say that the contention that there is a symbolic Sanhedrin in this verse is not convincing and certainly no grounds for concluding that the account in Acts 1:15 was created rather than historical. Luke is therefore relating that at this juncture in the life of the Jesus movement, a group of about 120 persons participated in the replacement of Judas.[64]

Through Peter's speech, Luke explains why the choice of a successor for Judas is to be made. Haenchen declares that nothing of the speech could possibly come from Peter himself, but that it is Luke's creation.[65] Barrett agrees with Haenchen.[66] Witherington, to the contrary, argues, "The persistent misreading of historical conventions in regard to speeches in ancient historiographical works by scholars today can in part be attributed to the enormous influence of the work of M. Dibelius."[67] He further argues,

> If Luke was, as I think, a careful historian in the mold of Thucydides and Polybius, we may expect from him adequate and accurate (so far as his sources allowed) summaries of what was said on one or another occasion, especially because he had opportunity to consult with various of the ear-witnesses who heard these speeches,

60. Lake and Cadbury, *Acts of the Apostles*, 12. Polhill, *Acts*, 91 n. 52 also accepts the symbolic meaning.

61. Zwiep, *Judas and the Choice of Matthias*, 134.

62. Barrett, *Commentary on the Acts*, 1:96. In agreement with Barrett are Conzelmann, *Apostelgeschichte*, 28, and Wilson, *Gentiles and the Gentile Mission*, 107n1.

63. *Str-B*, 2:595.

64. I use the term Jesus movement instead of church, because Luke does not designate the group as church until later in Acts (5:21).

65. Haenchen, *Die Apostelgeschichte*, 167.

66. Barrett, *Commentary on the Acts*, 1:94.

67. Witherington III, *Acts of the Apostles*, 117n11.

or in some cases with early Christians and ministers of the word to whom the first listeners had conveyed a brief summary of what was said.[68]

Peter begins his speech by addressing the group as ἄνδρες ἀδελφοί, "men, brothers." Plümacher asserts that Luke is casting this speech (as in other instances) in LXX style.[69] The combination of the two words occurs only in 4 Macc. and otherwise seems to be peculiar to the book of Acts. But if Luke is quoting people who were likely familiar with this expression, then there is no need to assume that Luke created a style that he himself apparently learned from Jewish speakers.[70] People are addressed with the appellation ἄνδρες in twelve other passages in Acts (1:11; 2:14, 22; 3:12; 5:35; 13:15–16; 14:15; 15:7; 17:22; 19:35; 21:28; 22:1; 27:10). Bock notes, "In some of the cases in Acts where this generic term is used, it may be that not just men are addressed but the crowd as a whole."[71] Certainly in Peter's speech in Acts 2, the crowd is twice addressed with the appellation ἄνδρες, but the respondents were both male and female, designated as ψυχαὶ (here, meaning "persons"). As the plural ἀδελφοὶ can mean both men and women, the intended addressees are most likely the entire assembled 120 persons.[72] Luke, in fact, identifies the ἀδελφοὶ as the ὄχλος (the 120) one sentence earlier. One would need to dissect the speech into various parts in order to understand Peter's addressees as anyone other the 120 believers.

Peter based the action of replacing Judas on the fulfillment of Scripture: "Brothers, the Scripture had to be fulfilled, which the Holy Spirit spoke beforehand by the mouth of David concerning Judas" (Acts 1:16). He was not referring to just one Scripture passage, because he strings two

68. Ibid., 117–18.

69. Plümacher, *Lukas,* 47.

70. Longenecker, *Biblical Exegesis in the Apostolic Period,* 88–89, responding to the view that Luke's use of the LXX for quotations negates the authenticity of the recorded speeches, says, "Whatever the final resolution of the problem, it seems that we are faced with at least two issues regarding the text-form of the quotations in Acts . . . 1) the variety of biblical versions in the first century, and 2) assimilation for the sake of a Greek-speaking audience. In addition, the possible presence of a testimonial collection(s) and the activity on an amanuensis (in the case of the Epistles) add further complications. Until additional evidence is available, we are well advised to leave the questions of textual source and deviations in early Christian preaching open."

71. Bock, *Acts,* 69.

72. BDAG, 18c.

together (Pss 69:25 and 109:8).[73] Longenecker evaluates Peter's use of these two passages as midrashic interpretation, saying,

> A midrashic treatment of Scripture also appears in the Acts of the Apostles. The exegetical rule *qal wahomer* (light to heavy) under-lies the use of Ps 69:25 (MT=69:26) and 109:8, allowing Peter to assert that what has been said of false companions and wicked men generally applies, *a minore ad majorem*, specifically to Judas, the one who proved himself uniquely false and evil.[74]

The use of quotations from the Old Testament to substantiate an argument was a common practice in rabbinic Judaism.[75] Quoting ancient sources for the sake of argument was also a practice of Graeco-Roman rhetoric, which formed a major part of Graeco-Roman education (Aristotle, *Rhet.* 1.15.1–19; Quintilian, *Inst. Orat.* 1.18.12).[76] The pervasive impact of Greek training in Rhetoric in Palestine among the Jewish people, even among those who opposed the inroads of Hellenism, is well-documented.[77] The combining of two passages of Scripture, as in Acts 1:20, is common in the New Testament. Thus, there is nothing unusual about the form of Peter's speech in Acts 1, according to norms existing in his day, nor is there any-thing unusual if the speech as written is simply a synopsis of what Peter said, as formulated by Luke.

The source for Peter's interpretation, using portions of two different psalms to argue for a substitute for Judas, is well explained by Gooding:

> But where, we ask, did Peter get the idea . . . that these Psalms had anything to do with Judas, or that their details could supply an authoritative directive as to what should be done about his defec-tion? Luke has already told us (Luke 24:27, 44–47). Peter got it, not from his prior knowledge or rabbinic principles of Old Testament interpretation, nor from the Holy Spirit given at Pentecost, but

73. Lake and Cadbury, *Acts of the Apostles*, 13, say that the quotation of Ps 69:25 is inaccurate.

74. Longenecker, *Biblical Exegesis in the Apostolic Period*, 97. Zwiep, *Judas and the Choice of Matthais*, 137, asserts that Peter is quoting one psalm. He does this, however, by asserting that τὴν γραφὴν means "a scripture" in this instance, and by relocating the first quote of verse 20 to verse 17. Both assertions are difficult to defend. Later, Zwiep says that Luke was well aware that he was quoting two separate Scriptures, ibid., 154.

75. The practice is easily discernible from perusing *Str-B*. See also Barrett, "The Inter-pretation of the OT in the New," 1:386–89.

76. Stamps, "The Use of the Old Testament," 27.

77. Hengel, *Judentum und Hellenismus*, 108–98.

from the Lord Jesus himself. It is unthinkable that in his survey of the Law, the Prophets and the Psalms Christ should have omitted all reference to David, the prototype king of the royal line of Judah, when, as Messiah, he was David's physical and spiritual heir. . . . And then again, during Absalom's rebellion . . . his close friend and adviser Ahithophel proved a traitor . . . in the same way as Judas advised the high priest how Jesus could be found and arrested.[78]

He concludes, "Not one of the one hundred and twenty disciples in the upper room could have read this lament of David's without seeing its immediate relevance to the situation that faced them."[79] The forty days Jesus spent with his disciples explaining the kingdom of God (Acts 1:3) would also have been a source of Peter's understanding of the Messianic interpretation of the Old Testament.[80]

Two qualifications were necessary to assume the role of apostle:

1. The candidate had to be "one of the men who have accompanied us during all the time that the Lord Jesus went in and out among us" (v.21).

2. He had to be a "witness of his resurrection" (v.21).

The first requirement describes Jesus in the time that he "went in and out," (εἰσῆλθεν καὶ ἐξῆλθεν) which is a Semitism, referring to a person's daily work (וּלְבֹא לָצֵאת, see Deut 28:6; 31:2; 2 Sam 3:25; 2 Kgs 19:27; Ps 121:8; Isa 37:28).[81] Thus, the candidate had to have been with Jesus enough to experience his daily activity during the course of his ministry and to see the resurrected Jesus.

In response to Peter's recommendation, two men were put forward: Joseph Barsabbas and Matthias. For purposes of understanding group decision-making in this passage, a great deal depends on the reference of the word ἔστησαν. There are essentially five views of the action:

1. Peter put the two forward (which would require the reading, ἔστησεν— found in MSS D, but otherwise not well attested).[82]

78. Gooding, True to the Faith, 47.

79. Ibid., 48.

80. Pelikan, Acts, 38–41, says that many teachers in the early history of the church regarded these forty days as a special time of indoctrination for the church.

81. BDB, 97d.

82. Other manuscripts which have this reading are Lectionary 156 (tenth century), early Latin versions d (fifth century) and gig (thirteenth century), and Augustine. The amount of early witnesses for ἔστησαν (including a, A, B, C, and early Latin versions)

2. There were only two candidates in the group, who then put themselves forward[83] (which would require the reading, ἐστῆσαντο, which is unattested).

3. The apostles put the two forward.

4. The group of 120 disciples put the two forward.

5. It cannot be determined from the text who did the choosing.[84]

Since the first two choices listed above have little or no textual support, they will be eliminated from this discussion. Longenecker holds to the third view, that the nominations were done by the apostles. He argues for this interpretation on the basis that the word "us," referring to the apostles, is emphasized (used three times in vv. 21–22).[85] Getz agrees with Longenecker, though he does not give any arguments from the text for his choice.[86] Those taking the fourth view that the entire group chose the candidates include Calvin, Alford, Turretin, Lake and Cadbury, Shepherd, Bruce, Kistemaker, and Barrett.[87] Bruce says that the election recorded in Acts 1 compares with the election of magistrates in ancient Athens.[88] Zwiep responds, "If this indeed provides the background to the election of the new apostle, it probably tells us more about Luke than about the historical context of the events narrated, since a Greek election procedure is not very likely in the given Palestinian context."[89] But this response is only true if Luke is not recording history, but instead recreating it. The familiarity of Palestinian Jews with Graeco-Roman democracy and the practice of the

are, by comparison, massive. Interestingly, the D manuscript was later corrected to read ἔστησαν. Metzger, *A Textual Commentary on the Greek New Testament*, 288, infers that the D text reading (singular) was deliberately written to magnify the role of Peter. Barrett, *Critical and Exegetical Commentary on the Acts*, 1:102, answers, "It is tempting but would be precarious to argue that the Western text was concerned to magnify the authority of Peter."

83. Schnabel, *Early Christian Mission*, 1:393.

84. Zwiep, *Judas and the Choice of Matthias*, 159–60.

85. Longenecker, *Acts*, 265.

86. Getz, *Elders and Leaders*, 56.

87. Calvin, *Commentary on the Acts*, 86; Alford, *The Greek New Testament*, 2:23; Turretin, *Institutes of Elenctic Theology*, 3:229; Lake and Cadbury, *Acts of the Apostles*, 14 (if the plural reading is chosen); Shepherd, "The Development of the Early Ministry," 142; Bruce, *Acts of the Apostles: Greek Text*, 112; Kistemaker, *Acts*, 67; Barrett, *Commentary on the Acts*, 1:102.

88. Bruce, *Acts of the Apostles: Greek Text*, 112.

89. Zwiep, *Judas and the Choice of Matthias*, 160.

Qumran community in using votes have already been demonstrated in chapter 2. In this instance, however, Peter was most likely following a tradition of Jewish life tracing back through the records of the Old Testament up to their own day: namely, that assemblies of the people were held for special events and decisions (see chapter 2).

The word ἔστησαν should be taken to refer to the whole 120 for several reasons. First, the multitude is the natural antecedent. In v. 15, it was the multitude, or 120, who were addressed. This was the group, Luke wants his readers to understand, that Peter called "brothers." Second, though the eleven apostles were named in v.13, Luke takes special pains to note that others were included with the eleven in the upper room, and who they were in v. 14. From vv.16–22, the narrative is taken up with Peter's speech. From vv.24–26, the narrative deals with the choice by lot. There would be little point in presenting the whole number of people in the narrative if the apostles are meant in v. 23. Third, Longenecker emphasizes that the eleven were denoted three times in vv. 21–22 by the word "us"; therefore, they are addressed. However, simply because the eleven, with Judas, were the subject of Peter's speech does not mean they were the exclusive ones to take action when the speech was finished. How else would Peter refer to the eleven, of which he was a part, when speaking to the whole 120, than to say "us" (ἡμεῖς)? What other word was at his disposal? Fourth, if the addressees of Peter's speech were only the eleven, then Peter only meant for the other one hundred plus persons in the room to overhear his speech (the candidates would be selected from them). This would be a unique way of talking to the disciples of Jesus, a method otherwise not repeated in the New Testament. Fifth, the principle from Jesus that his disciples were all brothers (see chapter 3) would lead one to expect that Peter would include all of Jesus' followers in the proceedings.

Finally, the means by which the new twelfth disciple was chosen was the lot (ὁ κλῆρος). According to Strack and Billerbeck, the giving of lots was a common practice in the time of the second temple to determine which priest would take care of a particular ministry for that day, including the slaughter, the sprinkling of blood, the carrying away of the ashes, the removal of the ashes from lamps, the taking of the pieces of the victim to the altar, the taking of bread or wine to the altar.[90] Likewise, the use of lots was practiced widely among the Greeks and the Romans, both for social

---

90. *Str-B*, 2:596–97.

and religious purposes.[91] The expression "to cast lots" (βάλλειν κλήρους) is found frequently in the LXX and Josephus' *Antiquities*.[92] Beardslee does not see the explanation of Strack and Billerbeck as having any meaning for Acts 1:26. Rather, it is the casting of lots in the Qumran community which is similar to the choice of Matthias. For the Qumran community, the casting of lots was metaphorical, not literal. This is how Beardslee takes the meaning of Acts 1:26.[93] Though similar, the Qumran use of the κλήρους is not the expression in verse 26, which makes Beardslee's explanation tenuous. Here the verb is δίδωμι. The observance of the difference in the verbs causes Lake and Cadbury to suggest that the expression in verse 26 means to give their votes.[94]

Zwiep explains the four ways in which the giving of lots in Acts 1:26 is understood:

> First, αὐτοῖς may be understood as an indirect object, "they gave lots *to them* (to Barsabbas and Matthias)." If so, the two candidates would put their lots into the vessel and the one whose lot would fell [*sic*] out first would be elected. Second, Matthew Black thinks αὐτοῖς may represent the Aramaic ethical dative "they (the apostles) gave themselves lots." Third, "they (Barsabbas and Matthias) gave the(ir) lots to them (the apostles)." Fourth, Gerhard Lohfink, Gerhard Schneider and Joseph Fitzmyer take it as a *dativus commodi* (cf. Lev 16:7–10) "they gave lots *for them* (for Barsabbas and Matthias)" (NRSV).[95]

To support the fourth interpretation, Zwiep also points out that δίδωμι κλήρους τινι is a correct translation of נָתַן גּוֹרָל לְ. There is, however, not a 1:1 correspondence in the translation to the action in Acts 1:26.[96] The LXX uses the expression ἔδωκαν ἐν κλήρῳ in 1 Chr 6:50 to describe the assigning of cities. But this is not the same as ἔδωκαν κλήρους αὐτοῖς in Acts 1:26. The most likely explanations are either the first (Barsabbas and Matthias

91. Barrett, *Commentary on the Acts*, 1:104.

92. *BDAG*, 548c.

93. Beardslee, "The Casting of Lots at Qumran," 245–52.

94. Lake and Cadbury, *Acts of the Apostles*, 15.

95. Zwiep, *Judas and the Choice of Matthias*, 171.

96. Ibid. The instance Zwiep gives, Lev 16:8, is not so translated by the LXX. Instead, the verb used is ἐπιτίθημι. Correct examples are Deut 31:28; Josh 14:3; 17:4, though they do not mean "choose a person." Block, *Acts*, 90 offers the examples of Josh 18:6 and 19:51. Again, the LXX translation is not βάλλειν κλήρους or δίωμι κλήρος. In fact, the Hebrew verb is not נָתַן in either passage.

were given lots, which they put in a bag to be shaken) or that the group voted by giving lots. The action of giving lots for a ministry, however, is not repeated in the New Testament. Whichever method of selection was used, the disciples looked to God to do the choosing (v. 25). The replacement of Judas was interpreted as God's direct choice: as the first apostles were chosen directly by Jesus, so must the new twelfth apostle.

The choice of Matthias, the replacement of Judas as the twelfth apostle, involved the action of the whole group of about 120 disciples, gathered in the upper room. It was not a willful action on the part of Peter, or Peter and the disciples together. For their readiness for the coming Messianic age, the eleven needed a twelfth apostle. For the spread of the gospel, the Jesus movement needed one more witness of the resurrection. The basis of the action was the Old Testament, which had been interpreted for the disciples by the Messiah himself. The entire group present was instructed and prompted to take action. At the least, the group put forward two candidates for the apostleship. At the most they voted between the two.[97]

Acts 6:1–6

Luke's narrative includes the words and actions of two of the more illustrious personalities of the early church: Stephen and Philip. To rightly introduce them, Luke has to tell the historical background of their rise to prominence in the church. In so doing, Luke relates one of the more colorful accounts of corporate decision-making in the book of Acts. At the same time, he reveals the beginning of a new ministry.[98]

For centuries, this passage in Acts was taken as the origin of the Diaconate in the church. Irenaeus was the earliest to assert the connection (*Adv. Haer.* 1.26; 4.15). He also called Stephen "the first deacon" (*Adv. Haer.* 3.12). That the early Roman church regarded Acts 6 as the beginning of the Diaconate is reflected in Eusebius' comment that the Roman church

97. Hammett, *Biblical Foundations*, 148, says that this passage is questionable as an indication for corporate decision-making in the church, since the church was not born until Pentecost. However, Hammett's view is somewhat simplistic in that the Jesus movement was well in place at this historical moment and the structure of the movement did not change as it became the church.

98. Lake and Cadbury, *Acts of the Apostles*, 63, assert that Luke's aim in this passage was to relate how the communistic system of the first church broke down. Their idea, however, is not followed by many. In fact, the passage demonstrates how the system continued through the solution of the problem.

insisted on the number of seven deacons (Eusebius was writing about an instance in the days of Novatian, ca. 250 CE; *Hist. Eccl.* 6.46).

The viewpoint that Acts 6 records the origin of the Diaconate began to change through German higher criticism in the mid-1800s. Alford, for instance, was wary of saying that Acts 6 marks the beginning of the first deacons of the church.[99] The majority of theologians in Alford's day still viewed Acts 6 as the beginning of the diaconate. This is evidenced, for example, by the comments of Knowling and Hort at the turn of the twentieth century, who both asserted that Acts 6 records the beginning of the regular ministry of deacons in the church.[100]

The former confidence has eroded over the last one hundred years, and today, "There is a general consensus of opinion that their [the seven] appointment does not constitute the origin of the diaconate."[101] Joseph Lienhard's statement, "Older views, which facilely saw in this text the establishment of the order of diaconate, have been abandoned" is, however, an exaggeration.[102] L. Roy Taylor asserts the opposite, that "most regard Acts 6 as the institution of the office of deacon mentioned in Paul's letters to the churches at Philippi and Ephesus."[103] The primary argument against the interpretation that Acts 6 explains the origin of the diaconate is that the word διάκονος is not used at all in the account. Barrett, for instance, argues, "But the word *diakonos* is not used, and to set out to describe the origin of the deaconate without using the word deacon is a scarcely credible undertaking."[104] The second argument against the identification of Acts 6 with the beginning of the diaconate is that Stephen and Philip were afterwards primarily involved in preaching activity.[105] A third argument advanced is that all the men's names were Greek.[106] A fourth argument is that the role of deacons is not mentioned anywhere again in the book of Acts.[107]

99. Alford, *The Greek New Testament*, 2:63.

100. Knowling, *Acts of the Apostles*, 169; Hort, *The Christian Ecclesia*, 50.

101. Fung, "Ministry in the New Testament, " 164.

102. Lienhard, "Acts 6:1–6," 228.

103. Taylor, "A Presbyterian Response," 162.

104. Barrett, *Church, Ministry, and Sacraments*, 49. See also MacArthur, *The Master's Plan*, 208.

105. Küng, *The Church*, 400–401; Wikenhauser, *Die Apostelgeschichte*, 81; Gordon Fee, *1 and 2 Timothy, Titus*, 86.

106. MacArthur, *The Master's Plan*, 208. The significance of the names is discussed elsewhere in this section.

107. MacArthur, *Acts 1—12*, 182.

There are, however, good reasons for viewing Acts 6:1–6 as the origin of the diaconate. First, after surveying the use of διάκονος, διακονία, and διακονεῖν in the New Testament, Cranfield observes, "There is in the NT a specialized technical use of *diakonein* and *diakonia* to denote the practical service of those who are specially needy 'in body, or estate,' and that it is highly probable that the specialized technical use of *diakonos* also has the same reference."[108]

A second reason is offered by Longenecker: "The ministry to which the seven were appointed was functionally equivalent to what Paul covered in the title, 'deacon' (cf. 1 Tim 3:8–13)—which is but to affirm the maxim that in the NT 'ministry was a function long before it became an office.'"[109]

To argue that the seven did not fulfill the role of deacon because two of the seven engaged in preaching is to misunderstand the meaning of their ministry. The role of preaching is not limited to a particular office in the New Testament. This is to confuse New Testament ministries with later ecclesiastical demarcations.[110] In fact, the responsibility to proclaim the gospel was given to all disciples (Luke 24:33–48). As the seven were selected, the apostles were not simply the evangelists of the church, they were also its primary teachers (Acts 2:42). It is in this teaching ministry that they wanted to distinguish their own from that of the seven, not in evangelistic proclamation (6:4).

Finally, Luke was writing history. His writing would naturally include the origin of institutions:

> St. Luke, from the prominence given to the narrative, may fairly be regarded as viewing the institution of the office as establishing a new departure, and not as an isolated incident, and the emphasis is characteristic of an historian who was fond of recording "beginnings" of movements.[111]

It is unlikely that the office-title *deacon* was used at that time in the church's history. Luke avoided the temptation of writing anachronistically.[112]

For the reasons listed above, this study takes the view that Acts 6:1-6 records the beginning of the official ministry of deacon in the early church.

108. Cranfield, "Diakonia," 73.

109. Longenecker, *Acts*, 331.

110. Schnabel, *Early Christian Mission*, 1:428.

111. Knowling, *Acts of the Apostles*, 169. Strauch, *Minister of Mercy*, 45–49, presents this same argument in a fuller version.

112. Strauch, *Minister of Mercy*, 46.

For those who take the New Testament to be their guide for instituting offices in churches, this has important ramifications. With regard to how groups in the New Testament went about making corporate decisions, it is less crucial.

The origin of the new ministry came out of a church problem: the neglect of the widows of the Ἑλληνιστῶν. This neglect arose, Luke hints, on account of the growth of the church in Jerusalem (ἐν δὲ ταῖς ἡμέραις ταύταις πληθυνόντων τῶν μαθητῶν). Some writers criticize the apostles in this passage, arguing that they were unwilling to get involved in helping the needy. They likewise argue that Luke was not being critical enough of the apostles.[113] Schnabel responds, "I find this critique incomprehensible. . . . The appointment of seven co-workers implies the admission of the Twelve that they had failed the widows and that the solution of the problem is not an intensified involvement on their part."[114] The cause of the problem is easily understood if one considers the previous five chapters of the book of Acts (see 4:34–35):

> It is impossible not to connect this act [the selection of the seven] with the laying of the contributions at the Apostles' feet. As being thus constituted stewards of the bounty of the community they were in a manner responsible for the distribution of the charitable fund. But the task had outgrown their powers, unless it was to be allowed to encroach on their higher Divinely appointed functions. They proposed therefore to entrust this special part of the work to other men."[115]

According to 4:4, the number of men belonging to the church was five thousand. If one would reckon women and children to the number, the church had grown to the size of a small city. The apostles were confronted with a conflict of two necessary ministries: instructing the church in the Word and meeting the temporal needs of those who lacked material substance. The disciples did not have enough time to do both effectively.

Luke's statement that "a complaint by the Hellenists arose against the Hebrews" (6:1) has led to significant discussion about the identity of the Hellenists. Cadbury states that the Hellenists in 6:1 were Greeks, i.e.,

---

113. Spencer, "Neglected Widows," 721–22. Roloff, "Konflikte und Konfliktlösungen in der Apostelgeschichte," 117–18.

114. Schnabel, *Early Christian Mission*, 1:429. His response is in particular to Roloff.

115. Hort, *The Christian Ekklesia*, 51.

non-Jews.[116] Few, however, have followed his suggestion. Ἑλληνιστής means "one who uses the Greek language."[117] Windisch says,

> Ἑλληνιστής derives from ἑλληνίζειν, as does βαπτιστής from βαπτίζειν . . . . If ἑλληνίζειν means "to speak Greek," but also "to live as a Greek," (cf. ἀττικίζειν, "to speak Attic" and "to have the Attic outlook" . . .) then the Ἑλληνιστής includes not only the Greek language but also a Greek or non-Jewish mode of life.[118]

That the church was made up of Jews, not Jews and Gentiles, needs little explaining. Until this point in the history of the early church, neither Samaritans nor Greeks were included in the group (unless as Jewish prose-lytes, v. 5). Hengel says that by the middle of the third century BCE, all of Judaism should be classified as Hellenized Judaism. It would be better to differentiate between Greek-speaking and Hebrew/Aramaic speaking Jews. However, even this is somewhat problematic, as many in Jerusalem spoke Greek.[119] It is estimated that between ten and twenty percent of the population of Jerusalem spoke Greek as their mother tongue.[120] Some distinguish the Hellenists and Hebrews as those who came from the Diaspora as opposed to those who came from Palestine.[121] This cannot be the case, however, since Paul, whose origin was in Asia Minor, calls himself one of the Hebrews (Phil 3:5). Porter argues that the use of the two terms in Acts 6:1 is ". . . probably a linguistic distinction made between Jews who spoke mainly Greek and those who spoke mainly Aramaic or who also spoke Aramaic. Before the third century AD these terms were virtually exclusively linguistic terms referring to language competence."[122]

---

116. Cadbury, "The Hellenists," 1:59–74. Windisch, "Ἕλλην, κ.τ.λ.," *TDNT*, 2:511, explains reasons both for and against Cadbury's explanation, concluding that it is not convincing.

117. *LSJ*, 536.

118. Windisch, *TDNT*, 2:510.

119. Hengel, *Judentum und Hellenismus*, 193: "Das gesamte Judentum ab etwa der Mitte des 3.Jh.s.Chr. müsste im strengen Sinne als hellenistisches Judentum bezeichnet werden, und man sollte besser zwischen dem griechischsprechenden Judentum der westlichen Dispora und dem aramäisch/hebräischsprechenden Judentum Palästinas bzw. Babyloniens unterschieden."

120. Cornu and Shulam, *The Jewish Roots of Acts*, 316.

121. Gutbrod, "Ἰουδαῖος, κ.τ.λ. in the New Testament," *TDNT*, 3:389; Löning, "Der Stephanuskreis und seine Mission," 84.

122. Porter, "Did Jesus Teach in Greek?," 210.

The conclusion of Witherington is most likely the best. Speaking of its usage in the New Testament, he says,

> Thus we conclude that the term Ἑλληνιστής . . . means a Greek-speaking person, with the context defining more precisely what sort of Greek-speaking person Luke has in mind, ranging from Jewish Christians, to Jews, to pagans. This in turn means that Luke does not use "Hellenist" as some sort of technical term for a specific kind of Christian. Nevertheless, it is clear that the disagreements between Aramaic- and Greek-speaking Jewish Christians referred to in Acts 6:1ff is important as a clue to the varied character of even the earliest Christian fellowship in Jerusalem.[123]

Jewish communities took care of the poor, the widows and orphans. They did so because Yahweh had commanded it in the Law (Deut 14:19; 16:24; 24:19–22; 26:12–13).

> Caring for the needy was part and parcel of being an Israelite, one who belongs to such a Lord who "executes justice for the fatherless and the widow, and loves the sojourner, giving him food and clothing" (Deut 10:18; James 1:27). Among the prophets "doing justice for the widows" was shorthand for covenantal loyalty. In the Rabbinic tradition "doing justice (*sedeka*) was spell out in terms of organized community almsgiving."[124]

The apostles had begun this ministry in the Jerusalem church (Acts 4:34–35). James, who according to Luke was a part of the Jerusalem church from its beginning, designates the action of helping the widows and orphans as a sign of possessing true faith in Christ (Jas 1:27). During the time of Jesus, the city of Jerusalem made a weekly distribution of food and clothing to the poor: "There can be no doubt that these arrangements served as a model for the primitive Church."[125]

The choice of seven to take over the ministry of helping the needy of the church would not, in a Jewish context, be anything novel. Some scholars have claimed that the institution of the ministry of the seven in Acts 6:3 was based on the Jewish model of "the seven of the city."[126] However, the

---

123. Witherington III, *Acts of the Apostles*, 242.

124. Nagel, "The Twelve and the Seven," 115. Nagel's last sentence quotes Johnson, *Acts of the Apostles*, 105–6.

125. Jeremias, *Jerusalem in the Time of Jesus*, 131.

126. Daube, *The New Testament and Rabbinic Judaism*, 237. *Str-B*, 2:641: "Die Siebenzahl wohl nach Analogie der sieben Mitglieder, aus denen in den jüdischen Gemeinden

identification is not exact, because the care of the poor was designated to a committee of three persons, appointed by the governing board of the city.[127] The people who administrated the care of the poor were designated as גַּבָּאֵי צְדָקָה (alms-receiver) or מְחַלְּקִי צְדָקָה (alms-giver).[128] This is perhaps why no title is given to the seven in Acts 6. They would have been called "alms-givers" or "alms-receivers," not deacons.

To solve the problem, the apostles called together τὸ πλῆθος τῶν μαθητῶν ("the multitude of the disciples"). One view is to identify this group as the "Grecian disciples."[129] Strauch suggests that it was not the whole group of disciples that met together, but rather their representatives: "These were Jews, not Gentiles, so they were accustomed to having representative leaders, such as elders, act on their behalf (Acts 15:6–22; 21:17, 18)."[130] Strauch's statement, however, is only half true. As described in chapter 2, assembly of the people was a way of life in Israel historically. It was also part of the normal Jewish experience in Palestine in cities and villages during the time of Christ. The terminology of the passage does not lend itself to an event of only representatives, as the following paragraphs explain.

When used of people, the term πλῆθος can mean either a large group (either organized or unorganized), an assembly, or a populace. Instances of an unorganized group include Acts 2:6, "And at this sound the multitude came together"; 5:16, "The people also gathered from the towns around Jerusalem"; and 21:36, "the mob of the people followed." In these verses, the context clearly indicates an unorganized group. When τὸ πλῆθος is used of religious communities, "it is a technical term for the whole body of their members."[131] In Acts 4:32, the church in Jerusalem is called τὸ πλῆθος; in 15:12, 30 the church in Jerusalem is called τὸ πλῆθος. "This word, followed by a national name in the genitive, often signifies not *multitude* simply, but *people* in the official political sense. Thus we have τὸ πλῆθος τῶν Ἰουδαίων in 1 Macc. 8:20, 2 Macc. 11:16."[132] τὸ πλῆθος is also used to designate the

meist der Ortsvorstand sich zusammensetzte. Dieser hieß deshalb geradezu ‚die Sieben einer Stadt' oder ‚die sieben Besten einer Stadt.'"

127. Str-B, 2:643.

128. Ibid.

129. Gaechter, *Petrus und seine Zeit*, 128–30. Spencer, *Portrait of Philip in Acts*, 196, says he argues unconvincingly. Getz, *Elders and Leaders*, 57. Getz does not explain his reasons for the conclusion.

130. Strauch, *Biblical Eldership*, 282.

131. BDAG, 825d.

132. Deissmann, *Bible Studies*, 232.

assemblies of Rhodes and Lydia (first century CE).[133] Lake and Cadbury further define this usage of πλῆθος as "a body of persons regarded in their corporate capacity, almost equivalent to *demos* or to the American use of the word 'people.'"[134]

Luke uses τὸ πλῆθος τῶν μαθητῶν in a slightly different sense in Luke 19:37 ("the whole multitude of disciples"). Here, he is talking of the disciples of Jesus before his crucifixion, and therefore, not an organized entity. Nevertheless, the meaning is inclusive. He is not separating one part of the group of disciples from the rest or referring to a group of representatives by this expression. In Acts 6:2, Luke is talking about the church, thus by τὸ πλῆθος τῶν μαθητῶν he means all the disciples adhering to the church. Therefore, v.2 has to be talking about the entire assembly of the Jerusalem believers.[135] Various translations reflect the certainty of this meaning of τὸ πλῆθος τῶν μαθητῶν in v. 2: "Then the twelve called the multitude of the disciples *unto them*" (KJV); "And the twelve summoned the congregation of the disciples" (NASB); "So the Twelve gathered all the disciples together" (NIV); "Then the twelve summoned the multitude of the disciples" (NKJV); "And the twelve called together the whole community of the disciples" (NRSV); "And the twelve summoned the full number of the disciples" (ESV); "Da riefen die Zwölf die Menge der Jünger zusammen" (Luther).

The Twelve decided that the best course to remedy the problem in the church was for the whole church to take action. It is critical to take Luke seriously when he repeats that the disciples were "of one accord" (Acts 1:14; 2:1; 2:46; 4:24; 5:12). The murmuring of the Hellenists was directed at the Hebrews (v. 1). The division that had begun along cultural lines certainly threatened to disrupt the existing unity of the church. Thus, to heal the rift, the cooperation of the whole group was necessary, not simply the cooperation of the Hellenists. As Spencer notes, "These disciples represent more than mere 'extras' on the scene; they are very much involved in solving the

---

133. Ibid.

134. Lake and Cadbury, *Acts of the Apostles*, 48. They point out the technical usage in Plato *Politicus* 291d, Thucydides 1.125 and 2 Macc 11:16.

135. It might be objected that the number of disciples in Jerusalem would prohibit any full assembly. To this it may be answered that the disciples were at this point still meeting at Solomon's porch (Acts 5:12), which could easily accommodate ten thousand people. Second, it would be foolish to force the meaning that there were no absentees. Both Old Testament and New Testament use the word "all" with a comprehensive, rather than an absolute sense. If Getz and Gaechter were correct, one would expect the wording to. πλῆθος τῶν μαθητῶν τῶν Ἑλληνιστῶν, or similar.

crisis which threatens their fellowship."[136] As a part of their understanding of the involvement of the whole group, the apostles did not criticize the murmuring of the Hellenist disciples (v. 1). Instead, they determined to act upon what they viewed as the reasonable complaints of the Hellenists.

The apostles instructed the whole church, "Brothers, choose (ἐπισκέψασθε) seven men from among you" (v.3).[137] The KJV translation of the verb as "look out" (in the sense of look for) is certainly legitimate, as this is the frequent meaning in the LXX (but it was also used to mean "choose" in the LXX, e.g., Num 4:27, 32; 16:5; 27:6; Neh 7:1). In any case, the church interpreted the apostles to mean "choose," as they did precisely that in their subsequent action (v. 5).[138] MacArthur's view, "Here we see the congregation is to nominate certain spiritually qualified men to serve, with the final appointment resting with those already in position as teachers and spiritual leaders," appears to be a misinterpretation of both words ἐκλέγω and καθίστημι.[139]

It should not come as a surprise that the apostles would judge the multitude of the disciples as capable to help create a solution and choose

136. Spencer, *Portrait of Philip in Acts*, 196.

137. MSS B has the reading ἐπισκεψώμεθα, which is used by the middle Egyptian Coptic translation (third century) and the Latin translations h (fifth century) and p (twelfth century). This reading would mean that the apostles were including themselves in the selection process. Metzger points out that this is to be rejected, not only because of unconvincing manuscript support but also because it is inconsistent with v.6. Metzger, *Textual Commentary*, 337.

138. *BDAG*, 378c, lists two other meanings for ἐπισκέπτομαι: "to visit someone" and "God's gracious visitation bringing salvation." Parrott, "The Role of the Congregation in the Government of the Church," 12, says, "Again, the issuance of this command and the fact that it was apparently carried out without question enforces the claim that the spiritual leaders were in control, they were the decision-makers." This flatly contradicts vv. 3 and 5.

139. MacArthur, *Acts 1–12*, 182–83. ἐκλέγω never means "nominate." It means "to select, to choose" and takes special meanings of "to conceal" and "to levy taxes," *LSJ* 511. In Acts 1:23 the group "proposed two" (NIV, NAB, NKJV). The word used is ἵστημι, which would more likely have been used if Luke had only meant that the church had made nominations to the apostles. In fact, the multitude "set forth" the seven (ἵστημι), but unlike Acts 1:23, only after they had made their final choice. Unlike Acts 1:23, in 6:3–6 there was no reduction of the numbers. Nor was there substitution of any of the seven elected by the multitude. Finally the apostles said they would set the chosen men over the ministry (καθίστημι). The word can mean "ordain" or "appoint," but not to select one or more out of a group (which the apostles would have to have done, had the final choice of personnel been theirs). The Greek word normally used to mean nominate is ὀνομασία)

the right leaders for the task. They were all baptized in the Spirit. (Note the promise of God, announced by Peter on Pentecost in Acts 2:38: "And you will receive the gift of the Holy Spirit.") Therefore they possessed a new inward direction from God and a capacity for understanding spiritual matters that exceeded their previous experience (see chapter 3). One of the requirements of the men to be selected was to be "full of the Spirit." At the point in time of the events of Acts 6, this group of believers had openly confessed Jesus as the Messiah, were being taught in the Word of God daily, were firm in their spiritual direction in the face of persecution, spoke the Word boldly in spite of threats, shared their wealth to the point of selling their property so that no one in the church had any need, were living in the fear of God after watching his severe chastening of one of their number, maintained harmonious relationships, and were expecting the return of Christ. They were surely capable of discerning which people were full of the Spirit and which were not.

The Twelve explained that their own responsibility was to place the elected seven in their new task. The NIV translates the last phrase in v.3 as follows: "We will turn this responsibility over to them." The translation is not a literal rendering of καθίστημι,[140] but it does focus the reader on the fact that the Twelve were delegating responsibility. The ministry for the seven was not entirely new; previously it had been the work of the Twelve to manage. The Twelve were simply dividing their own work, giving a portion of it to the new ministers. The Twelve would devote themselves primarily to prayer and the teaching of the Word (v. 4—which, following Jesus' example, would have also included training others): an enormous task for Twelve men among a group of people who were the size of a small city.[141] This ministry was crucial: "What carries everything forward in Acts is the preaching of the Word of God."[142]

The entire group was obviously impressed with the sensitivity and wisdom of the apostles (καὶ ἤρεσεν ὁ λόγος ἐνώπιον παντὸς τοῦ πλήθους— "What they said pleased the whole community" NRSV). The multitude then chose (ἐξελέξαντο) seven men.[143] How the church did the choosing is

140. *BDAG*, 492c, gives the meaning "appoint, put in charge" for καθίστημι in Acts 6:3. This is followed by the ESV, NAS, NKJV, NRSV, NAB, and NEB.

141. With this in mind, the view of Getz and Gaechter that the discussion was between the Twelve and the Hellenists could hardly be right. It would require the Twelve to say that they would devote themselves to the Word and the care of the Hebrew widows.

142. Nagel, "The Twelve and the Seven," 118.

143. "Choose" is the only meaning of ἐκλέγω in the NT.

not stated. Some are insistent that no vote was taken in this event.[144] This is, perhaps, too hasty a conclusion. As has been demonstrated in chapter 2, vote-taking was actively practiced in the Qumran community, by Jews in the Diaspora, and in many cities of Palestine, including Tiberias, Sepphoris, and the Decapolis. It is not certain that the seven were chosen by vote, but the possibility should not be ruled out either. Whatever method was used, Luke clearly relates that the whole group did the choosing. Interestingly, nearly all exegetical commentaries are in agreement with this conclusion.[145]

Because the names of all the selected men were Greek—Stephen, Philip, Prochorus, Nicanor, Timon, Parmenas, and Nicolas, Witherington concludes, "This seems to suggest that the community as a whole, in order to avoid even the appearance of favoritism, named mostly if not exclusively Greek-speaking Jewish Christians to administer the food distribution."[146] Most commentaries view this event as a beginning of increased Hellenistic leadership in the church, but it cannot be said for certain that the Greek names inevitably mean all seven were Hellenists. Although Nicolas, a proselyte of Antioch, certainly would be classified as a Hellenist, three of the twelve apostles of Jesus—Andreas, Philip, and Didymus—also had Greek names. What is safe to conclude is that whether the men were all Hellenists or not, the choice of them was satisfying to the whole church.

Many exegetes cite the choice of the seven as a demonstration of an early church which functioned in a democratic way.[147] Knowling criticizes this view:

> The passage has been quoted in support of the democratic constitution of the Apostolic Church, but the whole context shows that the government really lay with the Apostles. The Church as a whole is under their direction and counsel, and the Apostles alone determine what qualification those chosen should possess, the apostles alone lay hands upon them after prayer.[148]

But Knowling appears to be overemphasizing his point. As mentioned in chapters 2 and 3, democracies during the time of the apostles and earlier had

144. Couch, et al., *Biblical Theology of the Church*, 184–85.

145. Garrett, "The Congregation-Led Church," 319–21n52, lists English language works (through 2004), which conclude that the entire church chose the deacons. The list runs a full two pages, single-spaced, fine print.

146. Witherington III, *Acts of the Apostles*, 250.

147. For example, see the discussion of Spencer, *Portrait of Philip in Acts*, 198.

148. Knowling, *Acts of the Apostles*, 167.

a βουλή, which strictly set the agenda for its meetings. Moreover, whether democratic or not, it would have only been proper for those presently conducting a charitable function of the group to turn over the function to the new administrators and explain how to carry out the work. Finally, Knowling does not address how the choice was made, which is crucial if he is to substantiate his assertion.

It is perhaps a misnomer to denote the choice of the seven as a democratic action. What is missing in the account of the assembly is any mention of discussion or debate, which would be expected from citizens of an assembly in a democratic meeting (contrast Acts 6:1–6 with Acts 15:5–22: in the latter there is, even in the compressed report, evidence of debate and divergent opinions). The entire evaluation of the problem and its solution is given by the Twelve. The verbal involvement of the body entails voicing approval of the Twelve's idea (though it must also be noted that Luke gives a synopsis of the event, not its details). What appears instead of a democratic discussion is an astute and sensitive pastoral initiative, issuing in a decision made by all members of the body. Dever comments perceptively about the apostles in this instance: "It almost seems that they were recognizing in the church assembly the same kind of ultimate authority, under God, that Jesus had recognized in His statement in Matthew 18:15–17."[149] Beyer's analysis is apt:

> The Process described is of decisive significance in the history of Christian organization, since here for the first time we have an appointment, not through a call of the incarnate or risen Lord, nor through the self-attestation of the charismatic Spirit in a Christian, but by the election of the members of the congregation.[150]

Luke presents the choice of the Seven in Acts 6 as the resolution of a crisis worthy of a church led by the Spirit and confessing Jesus as Messiah. A corporate decision of this kind required church leaders who were sensitive both to the Spirit and the people of the church. It worked when genuine grievances (which inevitably come in a sizeable group) were heard seriously and sensitively. It also required instruction to the group on how a decision was to be carried out. Because a major rift developed among the whole group, the effort of the whole group was necessary to mend it. This

---

149. Dever, *Nine Marks*, 222.
150. Beyer, "διάκονος," *TDNT*, 2:605.

last matter was no doubt a crucial factor for determining the necessity of a corporate decision.

Acts 8:14–17

The Samaritan mission began after the church in Jerusalem (including Philip) was scattered through persecution.[151] The apostles would clearly have anticipated this event after Jesus had told them they would be witnesses in Samaria (Acts 1:8). As the apostles heard of the conversion and baptism of many Samaritans, they sent Peter and John as their representatives. The parallels of this passage with Acts 11:22–24, including the choice of representatives to go to the new work, have led some commentators to the conclusion that Luke interpolated from an Antioch source into Acts 8. Spencer responds that "the iterative pattern may be viewed as characteristic of Luke's style, a means of interlocking various parts of his narrative. The pervasive Lukan language . . . confirms this perspective."[152] This account fulfills multiple objectives in Luke's narrative. One of those objectives was to provide a connection between the Philip and Stephen stories.[153]

The purpose of the visit by Peter and John to Samaria is not difficult to discern from the text and from the commission given by Jesus in Acts 1:8. MacArthur's statement, "That the Samaritans were included in the kingdom was shocking to devout Jews, who despised them as half-breed outcasts," though generally true of devout Jews, is perhaps too strongly worded in this instance. [154] The apostles had already witnessed the conversion of many Samaritans during Jesus' ministry (John 4). Likewise, Jesus had prophesied their further conversion. Alford notes, "Our Lord's command (ch. 1.8) had removed all doubt as to Samaria being a legitimate field for preaching, and Samaritan converts being admissible."[155] The apostles most

---

151. Haenchen, *Die Apostelgeschichte*, 288, says that Luke is in error to say that the whole church was scattered rather than the Hellenistic segment. He likewise argues that Luke, with his incorrect emphasis on the unified Jerusalem church, can only with difficulty connect Paul with the persecution. Haenchen is following the view begun by F. C. Baur, which has been shown to be erroneous (see first section of this chapter). Pesch, *Die Apostelgeschichte*, 1:271, by contrast, argues that there is a clear unity in the tradition underlying the story in Acts, and that it does not bear the marks of layering.

152. Spencer, *Portrait of Philip in Acts*, 33.

153. Ibid.

154. MacArthur, *Acts 1—12*, 244.

155. Alford, *The Greek New Testament*, 2:89.

likely understood the report of the mission in Samaria as a fulfillment of Jesus' prophecy. The apostles, then, visited the work of Philip to legitimatize it, to unify the expanding movement with the Jerusalem body, and to see to it that the Samaritan believers also received the gift of the Spirit (8:15–17).[156] This is not to minimize the differences between the Jews and the Samaritans, which were significant. Because of those differences, it was necessary for the Twelve to affirm the genuine conversions of the Samaritans: "The prayer of the apostles allows God to show his acceptance of the Samaritans so that the entire church can see it."[157] Likewise, the miraculous coming of the Holy Spirit on the Samaritan believers confirmed that they were part of the same body with the Jews.

James Dunn compares the fascination of the Samaritans with Simon the sorcerer and their attentiveness to Philip's message and miracles: the same word προσέχω is used in both instances. Dunn concludes that the Samaritans were not genuinely converted; true conversion then became the work of Peter and John.[158] Spencer responds to Dunn in the following way:

> I have already instanced their [the Samaritans'] less enthralled preoccupation with Philip's miracles. But more than this, the respective προσέχω-expressions are not the same. With respect to Philip, the Samaritans "listened eagerly to *what was said*" (προσεῖχον . . . τοῖς λεγομένοις, v. 6); in Simon's case, they "listened eagerly *to him*" (πορσεῖχον δὲ αὐτῷ, v. 11; cf. v.10). It was not Philip himself, but Philip's message about Christ, which arrested the Samaritans' attention; by contrast, the Samaritans' attachment to Simon was more of a personality fixation, an enchantment with a cult figure.[159]

Thus, the apostles did not correct the work of Philip; instead they affirmed it.

Roman Catholic theologians use v. 17 to prove that the communication of the Holy Spirit must take place through the laying on of hands by the apostles and their successors. This particular interpretation has a long history, following its first appearance in the writings of Hippolytus in the

---

156. Maynard-Reid, "Samaria," *DNLT*, 1076; Bock, *Acts*, 330; Meyer, *Acts of the Apostles*, 170; Wikenhauser, *Die Apostelgeschichte*, 97.

157. Bock, *Acts*, 330.

158. Dunn, *Baptism in the Holy Spirit*, 64–65.

159. Spencer, *Portrait of Philip in Acts*, 51–52.

third century C.E. (*Trad. ap.* 21).[160] The interpretation is problematic in that Acts 10:44, for instance, records the receiving of the Holy Spirit without any apostolic laying on of hands. Wikenhauser claims 10:44 is simply an exception which does not change the doctrine.[161] However, there are other exceptions to this alleged doctrine in the book of Acts, viz. 8:36–39, 9:17, and 16:30–34. Kistemaker responds, "Except for 19:6, the historical context in Acts fails to lend support to the teaching that the church must have a sacrament of confirmation that is administered by placing hands on every believer, so that he or she may receive the Holy Spirit."[162]

The group decision-making in this instance of the life of the early church was done by the apostles. They undoubtedly saw themselves as the shepherds of the young church, wherever it put down its roots. The entire church was not involved in the action portrayed in Acts 8:14–17. It is important to note the wording of v. 14: "Now when the apostles at Jerusalem heard that Samaria had received the word of God, they sent to them Peter and John," because it parallels 11:22 and helps identify who was involved in the group decision in that passage (the next one to be considered). The apostles viewed the work of confirming and unifying, in this instance, as their responsibility. Their sending of representatives was not for hierarchical activity, but rather to confirm the expansion of the mission Jesus commanded before he ascended to heaven.

Acts 11:22

The story of the beginning of the church in Antioch depicts a further stage of expansion in the spread of the Christian message. "The theme that Luke unfolds is one of ever-widening circles comparable to those created by a stone thrown into a placid pond."[163] The new church begun in Antioch was new in kind, in that it was not primarily Jewish:

> What this paragraph is going to describe is something altogether new: not the planting in Antioch of a Christian Jewish synagogue to which Gentiles might be admitted on becoming Jews, but the planting of a community in which Jewish believers and Gentile

---

160. Müller, *Katholische Dogmatik*, 672. Denzinger, *Sources of Catholic Dogma*, 165.

161. Wikenhauser, *Die Apostelgeschichte*, 98.

162. Kistemaker, *Acts*, 302.

163. Ibid., 299.

believers met on equal terms—so that a new name, "Christians,"
was invented to apply to the members of this community (11:26).[164]

Ruled according to a democratic constitution,[165] Antioch was the
third largest city in the Roman Empire in the first century CE, with a population of ca. 250,000,[166] and a large Jewish population, estimated at between
20,000 and 65,000.[167] Part of the uniqueness of Antioch in the Lukan narrative is that there is a tradition that Luke was originally a native of Antioch
(Eusebius, *Hist. eccl.* 2.4.6). According to Josephus, many of the Gentiles in
Antioch were attracted to the Jewish faith (*J.W.* 7.45). Schnabel proposes
the following scenario for the evangelism which took place at Antioch:

> It is a plausible assumption that they [the Diaspora Jews from
> Cyprus and Cyrene] attended the synagogues of Antioch and pro-
> claimed the message of Jesus the Messiah to the Jews, proselytes
> and God-fearers who attended the synagogue services. Before
> long they also reached the polytheistic inhabitants of the city with
> the gospel.[168]

Luke relates that the Jewish believers from Cyprus and Cyrene took a
new step and "on coming to Antioch spoke to the Hellenists also, preaching the Lord Jesus" (πρὸς τοὺς Ἑλληνιστὰς εὐαγγελιζόμενοι τὸν κύριον
Ἰησοῦν—11:20). The author accepts the reading Ἑλληνιστὰς rather than
Ἕλληνας, and follows Metzger, the "mixed population of Antioch in contrast to the Ἰουδαῖοι."[169] The passage is then understood, with most commentators, that the hearers of the evangel were non-Jews. "This enterprise,"
says Bruce, "met with instant success. The Gentiles took to the Christian
message as the very thing they had been waiting for."[170]

164. Gooding, *True to the Faith*, 187.

165. Kolb, "Antiochia in der früheren Kaiserzeit," 102.

166. Jones, et al., "Antioch," *OCD*, 197.

167. Schnabel, *Early Christian Mission*, 1:785.

168. Ibid., 787.

169. Metzger, *Textual Commentary*, 387–89.

170. Bruce, *Acts*, 239. Bruce states that a particular form of gospel presentation, sug-
gested by v. 20, made the gospel understandable to the Gentiles in Antioch: "To present
him as Messiah to people who knew nothing of the hope of Israel would have been a
meaningless procedure, but the Greek terms *Kyrios* ('Lord') and *Soter* ('Saviour') were
widely current in the religious world of the eastern Mediterranean. Many were attempt-
ing to find in various mystery cults a divine lord who could guarantee salvation and
immortality to his devotees." Meyer, *Ursprung and Anfänge des Christentums*, 3:390–95,
argues that the acceptance of the message in Antioch was also influenced by the fact that

The inclusion of many people as disciples of Jesus who had never assented to adhere to the commands of the Mosaic law created a serious problem for the Christians in Jerusalem which was not resolved until the events of Acts 15. Luke makes his readers aware of the problem in 11:1–18. In the conversion of Cornelius, however, Peter was present to preach the message and confirm the work of the Holy Spirit in the lives of God-fearing Gentiles. In the case of the mission in Antioch, no apostle did the evangelizing, nor was the mission restricted to Jews, proselytes, and God-fearers.[171] The news of the mission in Antioch, therefore, demanded a visit from the church in Jerusalem.

For this occasion, the church did not send an apostle, but instead, Barnabas. Luke gives several reasons for Barnabas's competence for the task. First, he had shown unusual generosity to the rest of the church in Jerusalem in its early days (Acts 4:36–37). The church in Jerusalem could attest that he was wholeheartedly committed to the work of Christ's church and would certainly be reliable as a representative to the distant new work. Second, as Luke introduces Barnabas, he gives the meaning of his Aramaic name, "son of consolation," as though he wants to emphasize how Barnabas lived up to the meaning. Third, he further describes Barnabas as "a good man and full of the Holy Spirit." A fourth reason was probably his origin from Cyprus (4:36). He would likely be quickly accepted by the Diaspora Jewish believers who had done the original mission work in Antioch.[172]

In contrast to 8:14, where the apostles made the decision to send messengers of their number to Samaria, in this instance, the whole church sent Barnabas to Antioch. Some theologians, however, are not convinced that the commissioning of Barnabas as its messenger was the action of the whole church. Bruce, for instance, says it was the leaders of the church who sent him.[173] Reymond adds, "I doubt very seriously whether the entire church

Julius and Augustus Caesar were called σοτήρ in the Graeco-Roman world. He points out the fact that neither Mark nor Matthew uses the word σοτήρ in his gospel. Luke, on the contrary, uses it both in his gospel and in Acts.

171. For an explanation of the identity of the "God-fearers" in New Testament times and why they played so small a part in the accounts of evangelism in Acts, see Levinskaya, *The Book of Acts*, 118–26.

172. Barrett, *Commentary on the Acts*, 1:552, says, "Luke clearly understands Barnabas . . . to have been sent as an official inspector on behalf of Jerusalem, charged to see what was going on in Antioch and presumably if necessary to put an end to it." But the negative cast to this evaluation hardly fits the evaluation given above, or Barnabas' subsequent actions.

173. Bruce, *Acts*, 239–40.

in Jerusalem, which numbered in the thousands by this time, was polled to see what it thought about Barnabas's assignment."[174] Instead, Reymond suggests that the word ἐκκλησία in this instance means "the elder/overseer representatives of several congregations."[175] Reymond would be hard pressed to find lexical support for his definition. Bock points out, "That the Jerusalem community is called the church (ἐκκλησία, *ekklesia*) testifies to a growing self-identity as a community, as the term has not been used since Acts 9:31 and now becomes more frequent."[176] However, the strong identity came much earlier, at the election of the Seven in Acts 6.

> But the appointment was not only a notable recognition of the Hellenistic element in the Ecclesia at Jerusalem, a prelude of greater events to come, but also a sign that the Ecclesia was to be an Ecclesia indeed, not a mere horde of men ruled absolutely by the Apostles, but a true body politic, in which different functions were assigned to different members, and a share of responsibility rested upon the members at large, each and all.[177]

It would be helpful at this point to compare the passages 8:14 and 11:22. Note the parallels (translation NASB):

(8:14)   Now when the apostles in Jerusalem
         (δὲ οἱ ἐν Ἱεροσολύμοις ἀπόστολοι)

(11:22) the church at Jerusalem
         (ἐκκλησίας τῆς οὔσης ἐν Ἱερουσαλὴμ)

(8:14)   heard that Samaria had received the word of God
         (Ἀκούσαντες ὅτι δέδεκται ἡ Σαμάρεια τὸν λόγον τοῦ θεοῦ)

(11:22) And the news about them reached the ears of
         (Ἠκούσθη δὲ ὁ λόγος εἰςτὰ ὦτα τῆς περὶ αὐτῶν)

(8:14)   they sent them Peter and John
         (ἀπέστειλαν πρὸς αὐτοὺς Πέτρον καὶ Ἰωάννην)

(11:22) and they sent Barnabas off to Antioch
         (καὶ ἐξαπέστειλαν Βαρναβᾶν [διελθεῖν] ἕως Ἀντιοχείας)

---

174. Akin, "The Single-Elder-Led Church," 80. This quotation is Reymond's response to Akin.

175. Reymond, "The Presbytery-Led Church," 112–13.

176. Bock, *Acts*, 415.

177. Hort, *The Christian Ecclesia*, 52.

The recipients of the report in both instances are clearly denoted: in the first, "the apostles in Jerusalem"; in the second, "the church at Jerusalem." The same verb for receiving the news is used in both instances (ἀκούω). In the first, it appears as an aorist circumstantial participle, expressing the temporal idea.[178] In the second, it is an aorist passive, "it was heard." In Luke's use of a Semitism in 11:22, Ἠκούσθη δὲ εἰς τὰ ὦτα, "Luke," Haenchen asserts, "is true to the biblical idiom."[179] The expression εἰς τὰ ὦτα occurs frequently in the LXX as a translation of בְּאָזְנֵי (e.g., Gen 23:16; Num 14:28; Deut 32:44, and with ἠκούσθη in Isa 5:9).[180] Finally, in both passages, one or more representatives were sent: the verbs for "sent" differ in each case but are synonyms (ἀποστέλλω and ἐξαποστέλλω).

Luke portrays very similar actions of group decision-making. The group received information and the group sent in both instances. If in Acts 8:14 the apostles both heard news and sent representatives (with which there is almost no dispute among commentators), then in Acts 11:22 the Jerusalem church both heard news and sent a representative. If the apostles or the elders of the Jerusalem church had been intended (the elders are not mentioned until v.30), they would likely have been so noted (e.g., 11:30; 15:6; 21:18). Whether some of the church acted in representative capacity for the whole body is certainly possible, but the text does not indicate it happened. Luke's intent in 11:22 is to make plain that the sending of Barnabas was a church action.

That the whole church should be consulted for the sending of Barnabas makes sense. Surely the main thought of the Jerusalem church was that they wanted the new work in Antioch to succeed. However, a large faction of the Jerusalem church, designated as οἱ ἐκ περιτομῆς, "those of the circumcision" (NKJV), had considerable difficulty with Peter's eating with uncircumcised Gentiles (11:2). After hearing Peter's explanation and revelation, they were convinced of the rightness of his actions. But the mission activity in Antioch included neither apostles nor revelation about eating. The entire church would need to be involved in the choice of a representative to Antioch in order for all sides to be confident about the outcome of the visit. The members of the Jerusalem body were believer-priests. Consideration of

178. See Wallace, *Greek Grammar beyond the Basics*, 622–25, for an explanation of this type of participle.

179. Haenchen, *Die Apostelgeschichte*, 352.

180. The expression occurs thirty-five times in the LXX as a translation of the Hebrew בְּאָזְנֵי. Luke uses it two other times in his gospel (1:44, 9:44). James also uses the expression (5:4).

their differing views had to be taken into account by hearing them out. This could not be done by executive action or word from a governing board. The most sensible interpretation of Acts 11:22 is, therefore, that the entire church chose Barnabas as its representative to the new work Antioch.

Acts 11:30

The action in Acts 11:30 is similar to that in 8:14 and 11:22; in this case, however, the Christians in Antioch heard the information and sent messengers to Jerusalem. In addition, the information came not through a report from an eyewitness, but rather from the prophet Agabus. Likewise, the group in Acts 11:29 was not denoted as the ἐκκλησία, but as the disciples (τῶν μαθητῶν). However, for this last difference, the use of ἐκκλησία was unnecessary, since the believers were already described as the ἐκκλησία in v.26. The church in Antioch is also designated as "the disciples" in Antioch.

The occasion for the action of sending messengers was the visit of multiple prophets from the church in Jerusalem (v.27). Not only Barnabas but also others from the church in Jerusalem were interested in the healthy advancement of the mission work in Antioch. The prophecy of Agabus (ἐσήμανεν, "to signify ahead of time")[181] was most likely given at a public meeting of the church, or a part of the church, since Agabus was described as standing up (v.28, ἀναστὰς δὲ, see Acts 1:15; 5:17; 13:16; 15:7).[182] Paul, a leader in the church in Antioch, saw the public meeting of the church as the place for spoken prophecy (1 Cor 12:28; 14:29–23; although later Agabus spoke a prophecy to a small group of Christians, Acts 21:10–11). Agabus' objective was to inform the believers in Antioch of the coming famine in Judea, and thus encourage them to help their fellow-Christians.[183]

181. Bauer, *Wörterbuch zum Neuen Testament*, Sp.1495: "ein Vorzeichen geben." Barrett, *Commentary on the Acts*, 1:562–63, says that the verb points to the giving of oracles. Bauer cites Plutarch, Heraclitus, Epictetus, and Josephus for this use of σημαίνω.

182. MSS D and Augustine add, "and there was much rejoicing, and when we were gathered together . . . ." Lake and Cadbury, *Acts of the Apostles*, 131, claim that this account was inserted to the text in the middle of the second century, CE.

183. Haenchen, *Die Apostelgeschichte*, 359, says the mention of this famine is completely unhistorical, as no famine has ever encompassed the whole world. Bauer, *Wörterbuch*, Sp.1137 gives the definition of "the whole inhabited earth" for οἰκουμένη in v.28. Lake and Cadbury, *Acts of the Apostles*, 131, point out that ἐφ' ὅλην τὴν οἰκουμένην can mean "the whole land of Palestine." οἰκουμένη is a political, not a geographical word. Bock, *Acts*, 417, notes that one inscription in Asia Minor (*CIG*, 3973.5–6) speaks of a famine occurring in the whole world.

Since Antioch was a wealthy city populated with wealthy Jewish citizens,[184] the ability of the church in Antioch to help the church in Jerusalem in time of need seems obvious. The account in these four verses, Barrett argues, also marks the beginning of the independence of the Antioch church. Having been approved by a representative of the Jerusalem church, the church of Antioch acts "as an adult child . . . to care for its mother in need."[185]

The Christians in Antioch first heard the gospel through former members of the church in Jerusalem. They were also given effective spiritual assistance from Jerusalem in the person of Barnabas. It was only natural that they desired to aid the Jerusalem church in return. Bock notes,

> The famine relief indicates a complete reconciliation as needs are met across geographical and ethnic boundaries. The relief portrays the oneness and caring of the community, as did Acts 4 in Jerusalem, where goods were shared. Racial harmony and caring are possible. The church is one despite being in different locales.[186]

The Christians in Antioch responded individually to the prophecy: "So the disciples determined, everyone according to his ability, to send relief to the brothers living in Judea" (11:29). In v.30, however, there is a subject change from the individuals to the group (ὃ καὶ ἐποίησαν ἀποστείλαντες . . . διὰ χειρὸς Βαρναβᾶ καὶ Σαύλου).

The church decided to send two representatives with the money collected for the church in Jerusalem: Barnabas and Saul. It may be that Barnabas and Saul resemble the pairs sent by Jewish communities, entrusted with the transport of money.[187] There is no mention of how Barnabas and Saul were chosen, however. They may have simply recommended themselves, which was acceptable to the entire group. On the other hand, they may have been nominated and chosen by the body. Since the choosing of messengers by a body has already been noted in 8:14 and 11:22, there is little need for Luke to repeat the information regarding how another church selected its messengers. The following discussion of the 1 Cor 16:3–4 and 2 Cor 8:18–19 passage, however, will also shed light on the sending of Saul and Barnabas.

---

184. Schnabel, *Early Christian Mission*, 1:785.

185. Barrett, *Commentary on the Acts*, 1:558–59.

186. Bock, *Acts*, 418.

187. Barrett, *Commentary on the Acts*, 1:566.

Acts 15:1–2 and 15:22

In the controversy over whether Gentile Christians needed to be circumcised, "the brothers" in Antioch "determined that Paul and Barnabas and certain others of them should go up to Jerusalem to the apostles and elders concerning this issue" (15:2, NASB). After a decision was made in Jerusalem, the Jerusalem church and its leaders "decided to choose representatives and to send them to Antioch with Paul and Barnabas" (15:22, NASB). The discussion of the selection of these messengers will be taken up in the section on Doctrine and Practice in Acts 15.

1 Corinthians 16:3–4 and 2 Corinthians 8:18–19

As in the Acts 11:27–30 passage, 2 Cor 8:18–19 relates the collection and transport of a donation by Christians to the church in Jerusalem. Paul was fulfilling the admonition given him to remember the poor (Gal 2:10). Unlike the Acts 11:27–30 passage, the endeavor included many churches (in Galatia, Macedonia, and Greece) instead of one church (Antioch). As in the contribution from Antioch to Jerusalem, the offerings were an individual matter (1 Cor 16:2, ἕκαστος ὑμῶν παρ' ἑαυτῷ). The offerings were to be received by Paul as one collection at each church. Paul, however, was not to be the bearer of this gift alone, which occasioned the choosing of a representative(s).[188]

First Corinthians 16:3 says that the bearers of the gift were to be approved by the church (οὓς ἐὰν δοκιμάσητε). As Paul had been addressing the entire church in Corinth throughout his letter, so in this passage he expected the entire church to approve of its messenger. δοκιμάζω has generally two meanings: "to test" and " to approve, sanction."[189] A person who was δόκιμος, was "a man who is tested, significant, recognized, esteemed, worthy."[190] In particular, it was frequently used with the idea of approved as fit for office.[191] Plato used δοκιμάζω with reference to officials nominated by the citizens, who afterward, he instructs, need to be scrutinized (*Laws* 754d). Later, he recommended the same for priests who were either cho-

---

188. 1 Cor 16:3 mentions a plurality of representatives. 2 Cor 8:18–19 mentions one.

189. *LSJ*, 442.

190. Grundmann, "δόκιμος, κ.τ.λ." *TDNT*, 2:255. Aristotle uses it to mean "a citizen of repute" (*Politics* 3.4.1277a).

191. *LSJ*, 442.

sen by popular election or by lot: "The man whom the lot favors must be screened (δοκιμάζειν)" (*Laws* 759c). Moulton and Milligan state that "in the inscriptions indeed the verb is almost a *term. techn.* for passing as fit for a public office."[192] In this particular passage, 1 Cor 16:3, selection and approval seem to be one and the same process, but the expression οὓς ἐὰν δοκιμάσητε, "those whom you have approved" (NASB) or "those whom you consider qualified,"[193] is particularly apt in this case, since the people chosen would be handling a large sum of money.

It is important to note that Paul does not instruct the elders (or another group) of the church in Corinth to approve of or scrutinize the chosen messengers. In 1 Cor 16:1–4 Paul mentions neither πρεσβύτεροι nor ἐπίσκοποι. Nor does he use the expression, οἱ προϊστάμενοι ὑμῶν. By the time Paul wrote 1 Corinthians, the church in Jerusalem had πρεσβύτεροι, as did the churches in Lystra, Iconium, Antioch in Psidia, and, most likely, the church in Ephesus (Paul had visited them several months later). Philippi had ἐπίσκοποι. Thessalonica had leaders, whom Paul denoted as οἱ προϊστάμενοι ὑμῶν. It is unlikely that the Corinthian church had no leaders at the time of the letter (see chapters 1 and 3). But Paul does not denote or address leaders in the passage. The choosing and/or approving of the messengers was the task of the whole church. For people who were a part of Greek culture, this method would have been expected.

To have a group of people accompany the gift to Jerusalem would certainly be wise, as there would be less chance of robbery enacted against a large number of people.[194] In addition, as Fee notes, "It would be a practical way of assuring the various churches of the basic integrity of the entire enterprise."[195] In fact, Acts 20:4 names seven men who accompanied Paul and Luke to Asia, but no one from Corinth. No doubt changes took place between Paul's first appeal in 1 Corinthians 16 and the final gathering and transport of the donation of Corinth. Likewise, Paul's insistence that the representatives be approved by letter (δι᾽ ἐπιστολῶν) was a common practice in antiquity for people held responsible for money.[196] His explanation

192. Moulton and Milligan, *Vocabulary of the Greek Testament*, 167.

193. *BDAG*, 255d.

194. Garner, "Travel in Biblical Times," in *NBD*, 1213, says that "by NT times the Roman peace and authority had made travel relatively safe and constant." On the other hand, Purcell, "Travel," *OCD*, 1547, notes, "the risks from robbers and brigands remained real, even in Italy."

195. Fee, *First Corinthians*, 815.

196. Ibid.

in many ways fits the typical scheme in the classical world of representatives officially designated by a group of people (e.g., citizens).

Within a year after the writing of 1 Corinthians, Paul addresses the Corinthian church again on the matter of the collection for the church in Jerusalem (2 Cor 8:1–24).[197] Since Paul's first letter, controversy had taken place and he needed to motivate the Christians in Corinth anew to participate liberally in the offering (8:10–12). Evidently, in the meantime, Paul instituted or agreed to a different procedure than he had instructed in 1 Corinthians 16. Instead of being accompanied by representatives from Corinth on the trip, Paul and Timothy were sending Titus and another brother to receive the collection from the church (8:16–18). Just who the other brother was has generated a fair amount of speculation on the part of commentators at least from the time of Origen, who believed it was Luke.[198]

Paul emphasizes two things about the second brother who is coming with Titus. First, he was well-respected in all the churches (οὗ ὁ ἔπαινος ἐν τῷ εὐαγγελίῳ διὰ πασῶν τῶν ἐκκλησιῶν).[199] Because he is described as being praised ἐν τῷ εὐαγγελίῳ, he was doubtless a co-worker in Paul's mission work. That the man was known and respected would give him credibility for the task of handling money. Second, the man had been selected by the other churches to be Paul's traveling companion (συνέκδημος) for this ministry of generosity.[200]

The word for choosing in v.19, χειροτονηθεὶς, the passive, aorist participle of χειροτονέω, is important for the discussion of group decision-making. LSJ gives three meanings for χειροτονέω:[201]

1. "to stretch forth the hand" in order to vote (w. accusative of persons, "to elect")

2. "to appoint," irrespective of election

3. "to span with the hand" (thus, measure)

---

197. Guthrie, *New Testament Introduction*, 457–59.

198. See the explanation in Plummer, *Second Corinthians*, 248.

199. BDAG, 357b, defines ἔπαινος as "praise, approval, recognition."

200. Aristarchus is called Paul's συνέκδημος in Acts 19:29, which describes events prior to Paul's sending Titus and the second man. The fact that Aristarchus accompanied Paul all the way to Jerusalem and then to Rome lends credence to the idea that he is the man Paul had in mind in 2 Cor 8:18–19.

201. *LSJ*, 1986.

The third would obviously have no meaning in the context of 2 Cor 8:18–19. Thus, the question becomes, was the process one of election, or a selection (without reference to how the process was carried out). From its original sense, the understanding of "to stretch forth the hand" increased in its meanings. Eventually, χειροτονέω came to mean generally, "to vote," without any designation of how to vote was taken.[202] The second meaning of χειροτονέω is evidenced in several ancient authors. Josephus uses the term to refer to God's choice of David as king (*Ant.* 7.53) and Alexander's appointment of Jonathan as High Priest (*Ant.* 13.45). Philo uses χειροτονέω thirty-three times in his writings, most often with the meaning "appoint" (e.g., *Sacr.* 9; *Agr.* 130; *Mos* 1.156). The meaning would therefore be a simple appointment of one person by another. Hatch says, "Its meaning was originally 'to elect,' but it came afterwards to mean, even in classical Greek, simply 'to appoint to office,' without itself indicating the particular mode of appointment."[203]

The shift in meaning of χειροτονέω, however, did not eliminate its original meaning. It was used for voting for city magistrates in the time of the Roman Empire.[204] χειροτονέω was used in the LXX to refer to election of officials (*Baruch* 2.2; *Susanna* 1.62). It was employed in post NT writings to refer to the choice of church officers and representatives, decided by the whole church (*Did.* 15.1; Ign., *Smyrn.* 11.2; Ign., *Phild.* 10.1) or by a council (Ign., *Pol.* 7.2). It was also used by Josephus as he told how the assembly of Jews wanted to choose ambassadors to send to Nero (*J.W.* 2.342–43; 4.256) and for the election of Tiberius to counsel the second time (in this case, clearly "elect," *Ant.* 19.287). Philo uses χειροτονέω to mean the election of ambassadors by cities (*Spec.* 1.78, discussed later). Likewise, Plutarch (ca. 100 CE) uses χειροτονέω in its original, literal sense (*Arist.* 4.4; *Demetr.* 13; *Dio* 48; *Phoc.* 34), as does Diodorus Siculus (ca. 60 BCE, 19.9.4), Dionysius of Harlicarnassus (*Dem.* 9), and Lucian (*Abd.* 25). Two church fathers who wrote after 400 CE—Philostorgius (*h.e.* 7.6) and Sozomenus Salaminus (*h.e.* 6.8.6)—use χειροτονέω to mean the election of bishops, including laying on of hands.[205] Thus, the two meanings of the word—elect by vote or select—existed side by side. This would not be unusual in the Greek language. An almost identical phenomenon, for instance is seen in Josephus'

---

202. Brandis, "ἐκκλησία," 5:2194.

203. Hatch, "Ordination," 2:1501.

204. Jones, *The Greek City*, 182–83.

205. Lampe, *Patristic Greek Lexicon*, 1523.

use of the word προτεινέω. In his writings it can be used in multiple ways, including to mean "extend the hand, propose, put forward."[206] It should also be noted that in the instances given, where χειροτονέω meant merely to select, the occasion was one person selecting another, not a group selecting an individual.

Opinion is divided as to which of the two meanings is intended for Paul's fellow traveler in 2 Corinthians 8. Calvin argues,

> We must observe, however, the mode of election—that which was customary among the Greeks—χειροτονία (a show of hands), in which the leaders took the precedence by authority and counsel, and regulated the whole proceeding, while the common people intimated their approval.[207]

On the other hand, Murray Harris says, "Originally the verb *cheirotoneo* indicated election by 'stretching the hand' (i.e. voting), but this meaning cannot be pressed in NT usage where the term simply denotes appointment (Acts 14:23)."[208] Writers favoring the meaning of "voting" include Barrett, Bernard, Alford, Lenski, H. A. W. Meyer, and BDAG. [209] Writers favoring the meaning of "select" include Lohse and Harris.[210]

The activity of Jewish communities in the Diaspora, who sent temple offerings and financial aid to the citizens of Jerusalem, no doubt played a role in forming Christian thought regarding their assistance to the brethren in Jerusalem. Strack and Billerbeck point to similarities between the action in 2 Cor 8:16–24 and the collection for Jewish teachers in the Holy Land who were impoverished after the destruction of Jerusalem in 66 CE. Rabbinical accounts do not identify definitively who appointed the collectors (who themselves were Jewish teachers), but Strack and Billerbeck assume it was the "Patriarchate" (*gerousia?*) that selected the collectors.[211] Philo gave an account of the selection of ambassadors by Jewish communities in the Diaspora for delivering the first fruits to the temple during the time of Christ. This account seems to parallel Paul's collection much more closely

---

206. *LSJ*, 1534.

207. Calvin, *Commentary on Corinthians*, 2:301.

208. Harris, *2 Corinthians*, 372.

209. *BDAG*, 1083c; Alford, *The Greek New Testament*, 2:683; Barrett, *Second Corinthians*, 228–29; Bernard, *Second Corinthians*, 3:89; Lenski, *Interpretation of 1 and 2 Corinthians*, 1151.

210. Lohse, "χειροτονέω," *TDNT*, 9:437. Harris , *2 Corinthians*, 372.

211. *Str-B*, 3:317, 523.

than do the instances of helping the impoverished teachers after 66 CE. Philo states,

> And since the nation is the most numerous of all peoples, it follows naturally that the first fruits contributed by them must also be most abundant. Accordingly there is in almost every city a storehouse for the sacred things to which it is customary for the people to come and there to deposit their first fruits, and at certain seasons there are sacred ambassadors selected on account of their virtue, who convey the offerings to the temple. And the most eminent men of each tribe are elected (χειροτονοῦνται) to this office, that they may conduct the hopes of each individual safe to their destination; for in the lawful offering of the first fruits are the hopes of the pious. (*Spec.* 1.78)[212]

The use of χειροτονέω to mean only "select," without the idea of a group decision, normally is denoted by the context as one chosen by another. Where it can be determined, its use with a group normally has the meaning "elect (by vote)." Since a group, or rather groups, are in view in 2 Cor 8:18–19, the most likely meaning is that the various churches, each as a body, elected the brother who accompanied Titus. Paul thus afterward regards this man as one of the "messengers of the churches" (ἀπόστολοι ἐκκλησιῶν, 8:23: "the commissioned representative of the congregation").[213] The best interpretation of the passage is, therefore, that the messenger was elected. The assertion that the translation "elect" in 2 Corinthians 8:19 is exaggerated literalism[214] cannot be harmonized with an historical understanding of the meaning of χειροτονέω.

Acts 13:1–3 and 15:36–41

Acts 13:1-3 marks the beginning of a new section of Luke's record of the early church. From this point forward in Acts, the center of Christian mission activity shifts away from Jerusalem, and mission work becomes increasingly Gentile-oriented (while never departing from its goal to reach Israel). Witherington says, "Luke's intent is to portray this missionary journey as

212. *The Works of Philo*, 541.

213. Rengstorf, "ἀποστέλλω, κ.τ.λ." *TDNT*, 1:422. Rengstorf says that in this instance and in Phil 2:25, "ἀπόστολος has a religious rather than legal significance." On the other hand, as they were carrying money, ἀπόστολος probably has both meanings in 2 Cor 8:23.

214. MacArthur, *The Master's Plan*, 191.

being the inaugural efforts by a church . . . at overseas missions."[215] Most writers regard the sending out of Barnabas and Saul as an action of the church in Antioch. Bock, for example, notes, "Here is a church that has seen the need to reach out to the world as its members draw near to God. Their heart has become wedded to God's calling as a result."[216] Other commentators regard the sending of Saul and Barnabas as an action completed by only the first five people mentioned in the passage. The differences of interpretation relate to how the events in vv. 1–3 proceeded. After naming five leaders in the church in Antioch,[217] Luke says that they "were worshiping the Lord and fasting" (v. 2). The word for "worshiping," λειτουργούντων, may also be translated as "ministering" (KJV, NASB, NKJV, Luther). The interpretation of the passage is, to a fair extent, determined by the meaning of this word. λειτουργέω occurs three times in the New Testament and frequently in the LXX. BDAG states that it originally meant service of the individual for the state. In Christian literature, λειτουργέω has a three-fold usage:

1. to denote the service of priests and Levites

2. figuratively: of the various ways in which religious people serve God

3. speaking generically of Christian service[218]

Haenchen states that Luke here has taken "an especially ceremonial-sounding term" from the LXX.[219] In addition, he says, in the *Did.* 15.1, λειτουργέω is used to mean "hold a Christian service."[220] Hort argues that λειτουργούντων τῷ κυρίῳ would denote that the church was holding a solemn service. He then elaborates,

> The service here denoted by the verb λειτουργέω was probably a
> service of prayer. The context suggests that it was not a regular and
> customary service . . . but a special act of worship on the part of a

---

215. Witherington III, *Acts of the Apostles*, 390. Lake and Cadbury, *Acts of the Apostles*, 141, view this account as coming from a Jerusalem tradition. As in other judgments of this type, the tracing of origin is almost impossible to prove.

216. Bock, *Acts*, 440.

217. Roloff, *Apostelgeschichte*, 193, says that the prophets mentioned in 13:1 were traveling prophets who had settled in Antioch. However, there is no way to establish his statement. The New Testament does not indicate that prophets must have an itinerant ministry.

218. *BDAG*, 591a.

219. Haenchen, *Die Apostelgeschichte*, 380.

220. This second point is debatable.

solemn meeting of the whole Ecclesia, held expressly with reference to a project for carrying the Gospel to the heathen.[221]

Kistemaker argues that the passage must be referring to a public service, since that is the meaning of λειτουργέω in Christian literature;[222] he bases his statement, in part, on Strathmann's explanation.[223] Strathmann points out, however, that the noun λειτουργία has a broader meaning than merely public service. In Acts 13:2, he says that λειτουργέω "is used for a fellowship of prayer."[224]

The argument of Haenchen, that *Did.* 15.1 was speaking about a public worship service, is certainly questionable. The *Didache* is discussing bishops and deacons who could render the service of prophets and teachers. Prophets and teachers, of course, had primarily a public ministry, but Haenchen's example does not prove that Acts 13:2 was a public worship service. It would seem best to understand λειτουργέω as "spiritual, or Christian service" in a general sense (with a likelihood of public ministry).[225]

Witherington points out correctly that the natural antecedent to "they were worshiping the Lord" is the five teachers named in v.1.[226] In that case, it was while the five were praying and fasting that the Holy Spirit spoke to one of them about Barnabas and Saul; the remaining three separated Barnabas and Saul from themselves and sent them away. The church learned about the prophecy indirectly and was informed afterward about the action. In view of other events involving the church in the book of Acts, a scenario of Acts 13:1–3 as a private event would be unusual. Witherington says that the action of sending out Barnabas was the conscious action of the church.[227] If, however, only five people were involved, the action can only be described as that of a small part of the church.

Ramsay solves the difficulty by claiming that Luke makes an awkward change of subject in v.3 from the five to the whole church.[228] Ramsay further

---

221. Hort, *The Christian Ecclesia*, 63.

222. Kistemaker, *Acts*, 455.

223. See Strathmann, "λειτουργέω, λειτουργία," *TDNT*, 4:228.

224. Ibid. Lake and Cadbury, *Acts of the Apostles*, 142, on the contrary, argue that the meaning of λειτουργέω cannot be narrowed to this meaning.

225. Thus, *BDAG*, 591a.

226. Witherington III, *Acts of the Apostles*, 393.

227. Ibid., 391.

228. Ramsay, *St. Paul the Traveller*, 66–67.

argues that the whole church laid hands on Saul and Barnabas.[229] Longenecker argues that on the basis of the other actions of churches throughout the book of Acts, the laying on of hands and sending out was a public action.[230] Knowling views the most likely scenario as involving the whole church present. This, he contends, in answer to Ramsay, does not mean that they had to take part in the laying on of hands:

> But if the whole Church was present, it does not follow that they took part in every detail of the service, just as they may have been present in the public service of worship in ver.2. . . . There is therefore no reason to assume that the laying on of hands was performed by the whole church, or that St. Luke could have been ignorant that this function was one which belonged specifically to the officers of the Church.[231]

The laying on of hands had an ancient history in Israel (Gen 48:14, Jacob laying his hands on his grandchildren; Num 27:23, Moses laying his hands on Joshua). Its meaning was evidently understood among early Christians (Heb 6:1–2). It was also a standard practice of Jewish scribes upon their successors and conveyed authority to teach. Among the scribes, this act of ordination was always public.[232] Though the laying on of hands in Acts 13:3 had nothing to do with successors in teaching, if similar to the practice among the scribes, it also would have taken place publicly.

The likelihood that the whole church was involved in the event is indicated by the fact that upon their return, Barnabas and Saul reported directly to the church in Antioch, not to the other three alone (14:27).[233] The likelihood that the whole church took part in the action of Acts 13:1–3 is increased by the account of the second missions trip to the Gentiles in Acts 15:36–41. When Paul left Antioch for his second missions trip with his new partner, Silas, the two were "commended by the brothers to the grace of the Lord" (Acts 15:40). "The brothers" (οἱ ἀδέλφοι) is frequently used to denote a group of Christians in an area, and at times all the believ-

229. Ibid., 67.

230. Longenecker, *Acts,* 417.

231. Knowling, *Acts of the Apostles,* 283.

232. Lohse, *Ordination im Spätjudentum,* 29–30; 65. Lohse says that the laying on of hands in this instance was no ordination (Barnabas and Saul were already teachers), but a signification of the release (ἀφορίζειν) to the new ministry by the church in Antioch, 73–74.

233. So, accordingly argue Ramsay, *St. Paul the Traveller,* 67; Longenecker, *Acts,* 417; Kistemaker, *Acts,* 455; Bruce, *Acts,* 261.

ers in a local church (e.g., Acts 1:15; 11:1; 12:17; 15:32; Phil 1:12; 1 Thess 5:27; 1 Tim 4:6). As this expression was used to signify the people of the church in Antioch eight verses earlier, it is the obvious meaning of Acts 15:40. "The brothers" (i.e., the church of Antioch) commended (or "gave up" παραδίδομι) Paul and Silas to God's grace for the new mission work.

The act of laying on of hands in Acts 13:3 is not an impartation of a gift or an office (thus a sacrament). The Holy Spirit had declared, "Set apart for me Barnabas and Saul for the work to which I have called (προσκέκλημαι) them." προσκέκλημαι is the perfect middle form of the verb προσκαλέω. Thus, the action had already taken place. Paul had been called to a special work among the Gentiles already in Acts 9:15. The Roman Catholic exegete Wikenhauser says, "One must really question whether this was a sacramental ordination. . . . Would Paul, who was directly called by Christ to be an apostle, need an ordination from a bishop?"[234]

There are two possible scenarios for Acts 13:1–3, both of which involve group activity. The first is that five teachers and prophets were together fasting and praying. The Holy Spirit spoke through one of them to separate Barnabas and Saul for their ministry to the Gentiles. The small group fasted and prayed more, then three of the group laid their hands on the two and sent them away. Sometime later the three related to the church in Antioch what they had done. The second scenario is that either from the outset (v. 1) or in the course of the events, the entire church in Antioch was or became involved. Whether the whole church laid hands on Barnabas and Saul, or only the ones designated did so, the entire church sent out the two missionaries. The second scenario seems much more likely because of the usual public nature of λειτουργέω, the reporting of Barnabas and Saul to the whole church in 14:27, the identical action for Paul's second journey which involved the giving over of Paul and Silas to the Lord for the mission by the whole church in 15:40, and the unlikelihood that an act of such consequence would be performed in a sequestered fashion or that two of the most important leaders of the church would depart without explaining why.

Acts 14:21–23

Acts 14:23 is the one instance in Luke's narrative in which he describes how elders were designated in the Pauline churches. Longenecker says that Paul

---

234. Wikenhauser, *Die Apostelgeschichte*, 148. Translation by the author.

and Barnabas left the churches "with spiritual guides and an embryonic ecclesiastical administration."[235] Haenchen sees the event as an interpolation from church structure at a later time, which was not Pauline.[236] His assertion is answered, however, in the first section of this chapter.[237] Saul and Barnabas spent about eighteen months on their first journey,[238] traveling first to Cyprus to minister (during which time they traversed 181 km of the island, from Salamis to Paphos),[239] then sailing to Perga, then traveling to Antioch in Pisidia, Iconium, Lystra, and Derbe, then retracing their steps to the Pamphylian coast (a total of over 1250 km,[240] most likely all on foot), then returning by boat to Antioch. The total walking time (avg. ca. 25 km per day) would have been sixty days.[241] The two missionaries could not have spent longer than a few weeks to a few months in any one place. The establishment of defined gatherings, which were churches, in such a short time is in itself phenomenal. That the churches would have credible leadership with doctrinal understanding is even more so. Just as phenomenal is Luke's recording of the appointment of elders, in matter-of-fact style. The appointment (χειροτονήσαντες is an aorist circumstantial participle) is not the main thrust of his sentence in v.23. Luke emphasizes, rather, "they committed them to the Lord in whom they had believed."

As mentioned in chapter 2, Campbell and others explain that the elders in Pauline churches were primarily heads of households. The heads of households who became Christians would be followed automatically as the leaders of house churches. As has been explained in chapter 2, this scenario is very unlikely for a number of reasons. At this juncture, it is important to emphasize that Paul's view of an elder included competence in teaching the Scriptures (Acts 20:28-30; 1 Tim 3:2; Titus 1:9). It may be that the elders, whose selection is recorded in Acts 14:23, had spent significant time in the

235. Longenecker, *Acts*, 438.

236. Haenchen, *Die Apostelgeschichte*, 419.

237. Ramsay, *St. Paul the Traveller*, 121, comments, "It is clear, therefore, that Paul everywhere instituted Elders in his new Churches; and on our hypothesis as to the accurate and methodical expression of the historian, we are bound to infer that this first case is intended to be typical of the way of appointment followed in all later cases."

238. Reymond, *Paul, Missionary Theologian*, 115. Alexander, "Chronology of Paul," 122–23, reckons the time of the trip to be one year. Hemer, *Acts in Its Historical Setting*, 269, reckons the maximum amount of time to have been eighteen months.

239. Schnabel, *Early Christian Mission*, 2:1074.

240. Ibid.

241. Ibid., 2:1076.

synagogues before hearing the gospel from Barnabas and Paul. It would be hard to guess how they might otherwise have gained their capability to understand and communicate correct teaching.

Acts 14:23 explains the appointment of elders in the churches in the following manner: χειροτονήσαντες δὲ αὐτοῖς κατ᾽ ἐκκλησίαν πρεσβυτέρους, ("And when they had appointed elders for them in every church"). The κατὰ is distributive, meaning they were selected at each of the churches in Lystra, Iconium, and Antioch.[242] This phrase is not, in itself, a proof that Barnabas and Paul appointed multiple elders in each church.[243] It is passages such as Acts 20:17, 21:18, and Phil 1:1 that make multiple elders in a church likely.

The meaning of the word for "appoint," χειροτονέω, has already been explained in the discussion of 2 Cor 8:18–19. It means either "to select," when referring to one person doing the selecting, or "elect," when a group of people does the selecting.[244] The meaning of χειροτονήσαντες in Acts 14:23 is, as in each case, determined by the context. The natural antecedent of the participle is τὸν Παῦλον (14:19) and τῷ Βαρναβᾷ (14:20—note that Paul and Barnabas "returned to Lystra, Iconium, and Antioch," v. 21). Furthermore, the main verb of v. 23 is παρέθεντο, referring to Paul and Barnabas. Thus, "And when they had appointed elders for them in every church, with prayer and fasting they committed them to the Lord in whom they had believed." It is Paul and Barnabas who did the appointing in Acts 14:23.

There are essentially two interpretations of the selection of elders in Acts 14:23. The first is that this event was solely the action of Paul and Barnabas.[245] The second is to view the action as an election of the church body (even if Paul and Barnabas did the appointing).[246] The basis of the

242. BDAG, 512b.

243. A similar sentence, with a distributive use of "all" could be so formulated in English: "The virtuoso gave concerts at all the universities." This does not imply more than one concert at each university.

244. It is unfortunate that some commentaries in their discussions of 2 Cor 8:18–19 or Acts 14:23 merely point out the change in the meaning of χειροτονέω from "elect by the show of hands" to "select" without observing that the original meaning of χειροτονέω, "to elect," continued in use as well, long after all the apostles were deceased.

245. Holding this position are BDAG, 1083a; Lohse, TDNT, 9:437; Jackson and Lake, The Beginnings of Christianity, 1:168; Haenchen, Acts of the Apostles, 419; Bock, Acts, 482–83.

246. Holding this position are Calvin, Commentary on the Acts, 2:27–28; Meyer, Critical and Exegetical Handbook of the Acts, 275; Alford, Greek Testament, 2:160–61; Brown, Acts of the Apostles, 3.2:99; Lenski, Interpretation of the Acts of the Apostles,

first view is the (correct) evaluation of the grammar: Paul and Barnabas appoint. The basis of the second view is that this is a summary account, not telling the details of how the choice of the elders took place. One must look to other New Testament passages to find details about the choosing of leaders in churches. Kistemaker, expressing this idea, says,

> By following the analogical rule of comparing Scripture with Scripture, we learn that in Acts Luke presents "three typical pictures of election and ordination in the cases of Matthias (1:23–26), the Seven (6:1–6), and Paul and Barnabas (13:1–3)." These analogies demonstrate that the assemblies chose the candidates, then prayed and fasted, and afterward ordained them. Likewise, in the case of the elders in Lyconia and Pisidia, the apostles approved the selections made by the churches and, after prayer and fasting appointed them.[247]

Following the same vein, Ridderbos comments,

> When one surveys the whole . . . it is evident that in each investiture with and acceptance of official power to act and authority two different elements are present: first, Christ himself, who will not only have the office established and maintained in the way of the transference of power once given, but works in the church through his Spirit, so that the work of the Lord on earth may be done, his church be built up, and his power to act invested in persons qualified to that end. Second, the church itself, which designates and chooses these persons and in the name of the Lord enables them to enter upon the work charged to them.[248]

Alexander Strauch's evaluation is similar:

> Luke simply does not reveal what part the congregation played in the process of appointing these new elders. It is possible that Luke expected his readers to understand that the appointing of the Seven in Acts 6:1–6 established the pattern followed by all later appointments to church offices. Thus the verb "appointed" summarizes the whole process of selecting, examining and installing into office.[249]

585–86; Longenecker, *Acts*, 439; Kistemaker, *Acts*, 525–26; Barrett, *Commentary on the Acts*, 1:687.

247. Kistemaker, *Acts*, 525.

248. Ridderbos, *Paul: An Outline of His Theology*, 476.

249. Strauch, *Biblical Eldership*, 136.

Calvin claimed that the actions of Barnabas and Paul show obvious similarity with the election of magistrates in the Graeco-Roman world, in which two *douviri* managed the municipal election. In the end, although the people cast the actual vote, the *douviri* were said to have elected the magistrates. Thus, Calvin said, the elders were chosen in each church "by the consent of all" (*Omnium suffragiis*).[250] Hatch, though speaking about ecclesiastical votes later in church history, affirms Calvin's view.[251] Though one cannot prove the identical function of Barnabas and Saul with the actions of the *Douviri* (*duumviri*), Calvin's point is legitimate. In fact, "The *duoviri* convened . . . the popular assembly, conducted the election of other officials and functionaries . . . and represented the city before the emperor."[252] The new converts would have been familiar with this practice, since the *polis* government was in force in the cities where the churches had been established. A second factor supporting Calvin's interpretation is the fact that χειροτονέω can take the meaning, "confirm an election."[253] A third phenomenon would make Calvin's explanation likely, namely: the new congregations would have looked to the missionaries for guidance in organizing themselves.

When Paul instructs Titus to do the same thing that he and Barnabas have done in Galatia (Titus 1:5), he cites a series of character qualities and one ability (expound the Word of God) that are necessary for the task of elder (Titus 1:6–9). Character qualities are observed over a period of time; one cannot discern within several weeks the full catalog of traits Paul required. Nor can one be sure of a candidate's teaching ability until one has observed him in practice a few times. Paul and Barnabas needed assistance of the congregations, if not the vote of the congregations, to evaluate candidates for the task of elder. The missionaries did not have adequate time to judge the character of the potential elders. Only the people from the

---

250. Calvin, *Commentary on the Acts*, 27–28.

251. Hatch, *Organization of the Early Christian Churches*, 127, "The conditions of ordinary appointment to civil office in the Roman municipalities are known to us from many and unimpeachable sources. Those sources show that, though election prevailed, it did not of itself constitute an office, that any one who was so elected had to pass a preliminary examination as to his possession of the required qualifications. . . . In Rome itself, especially during the Republican period, the person appointed is said to be appointed, not by the people who elected, but by the officer who presided at the election."

252. Gizewski, "Duoviri, Duumviri," 4:739.

253. Rost, et al., *Handwörterbuch der Griechischen Sprache*, 2/2:2440.

churches, who had known their fellow-members and sat under their teaching, would have been able to discern who was fitting.

James White argues against the idea that the New Testament teaches congregational selection of elders:

> Titus was to appoint the elders. The position is divinely ordained. It does not derive its existence or authority from the congregation. The elder's authority comes from Christ, and the congregation's role is that of recognition of God's gifting and calling. This may seem like a small point, but it is not. If one believes the elder's authority becomes the "consent of the governed" in essence, that authority becomes merely an extension of the gathered congregation.[254]

White makes a good point by emphasizing the calling of Christ in eldership. This does not, however, answer the question of how candidates were chosen for the ministry of elder. If he means that they were chosen exclusively by Paul, Barnabas, and Titus, how was this order of choosing elders extended? Was it then exclusively the right of apostles (and their assistants)? Was it the role of any missionary? Who fulfills that role today in the absence of apostles? Who fulfills it in the absence of both apostles and missionaries who begin churches? If the congregations of the New Testament voted for their elders, how was this in any way *not* a recognition of God's gifting and calling? John Suggit's comment is very helpful in this context: "Any community needs officially appointed and recognized leaders. The Christian church is no exception, but though the appointment is made by human beings, Acts considers it always as due to the action of the Spirit."[255]

White's emphasis on the calling and gifting of Christ for the office of elder is also decidedly incomplete. Just as the elders are called and gifted by Christ, so in the same way, the Seven in Acts 6:1–6 were called and gifted by Christ. But, at the same time, they were clearly chosen for their ministry by the congregation of Jerusalem. The example of Acts 6:1–6, as in other instances, "illustrates the perfect blending of charisma, office and function."[256] Reviewing Paul's statements about the contributions of the churches in Philippi and Corinth to Jerusalem, Ellis notes, "All this invites the conclusion that the appointed delegates from Philippi were engaging in an act of ministry pursuant to their charisms, charisms that were recognized and

---

254. White in Garrett, "Congregation-Led Church," 205. (This is James White's response to Garrett's chapter.)

255. Suggit, "The Holy Spirit and We Resolved," 44.

256. Fung, "Ministry in the New Testament," 166.

endorsed by the congregation."[257] As there is, in Paul's teaching, gifting for all ministries, the method of choosing elders would not necessarily be influenced by their kind of gifting, any more than choosing a church member to look after the poor or acting as a messenger would be. Instead, the determining factors for who chooses people for, and places them in ministry would need to be the nature and sensitivity of that ministry and the range of its authority.

PASSAGES WHICH TEACH CHURCH DECISION-MAKING FOR DISCIPLINE

Excommunication was practiced much more widely among the ancients than it has been in modern times. This was true both of non-Jewish organizations as well as in Jewish society. Schürer explains that "in continuous contact with a Gentile environment, the Jewish communities could only preserve themselves by constantly and carefully eliminating alien elements."[258] Levels of discipline included "the ban" (which involved forms of social ostracism), whipping, and exclusion.[259] For the final level, note John 9:22: "For the Jews had already agreed that if anyone should confess Jesus to be Christ, he was to be put out of the synagogue."

In harmony with other groups in the time of Jesus and the apostles, discipline (including excommunication) was crucial for church life. Laney emphasizes this truth in the following way:

> The New Testament contains abundant evidence of the practice of discipline by the apostolic church (Matt. 18:15-20; Acts 5:1–11; 1 Cor 5:1–5; 2 Cor 2:5–11; Gal 2:11–14; 6:1; 2 Thess 3:6–15). That church discipline was a prominent concern of the church in the post-apostolic period—through the first two or three centuries—is made clear by the debate over the possibility of forgiveness for sins committed after conversion. . . . By the fourth century the church had developed a rigorous system outlining the steps to restoration and the duration of penance.[260]

257. Ellis, *Pauline Theology*, 93.

258. Schürer, *History of the Jewish People*, 2:431.

259. Schmidt, "Discipline," 214–15.

260. Laney, *Guide to Church Discipline*, 41–42.

The above quote lists seven different texts which deal with church discipline. That there are so many New Testament disciplinary texts demonstrates the importance of discipline for the life of the early church.

1 Corinthians 5:1–13 and 2 Corinthians 2:5–11

The two passages under consideration in this section have traditionally been interpreted as belonging to the same controversy: the discipline of one particular member of the church in Corinth. David Brown, who titles his commentary of 2 Corinthians 2:1–17 as "The Incestuous Person ought now to be Forgiven," is typical of the earlier viewpoint.[261] In the past one hundred years, however, a number of scholars have taken issue with the traditional interpretation. Klauck, in fact, says that most writers "correctly" have given up the idea of combining the two.[262] Hughes explains,

> Many commentators (among them Godet, Moffatt, Plummer, Lietzmann, Bachmann, Robertson, Strachan) suppose that, probably during the hypothetical "intermediate" visit, Paul had been wantonly affronted to his face and his authority resisted by a particular member of the Corinthian church, who may also have been the ringleader of an insubordinate faction, and thereafter had written the hypothetical severe "intermediate" letter demanding the punishment of this offender.[263]

One suggestion is that the man in view in 2 Cor 2:5–11 "was probably a visitor . . . to Corinth."[264] Another is that the offender in 2 Corinthians 2 was a member of the church in Corinth who had misused the funds collected for the church in Jerusalem.[265]

James South lists the reasons for interpreting the instance of discipline as one and the same, the reasons against, followed by answers to the reasons against:

---

261. Brown, *Acts*, 3/2:340.

262. Klauck, *2 Corinthians*, 29.

263. Hughes, *Second Corinthians*, 59.

264. Barrett, *Second Corinthians*, 93; Harris, *2 Corinthians*, 328, gives the same explanation.

265. Thrall, *Commentary on Second Corinthians*, 68–69.

For:

1. There are a number of similarities between 1 Cor 5:1–8 and 2 Cor 2:5–11, including references to Satan and that both deal with communal discipline.

2. In 1 Corinthians 5 the offender was delivered to Satan; in 2 Corinthians 2 the fear is that Satan will gain the advantage if the discipline is taken too far.

3. In 2 Cor 7:9–12 Paul focuses on the repentance of the community, which would not have been the case if Paul were concerned with a personal offense.

4. The consensus view holds that the offense mentioned in 2 Corinthians 2 is a personal one against Paul, but it is this perception of a personal offense which Paul is trying correct, i.e. the offense was *not* personal.

Against:

1. The oldest objection was raised by Tertullian (*De Pudicitia* 13–16), who could not believe that if Paul had so completely condemned the sinner in 1 Corinthians 5, he could counsel forgiveness in 2 Corinthians 2. South answers: "This argument is a classic example of the manner in which the assumption of the curse/death interpretation of 1 Corinthians 5 skews our understanding of other texts and of the nature of early Christian discipline. . . . How can such understanding be squared with Paul's view of grace?"

2. There is no clear evidence in either 2 Corinthians 2 or 7 that any sexual offence is in view. South answers: "While this is without doubt the case, we must observe that *no* offence is clearly outlined in these chapters, so the possibility that a sexual offence is in view is as likely as any other."

3. Satan's role is not the same in both texts: in 1 Corinthians 5 he is the agent of punishment, in 2 Corinthians 2 he is a threat to Paul and the community. South answers: "This ignores the fact that in both OT and NT, Satan frequently has a dual role."

4. In 1 Corinthians 5 Paul is concerned about the purity of the congregation; in 2 Corinthians 2 he is concerned about unity and harmony. South answers: "In both texts Paul has a deep concern for the salvation

of the individual offender. . . . Any difference in emphasis between the two texts is sufficiently explained by the change in circumstances."[266]

This study accepts the arguments of South and views both texts as dealing with discipline of the same offender.

In the debate regarding Paul's guidelines for establishing church discipline, one position is that "Paul probably borrowed some notions from Jewish groups such as the Pharisees, whose disciplinary procedures he knew well from his early days."[267] While Paul's training as a Pharisee no doubt played a role in his understanding of discipline, his most likely source for church discipline came from Christ himself. Since discipline was commonly practiced in groups of his day, Paul would have been especially sensitive to what Christ had taught on the subject. The clearest outline for discipline among the followers of Jesus is given in Matt 18:15–20. Donald Hagner comments, "This is as close as we come in Matthew to an actual handbook of rules for the community."[268] Though discipline was practiced, this outline is not repeated anywhere else in the New Testament, which indicates that it had embedded itself in the thinking of the church, for whom there would be no perfecting of what the Lord of the church had explicitly instructed.

Jesus' instruction in Matthew 18:15–20 teaches discipline in four stages:

1. private confrontation (v. 15)

2. confrontation by two or three (v. 16)[269]

3. confrontation by the whole church (v. 17)

4. expulsion from the church if the offender remains unrepentant (v. 17–18)

There is a question of how the disciples would have comprehended εἰπὲ τῇ ἐκκλησίᾳ in v. 17, since this was only the second time that Jesus had

---

266. South, *Disciplinary Practices in Pauline Texts*, 95–101.

267. Schmidt, "Discipline," 214.

268. Hagner, *Matthew 14—28*, 530.

269. Ibid., 532, "The hope is for repentance and restoration. But in this intermediate stage at the same time the matter acquires the status of legality (2 Cor 13:1; 1 Tim 5:19), which can serve to bring the process to the third stage, including excommunication, if necessary." Gundry, *Matthew*, 369, sees this step differently than Hagner: "Their going does not have the purpose of establishing the original charge (the truth of which is taken for granted) or of enabling them to act as witnesses before the church in case of a second refusal, but of strengthening the reproof with a view toward restoration."

mentioned the ἐκκλησία. The meaning of the term here has significant bearing for the church on the subject of discipline, following the resurrection of Christ. If Jesus made the instruction about discipline in Aramaic, he would have used the word כְּנִישְׁתָּא to express the assembly.[270] Schmidt suggests that this can mean the whole divine community of the OT.[271] He concludes, "It [כְּנִישְׁתָּא] is to be understood in terms of a reference to the Synagogue, the OT community, which Jesus does not deny, but expressly affirms, which He and He alone fulfils, since as the Messiah He here and elsewhere places Himself under the Law."[272] Johnston says that after the resurrection, "The disciples of the risen Christ believed themselves to be the true people of God; they were the Messianic community. This could be expressed in the *Kenishta*, the Congregation of God."[273] Therefore, Jesus' disciples were to think of themselves as a community and later as the Christian ἐκκλησία.

It may be, however, that Jesus did not give this teaching in Aramaic. Though Aramaic was the language of the Jewish people in Palestine, Greek was also widely used. Because of the wide use of Greek in Galilee and its surrounding areas, Peter and Andrew would have probably learned Greek to carry on trade. James, the brother of Jesus, wrote his letter in excellent Greek, about twenty years after the speech of Matthew 18. Matthew most likely knew Greek in order to perform his customs work. Jesus (and the Sanhedrin) would have needed to speak in Greek to communicate with Pilate during Jesus' trial. Mark informs his readers that the Syrophenician woman who asked Jesus to heal her daughter spoke Greek (Mark 7:25–30). Porter points out that a majority of the Jewish funeral inscriptions from Palestine are written in Greek, not Aramaic, and concludes,

> The statistics for Greek may well be a conservative estimate of the percentage of people that spoke Greek in the Jewish population in Galilee and even of Palestine. At the most private and final moments when a loved one was finally to be laid to rest, in the majority of instances, Jews chose Greek as the language in which to memorialize their deceased. Greek was apparently that dominant, that in the majority of instances it took precedence over the Jewish sacred language, even at a moment of highly personal and religious significance.[274]

270. Schmidt, "ἐκκλησία," *TDNT*, 3:525.

271. Ibid.

272. Ibid., 3:526.

273. Johnston, *The Doctrine of the Church*, 43.

274. Porter, "Did Jesus Teach in Greek?," 222.

Porter further concludes that Jesus likely taught in Greek, in particular on the occasions recorded in Matt 16:18 and Matt 18:15–20:

> The Semitic words [קָהָל, עֵדָה, בְּנִישְׁתָה] are at best only general conceptual equivalents, and often not even that (in the light of the use of ἐκκλησία in ancient Greek). . . . It is plausible that the use of ἐκκλησία was adopted because of the use of this word by Jesus himself here in Matthew 16:18 and 18:17, the use of a common Greek word to refer to a group of people gathered for a purpose.[275]

If Porter is right, the disciples may have, in fact, understood εἰπὲ τῇ ἐκκλησίᾳ in the Greek sense of "assembly." (Though not in the sense of a political assembly, as the Greek word was also used by the Greeks themselves simply as "assembly," without any reference to political structures.)[276]

The teaching of Jesus was different than the established Jewish teaching and practice of discipline and excommunication, first, because for Jesus, excommunication from the ἐκκλησία was corrective but not permanent. Ferguson explains,

> The preceding parable [Matt 18:12–14] shows that Jesus' teaching in these verses is not to give a mechanical process to be followed in expelling an erring church member but is to emphasize the effort to be made to reclaim that person. The individual goes to the person; a small group goes; then the whole church goes and makes an appeal. The purpose of the activity is pastoral, not punitive.[277]

Second, the involvement of the entire community (or church) in the discipline of an erring member was unknown in the Jewish community (with exception of the Qumran community):

> There is in any case no trace in Jewish congregations of anything resembling the way in which the full assembly of the Christian church at Corinth (1 Cor 5), or the Qumran community (1QS 8:25—9:2), itself discussed and decided on individual cases of discipline and administration. Instead this was done by the appropriate bodies, i.e., the elders of the congregation.[278]

In 1 Cor 5:1–13 Paul addresses the church about sexual immorality: in particular, that a church member is living with his stepmother (v. 1).

---

275. Ibid., 233.

276. Ibid.

277. Ferguson, *The Church of Christ*, 383.

278. Schürer, *History of the Jewish People*, 2:431. *Str-B*, 1:787 states the same thing.

Fee notes that the language "his father's wife" is taken directly from the LXX of Lev 18:7–8.[279] The father's wife was probably not a Christian, since Paul did not address her in his instruction.[280] The act of marrying or living with a father's wife is condemned by the Law of Moses (Lev 18:18; 20:11; Deut 27:20), the Mishna (*Sanh.* 7.4), Philo (*Spec.* 3.21), and various Roman writers (Gaius, *Institutes* 1.63; Cicero, *Pro Cluentio* 5.27; Tacitus, *Ann* 6.19). Winter argues that the father was still living, and "the young man's offence suggests that it was the form of incestuous liaison for which Roman law provided no leniency, but rather provoked punishment."[281] His arguments, however, pay little regard to the statements already referenced.

The sinning man's arrogance is clear in that he thought he could be a Christian while deliberately disobeying the Lord (or perhaps he thought there was nothing wrong with the act).[282] However, South notes that the attitude of the church people, even more than the sin committed, aroused Paul's ire.[283] This interpretation is strengthened by the fact that Paul never addressed the man directly. The congregation simply accepted the man's sin (Thiselton translates v.2, "you remain complacent").[284] The instance is, no doubt, shocking to the 21st century reader, but the situation took place in part, because "the Judeo-Christian moral restrictions on human sexuality were not easily absorbed by pagan converts. Paul had to address this question regularly in the Gentile churches (cf. 1 Thess. 4:1–8; Col 3:5–7; Eph 5:3–13)."[285]

279. Fee, *First Corinthians*, 201.

280. MacGorman, "The Discipline of the Church," 74.

281. Winter, *After Paul Left Corinth*, 49. Winter thinks instead of an illicit marriage, the illicit love affair was perhaps going to be prosecuted, for which the father had sixty days to initiate criminal action, 50–51. But the chances of Paul pre-empting legal action for the young man would have been slim. Sixty days' time was not enough to be certain that the letters would make it forth and back to Corinth (particularly when Paul would need time to write such a long letter as 1 Corinthians). Winter's idea also seems to have little to do with the whole sweep of Paul's rhetoric in 1 Corinthians 5.

282. Dever, *Nine Marks*, 175.

283. South, *Disciplinary Practices in Pauline Texts*, 30.

284. Thiselton, *First Corinthians*, 387. Orr and Walther, *1 Corinthians*, 188, say, "The implication is that they were proud in the assumption that their Christian freedom was enhanced by their sympathetic understanding of this unusual sexual relationship." Bruce, *1 and 2 Corinthians*, 54, essentially agrees. Clarke, *Secular and Christian Leadership at Corinth*, instead looks at the Corinthian pride as simply a general attitude within the church.

285. Fee, *First Corinthians*, 196–97.

Without any hesitation, Paul tells the Christians in Corinth what they need to do (v.2): ἀρθῇ ἐκ μέσου ὑμῶν, "Let him who has done this be removed from among you." He describes the intended action metaphorically, with the phrase, "Cleanse out the old leaven" (v. 7).[286] Paul finishes his address of the problem in v.13 with a forceful restatement of the action they need to take: "Expel (ἐξάρατε) the wicked man from among you" (NIV). In this last command, it could be that Paul is making rhetorical use of a phrase that occurs in Deuteronomy (LXX) six times: καὶ ἐξαρεῖς τὸν πονηρὸν ἐξ ὑμῶν αὐτῶν.[287] "The Deuteronomic formula surely raises in Paul's mind, if not the minds of his Gentile readers, the vices against which the formula is invoked in Deuteronomy."[288] Since Paul twice uses the second person plural imperative verb form when addressing the church (ἐκκαθάρατε, ἐξάρατε), he expects them to act as a group.

Paul's role in the action is described in the following way: "For though absent in body, I am present in spirit; and as if present, I have already pronounced judgment on the one who did such a thing" (v. 3). The expression is somewhat difficult to interpret, and there have been various explanations for the meaning of παρὼν δὲ τῷ πνεύματι. Interpretations include that Paul is speaking of his "pneumatic ubiquity,"[289] that Paul means that he is present through his letter,[290] that he is using the idea of being present in a psychological sense,[291] that Paul is speaking about his own spirit being mediated to them by the power of the Lord,[292] or that τῷ πνεύματι refers primarily to the Holy Spirit.[293] South argues, "Exactly how he conceived of this 'spiritual presence' is impossible to say."[294] Surely much more is meant than the idea that the letter was written with Paul's authority. He writes as though he is present and tells them how he judges. In a similar way, Paul also said to the church in Colosse that "I am with you in spirit, rejoicing

286. Findlay, *First Corinthians*, 810, says that the aorist implies "a summary and ἐκ- a complete removal . . . leaving the Church clean: an allusion to the pre-Paschal removal of leaven (Exod. 12:15ff., 13:7)."

287. Zaas, "Cast out the Evil Man," 259. The instances are Deut 17:7, 19:19, 21:21, 22:21, 22:24, 24:7.

288. Ibid., 260.

289. Orr and Walther, *1 Corinthians*, 188.

290. Wolff, *Der erste Brief an die Korinther*, 103. Klauck, *1 Korintherbrief*, 42.

291. Barrett, *First Corinthians*, 123.

292. Wiles, *Paul's Intercessory Prayers*, 145.

293. Fee, *First Corinthians* , 204–5.

294. South, *Disciplinary Practices*, 34.

to see your good order" (Col 2:5). Fee is right to conclude, "This letter, of course, communicates his prophetic word to them on this matter; he probably therefore thinks of the reading of the letter in the gathered assembly as the tangible way in which the Spirit communicates his prophetic-apostolic ministry in their midst (cf. 2 Cor 10:10–11)."[295]

Paul speaks very authoritatively. South says, "Paul is not about to *pronounce* sentence on the Corinthian offender. He has already done that. Rather he will now *announce* to the community what that sentence is and what it is that they must do."[296] Meeks argues that this does not eliminate the responsibility of the whole church to take action:

> On the one hand, he presents a *fait accompli:* "I have already decided." On the other, he gives unmistakable directions for a solemn assembly of the whole congregation to expel the wrongdoer and "hand him over to Satan." Paul takes for granted that such a plenary meeting is the way such a solemn action is to be taken.[297]

Still Meeks sees the passage as emphasizing rather than limiting Paul's apostolic authority. Rather than deferring to local governance, he gives no room for doubt about the final decision. The tension is not just about moral laxity, but also a tension between local leadership and supralocal governance through the apostle.[298] Schmidt agrees, and sees a hierarchical scheme for handling New Testament discipline in which serious cases were handled by the church leaders and the most serious cases by the apostle himself. [299]

The views of Meeks and Schmidt, however, are hard to substantiate (and Schmidt admits that evidence for his scheme is slight). There is no mention of leaders in 1 Corinthians 5. Paul's controversy was not with the leaders, except in so far as they were a part of the church. Obviously it is up to leaders to assert leadership when a controversial issue arises in a church. But Paul does not focus on this principle at all. It is the whole church that he repeatedly blames: "there is sexual immorality among you" (v. 1), "And you are arrogant!" (v. 2), "Your boasting is not good" (v. 6), "I wrote to you in my letter not to associate with sexually immoral people" (v. 9). In addition, if this had not been a case for the church to handle all by itself, he

295. Fee, *First Corinthians,* 205.

296. South, *Disciplinary Practices in Pauline Texts,* 34.

297. Wayne Meeks, *First Urban Christians,* 128.

298. Ibid.

299. Schmidt, "Discipline," 216.

would not have criticized them for having failed to take action. Finally, if the controversy in 1 Corinthians 5 is primarily a conflict of authority, how were such discipline cases to be handled after Paul was dead? Instead, Paul is asserting his authority as an apostle (and the missionary-founder of the church) to admonish the local church to fulfill its role in taking corporate action against the sinning brother. In other words, Paul is not asserting his authority so much as he is forcing the whole church to act. Paul views the sin so seriously that he feels Satan is using it to destroy the church in Corinth.[300] Paul does not need the church to help him judge the erring brother himself. He does, however, need the church to act in assembly in order for the error to be removed from the church. South says that "Paul does not leave the decision in their hands."[301] This is true, in that he tells the Corinthians there is only one right decision; it is not true, however, in that he urges the whole church to act at their next assembly (συναχθέντων ὑμῶν—v. 4). "Otherwise, verse 13 loses its meaning, since by it the church is once again, expressly urged to expel the evil doer."[302]

In evaluating authority and responsibility in 1 Corinthians 5, most writers overlook one ramification of the process, i.e., they do not give proper consideration to all parties involved. As MacGorman notes, "This was not the kind of problem that could be turned over to a committee for resolution. It was a body problem, not simply an arm or a leg problem, and it required the participation of all members."[303] He later says, "For when immorality is condoned in a church, the moral fiber of the entire congregation is weakened."[304] The whole congregation needed to act in the disciplinary procedure to restore their own moral stature.

Since this study views 1 Corinthians 5 and 2 Cor 2:5–11 as addressing the same discipline event, 2 Cor 2:5–11 is viewed as a type of sequel to the urged proceedings of 1 Corinthians 5. The first point to note is that Paul's previous corrections, including his instructions in 1 Corinthians 5, were not a case of demanding submission to his authority: "Not that we lord it over (κυριεύομεν) your faith, but we work with you for your joy"

---

300. Wolff, *Der erste Brief an die Korinther*, 103.

301. South, *Disciplinary Practices in Pauline Texts*, 34.

302. Schrage, *Der erste Brief an die Korinther*, 374. "Dass V.13b sonst seinen Sinn verläre, denn dort wird die Gemeinde selbst ausdrücklich noch einmal aufgefordert, den Übeltäter auszustoßen."

303. MacGorman, "Discipline of the Church," 76.

304. Ibid., 78.

(2 Cor 1:24). Second, the church acted in a way pleasing to Paul and had acquitted itself (2 Cor 2:12; 7:11); the people had expelled the offender (2 Cor 2:6). Finally, there was a division in the church over the discipline, which should not be surprising. The offender was put out by the will of the majority (ὑπὸ τῶν πλειόνων) of the church (v. 6).

Most English versions translate ὑπὸ τῶν πλειόνων, "by the majority," including the ESV, NASB, NKJV, NIV, NAB, and NRSV.[305] The Vulgate translates it the same way: *a pluribus*. πλείονες is comparative. BDAG gives the meaning, "majority, most" for 2 Cor 2:6.[306] πλείονες is used with this substantival meaning also in 2 Cor 9:2, 1 Cor 9:19, 10:5, and 15:6. Furnish says, "In most, if not all of these instances, including the present passage, the use of the term seems to presume the existence of others, a 'minority,' not covered by it."[307] Some, however, take ὑπὸ τῶν πλειόνων to mean "the main body" in the sense of the הָרַבִּים in Qumran literature.[308] Thrall responds,

> The evidence for this viewpoint consists, in essence, of two items only, and becomes, on investigation, less compelling than it might initially appear. First, attention is drawn to the fact that in the LXX πλείονες (or the alternative form πλείους) is used on occasion to translate the Hebrew *rabbim*. In most of these instances, however, it is a true comparative, and irrelevant, therefore, to the alleged use in 2 Cor 2:6 as a term for the whole congregation. Secondly, there is a comment by Josephus in his discussion of the Essenes (*J.W.* 2.146). . . . The πλείονες here may be seen as the *rabbim*, i.e., the Qumran community as a whole. It is by no means clear, however, that this is what Josephus has in mind, for he goes on to say that "if ten sit together, one will not speak if the nine desire silence." This sounds much more as though οἱ πλείονες means "the majority" in the ordinary sense of the word. Moreover, it remains a plain linguistic fact that the precise Greek equivalent for *rabbim* would

305. The NEB translates v.6: "The penalty on which the general meeting has agreed has met the offence well enough." The NLT translates, "He was punished enough when most of you were united in your judgment against him." These both would convey the same sense as the translation, "This punishment by the majority" (ESV).

306. *BDAG*, 848b-c.

307. Furnish, *2 Corinthians*, 155.

308. Barrett, *Second Corinthians*, 91; Bruce, *1 and 2 Corinthians*, 184. See also Jeremias, "πολλοί," *TDNT*, 6:538–39.

be πολλοί not πλείονες. It is better to suppose, therefore, that in 2 Cor 2:6 οἱ πλείονες are "the majority" of the congregation.[309]

One can safely conclude, then, that after hearing Paul's letter of 1 Corinthians, the church in Corinth met together and decided the discipline of the sinning brother. The majority voted (or otherwise showed their view) to expel the man. The minority expressed themselves against this action or else did not express themselves at all. After hearing the news of the meeting and the aftermath, Paul needed to instruct the church to receive the repentant man back into fellowship.

In summary, church discipline, at its final stage, requires the corporate decision of the entire church. This principle is explicitly taught by Christ in Matt 18:17. It is also taught by Paul in 1 Corinthians 5, in that he makes toleration of immorality a church matter, not a church leadership issue or a debate about his authority (though he uses the moral force of his authority to declare there is only one right action to take). He also tells the church rather forcefully that they need to take action, and chides them for their reticence to do so (vv. 7, 13). Paul later acknowledges that a majority of the congregation voted to put the immoral man out of the church. Finally, the practice of immorality by church members eventually becomes a problem for the spiritual body, corrupting the whole, thus it needs to be handled by the whole body for the sake of their moral and spiritual rectitude.

Determination of Doctrine and Practice: Acts 15

The events recorded in Acts 15 hold enormous importance for the history of the Christian faith. Raymond Brown claims it was "the most important meeting ever held in the history of Christianity."[310] Witherington comments, "It is no exaggeration to say that Acts 15 is the most crucial chapter in the whole book. . . . It raises all the key questions of . . . what sort of history Luke was writing."[311] Bruce states, "The Council of Jerusalem is an event to which Luke plainly attaches the highest importance; it is as

---

309. Thrall, *Commentary on Second Corinthians*, 175.

310. Brown, *Introduction to the New Testament*, 306.

311. Witherington III, *Acts of the Apostles*, 439.

epoch-making, in his eyes as the conversion of Paul or the preaching of the gospel to Cornelius and his household."[312]

The occasion of the meeting in Jerusalem was the visit of members of the Jerusalem church to Antioch, who attempted to instruct the Christians there that they could only be saved if they were circumcised and followed the Law of Moses (15:1). Though Luke does not mention it here, as he does in Acts 11:1–3, Paul says that a major point of conflict in Antioch centered on Jewish believers eating at the homes of Gentile believers (Gal 2:11–13).[313] In that day Jewish prohibitions against eating in Gentile homes included eating only vegetables at the Gentile home, eating no meat offered to idols, or avoiding eating at a Gentile home altogether.[314] Strack and Billerbeck conclude, "Eating together as Jews and Gentiles was essentially out of the question: whether the Israelite or the Gentile gave the invitation"; still, they note that some rabbis did eat together with Gentiles.[315]

Some of the people in the Jerusalem church were never comfortable with Paul's evangelism of the Gentiles and wanted to correct it. Meyer explains what took place during the mission work at Antioch, which had distressed some of the Jewish believers in Jerusalem:

> The enormous success that Barnabas and Paul had during their mission activity in Antioch among the Gentiles was made possible through the abandonment of the requirement of the Jewish law and circumcision. Without the elimination of these, Christianity would always have remained a Jewish sect.[316]

Scott notes, "The geographical expansion related by the narrative of Acts . . . (1:8) is often noted. Less obvious, but no less important, is the cultural,

---

312. Bruce, *The Book of Acts*, 298.

313. This study will not concern itself with the chronological arguments of whether this visit refers to just before or just after the Jerusalem meeting of Acts 15. The conflict would have been the same in either case.

314. Slee, *The Church in Antioch*, 18–20.

315. *Str-B*, 4:374, "So konnte von einer Tischgemeinschaft zwischen Juden u. gojim kaum die Rede sein, gleichviel ob der Israelit der einladene oder der eingeladene Teil war."

316. Meyer, *Ürsprüng und Anfänge des Christentums*, 3:414. "Der reiche Erfolg, den Barnabas und Paulus bei ihrer Missionstätigkeit in Antiochia unter den Heiden erzielten, ist ermöglicht worden durch den Verzicht auf die Übernahme des jüdischen Gesetzes und der Beschneidung. Ohne einen solchen Verzicht wäre das Christentum immer eine jüdische Sekte geblieben." Translation by the author.

racial and social expansion."[317] It is possible that the process of incorporating the Gentiles began earlier than at Antioch: "It seems that Philip and other Greek-speaking Jewish Christians transitioned step by step to a Gentile mission free of the law in this region [the coastal plain, containing Ashdod, Gaza, and Caesarea] (Acts 8:26, 40)."[318] This may or may not have been true.[319]

In any case, those who were not at peace with evangelizing the Gentiles without the requirement of circumcision focused their displeasure primarily on Paul. The successes of Barnabas and Paul in Cyprus and Galatia would only have made them more concerned. Up to this point in the book of Acts, the controversy of including the Gentiles in the church had shown a progression from side issues to that which was essential: "Now at Antioch the main issue became clear: What is the nature of the new faith? On what basis is salvation imparted?"[320]

The teaching of the Judaizers in Antioch introduced a considerable amount of discord (στάσις) and debate (ζήτησις). Luke's expression, οὐκ ὀλίγης, "no small" is his oft-repeated *litotes*, thus meaning, there was a great amount of it in the church (15:2). The excessive amount of discord and debate required conflict resolution. The conflict extended beyond Antioch and ultimately encompassed all churches:

> It was not enough to indulge in "dissention and questioning" at Antioch; the whole issue had to be discussed and decided "at the highest level," for there was grave danger of a complete cleavage between the churches of Jerusalem and Judaea on the one hand and the church of Antioch and her daughter churches on the other hand. [321]

There was historical significance in Luke's portrayal of the resolution:

> The main way to resolve such a conflict in antiquity was to call a meeting of the ἐκκλησία, the assembly of the people (cf. vv. 12, 22), and listen to and consider speeches following the conventions of

317. Scott, "The Church's Progress to the Council of Jerusalem," 218.

318. Schnabel, *Early Christian Mission*, 2:1071.

319. Scott, "The Church's Progress to the Council of Jerusalem," 211–12, says that Philip's evangelism was among Jews, which would nevertheless have aroused suspicion among some of the Pharisaical party because of the large amount of contact Jews would have had with Gentiles while living and working in those areas.

320. Ibid., 219.

321. Bruce, *Book of Acts*, 304.

deliberative rhetoric, the aim of which speeches was to overcome στάσις and produce concord or unity.[322]

The response of the believers in Antioch was to send representatives to Jerusalem to clarify the matter.

There were two primary reasons for referring the matter to the church in Jerusalem. First, the Christians who had caused the dissention in Antioch had come from that church; it was, therefore, the responsibility of the church from which they had come to handle the matter. Second, the ramifications of any decision would be far-reaching. The spread of the gospel had started from Jerusalem, and the church in Jerusalem was still regarded as the mother church;[323] the Christians in other churches still looked to the Jerusalem church as the geographical source of their gospel. Christians were unified at a level not seen since. Bruce notes,

> It was unquestionable that a ruling from the church authorities there would carry more weight in the matter under dispute than anything else. Barnabas no doubt regarded himself as answerable to Jerusalem (cf. 11:22), and while Paul held himself answerable to none but the Lord who had commissioned him, he attached great importance to the maintenance of fellowship with Jerusalem.[324]

Another factor which would have directed the Christians of Antioch toward Jerusalem, perhaps in the background of their thinking, was that Christians at that time viewed Jerusalem as the literal center of the world. The geographical writings of Eratosthenes, Strabo, and Marcus Agrippa all placed the center of the world as just to the east of Jerusalem.[325]

Two more matters in the action of the church in Antioch need to be emphasized. First, it was the entire church that sent Paul and Barnabas: "*the brethren* determined (ἔταξαν) that Paul and Barnabas and certain others of them should go up to Jerusalem" (NASB). Bruce states, "There is no explicit subject for ἔταξαν, but it is plain from v. 3 that it was the church of Antioch that took this action."[326] Second, the representatives were sent to speak with "the elders and the apostles in Jerusalem" (v. 2).

322. Witherington III, *Acts of the Apostles*, 450.

323. Ibid., 451.

324. Bruce, *Acts of the Apostles: Greek Text*, 333. Barrett, *Commentary on the Acts*, 2:700, says, "It is best to render, 'They (the Christians at Antioch) appointed Paul and Barnabas and certain others to go up.'"

325. Bauckham, "James and the Jerusalem Church," 417–27.

326. Ibid. The Western text, as evidenced by D, reads that it was the visitors from

Many New Testament scholars have judged the account of the meeting in Jerusalem in Acts 15 as unhistorical. According to Dibelius, "Luke's treatment of the event is only literary-theological and can make no claim to historical worth."[327] Haenchen calls the account of the decree of the Jerusalem council impossible.[328] Pesch says that Luke puts two events together which historically did not occur together: the apostolic council and the apostolic decree. This, he explains, was done to present the mission to the Gentiles as a continuing part of the original history of the church.[329] Bock responds, "This is far too skeptical a reading of Luke's work. There is little doubt that such debate existed in the early church. We should not confuse selectivity with creativity and overplay the differences in the account."[330]

Can the meeting in Jerusalem rightly be called a "council"? Pesch says yes, that it is rightly called the Apostolic Council, as do Wikenhauser and Longenecker, calling it "the first ecumenical council."[331] John Meier names it "a prophetic harbinger of the ecumenical councils to come."[332] Reymond, while not calling the Jerusalem meeting an ecumenical council, evaluates it as "the Jerusalem Conference," which came up with a conciliar decree.[333] He further argues that Antioch did not have one church, but several churches which formed a synod. This synod sent Paul and Barnabas to Jerusalem. Likewise, Jerusalem did not have one congregation, but several, who also had a synod. These two synods met together with the presbyteries from Syria and Cilicia to act together at the Jerusalem general assembly.[334]

Jerusalem to Antioch who demanded Paul and Barnabas appear in Jerusalem. Metzger, *A Textual Commentary*, 426–27, demonstrates that the Western Text "has introduced several extensive alterations into the text of these verses."

327. Dibelius, *Studies in the Acts of the Apostles*, 100. Dibelius says, for instance, that "Peter's speech is founded upon the literary work of the author and can be understood only in the context of this work." 95.

328. Haenchen, *Die Apostelgeschichte*, 452–56.

329. Pesch, *Die Apostelgeschichte*, 2:72–74. As evidence, Pesch says, for example that a new account begins in 15:5, because the mood is no longer joyous, 76. Barrett, *Commentary on the Acts*, 710, responds, "It may be questioned whether such a precise delineation of sources is possible."

330. Bock, *Acts*, 488.

331. Pesch, *Die Apostelgeschichte*, 2:71; Winkenhauser, *Die Apostelgeschichte*, 171; Longenecker, *Acts*, 447.

332. Meier, "The Jerusalem Council," 465.

333. Reymond, *Paul, Missionary Theologian*, 151.

334. Reymond, "The Presbytery-Led Church," 96, 108.

Reymond's synods, of course, are nowhere to be found in the New Testament. If there were multiple congregations in Antioch and Jerusalem, their interactions are nowhere described. The book of Acts consistently refers to them as one church in each place. As has been mentioned earlier, Reymond has to redefine the word ἐκκλησία, without lexical support to substantiate his scenario. Quite a few writers do not see the meeting in Jerusalem as the Apostolic Council. Bock says that it should not be called a council "in the later technical ecclesiastical sense" but a "consultation."[335] Berkhof, though affirming the concept of inter-church assemblies, agrees, saying, "This council was composed of apostles and elders, and therefore did not constitute a proper example and pattern of a classis or synod in the modern sense of the word."[336] Fitzmyer adds,

"This meeting has often been referred to as the Apostolic Council. That is really a misnomer, because the meeting as described is not a solemn assembly of authorities from all over the church. Moreover, it is never counted as one of the councils in the history of Christianity."[337]

Farrar, an Anglican bishop, also argues against the idea that the meeting was a council:

It is only by an unwarrantable extension of terms that the meeting of the Church of Jerusalem can be called a "Council," and the word connotes a totally different order of conceptions to those that were prevalent at that early time. The so-called Council of Jerusalem in no way resembled the General Councils of the Church, either in its history, its constitution, or its object. It was not a convention of ordained delegates, but a meeting of the entire Church of Jerusalem to receive a deputation from the Church of Antioch.[338]

Another factor which makes this meeting in Acts 15 hard to equate with any other that followed is that apostles, witnesses to the resurrection of Christ, were involved.[339] Thus the authority would have been different than the kind seen in later gatherings. No doubt the presence of the apostles at the Jerusalem meeting was the main factor which motivated the churches

335. Bock, *Acts*, 486.

336. Louis Berkhof, *Systematic Theology*, 591.

337. Fitzmyer, *Acts of the Apostles*, 543. Fitzmyer nevertheless says that it led to the convening of official councils at a later date.

338. Farrar, *Life and Work of St. Paul*, 1:430–31.

339. Wiarda, "The Jerusalem Council and the Theological Task," 238, though Wiarda is discussing modern hermeneutics rather than reflection on church history.

in Antioch, Syria, and Cilicia to accept the conclusions of the Jerusalem meeting as authoritative.[340] The author finds the statements of Fitzmyer and Farrar convincing. The conclusion of the meeting was authoritative, but it was not made by a council, in the sense of a regional or an ecumenical council. It was a meeting involving two churches.

The next significant point in determining how corporate decision-making played out in Acts 15 is how the representatives were received in Jerusalem. Paul, Barnabas, and the others from Antioch were appointed to go to the apostles and the elders of the Jerusalem church. Luke says they were received (παρεδέχθησαν) by "the church and the apostles and the elders." The fact that at this juncture the church would be a part of the assembly should come as no surprise. First of all, the reception of church representatives by another church expressed the fundamental unity of the Christians.[341] It was the members of the church in Jerusalem who had been seriously controversial in Antioch; therefore, the church had a responsibility as a body to address the issue. In addition, the Jerusalem church was not, at this point, united in how it viewed the actions of its members in Antioch, nor in its view of the ministry of Paul and Barnabas. Immediately after Paul and Barnabas related the results of their mission in Cyprus and Galatia, the Jerusalem Christians from a Pharisee background raised objections: "It is necessary to circumcise them and to order them to keep the law of Moses" (v. 5).

The next phase was a gathering together of the apostles and elders (Συνήχθησάν τε οἱ ἀπόστολοι καὶ οἱ πρεσβύτεροι, v. 6). There is some question, however, how to fit this precisely into the course of events. Without mentioning the multitude (πᾶν τὸ πλῆθος) as Peter began his speech in v.7, the congregation was nevertheless present in v.12 as he concluded. Most likely, the apostles and elders met for a time and debated the issue, but the serious debate and speeches took place among the whole assembly. The Pharisaical party had very strong views and would not have been satisfied to simply receive a decision from their leaders in which they had no part in discussion. Luke precedes the account of Peter's speech with, "And after

---

340. Though this factor should make interpreters quite cautious about using the conclusions of later meetings in church history to be binding on churches, it does not eliminate the event as a pattern for church interaction and for dealing with doctrinal issues. Wiarda is countering the idea that Acts 15 teaches a particular "Spirit-led community interpretation." He concludes that Acts 15 does indeed give a model to guide our approach to theological decisions. Ibid., 248.

341. Kistemaker, *Acts*, 540.

there had been much debate" (v. 7). Bock points to the style of the account, saying, "That the full debate is not laid out in Acts 15 reflects Luke's choice not to drag the reader through everything that took place but to focus on the factors that led to resolution."[342] Kistemaker proposes "that the council met for many days to discuss the matter at hand and to come to a resolution that would maintain unity and unanimity in the church."[343] The debate, consultation, study, and argumentation of these days are not recorded. Instead, Acts 15 is a very condensed account of all that took place.

The next movement in the proceedings was the presentation of two speeches: Peter's followed by that of James. Fitzmyer notes that Peter's speech "is neither missionary nor kerygmatic, but rather a judicial or constitutive discourse, addressed to Christians, which enables the assembly to come to a doctrinal decision."[344] Witherington agrees, saying,

> This summary of the speech is clearly presented as an example of deliberative rhetoric in which Peter expects, after a brief *exordium*, that his *narratio* followed by two brief arguments (one in the form of a question) will be sufficient to silence the objectors to the Gentile mission.[345]

Peter's main argument is that God has created the acceptance of Gentiles in the church without circumcision: "And God, who knows the heart, bore witness to them, by giving them the Holy Spirit just as he did to us" (v. 8). "Peter had nothing to do with how Gentiles were to be included. God has acted and shown the way."[346] Therefore, those who wanted to require circumcision for salvation were tempting God (v. 10). This final point from Peter is a very serious warning, since Israel in the past had been severely chastened for the very same error (cf. Ex 17:2; Num 14:22). One may conclude that "Peter's speech was the influential moment in the discussion; it was his testimony that really turned the mind of the company."[347]

Following the speech, Luke writes, "And all the assembly (πᾶν τὸ πλῆθος)[348] fell silent" (v. 12). One suggestion is that perhaps this simply

342. Bock, *Acts*, 490.

343. Kistemaker, *Acts*, 543.

344. Fitzmyer, *Acts of the Apostles*, 543.

345. Witherington III,*Acts of the Apostles*, 453.

346. Bock, *Acts*, 500.

347. Proctor, "Proselytes and Pressure Cookers," 470.

348. The importance of this expression as a technical one, referring to the whole church, has been explained under the discussion of Acts 6:1–6. For those who would

means the meeting came to order.[349] Another is that this demonstrates that the Holy Spirit reigned in the assembly, so that "they yielded forthwith reason."[350] Most commentators, however, interpret the words as signaling that Peter's arguments were very convincing. There was no remaining argument against receiving the Gentiles without circumcision.

Peter's speech was followed by the report of Paul and Barnabas (this is a second report, see v. 5). Though it is curious to Dibelius that nothing was given of the content of this report, which should have been the most convincing, the omission is reasonable.[351] Luke has already given the account to the reader in chapters 13 and 14.

Concluding the meeting is James' speech, which gives scriptural arguments for the acceptance of Peter's conclusions. This speech, like Peter's, "is another clear example of deliberative rhetoric."[352] Lake and Cadbury conclude that James misquotes the Hebrew for his arguments.[353] This, however, is not at all the case:

> Careful attention to the text of the quotation in Acts 15:16–18 shows that it is far from simply a quotation of the LXX text of Amos 9:11–12 with small variations. It is a conflated quotation, combining Amos 9:11–12 with allusions to other, related texts (hence 'the prophets' in the introductory formula: 15:15), which assist its interpretation, and exhibiting a text-form which has been selected and adapted to suit the interpretation. These gestures are now familiar to us not only from the New Testament but also from the Qumran *pesharim*, and they must be understood as the product of skilled exegetical work. What appears to be merely a quotation of a scriptural text turns out to be in fact also an interpretation of the text.[354]

For the church, important decisions needed a scriptural basis. This was the chief effect of James' speech. "James's conclusion," says Bruce, "amounted to this: that all attempts to impose circumcision and its attendant

---

suggest that the term refers to the elders, Hort, *The Christian Ecclesia*, 70, says, "It is inconceivable that the body of Elders should be called 'the multitude.'"

349. Lake and Cadbury, *Acts of the Apostles*, 175.

350. Calvin, *Commentary on the Acts*, 61.

351. Dibelius, *Studies in the Acts of the Apostles*, 95–96.

352. Witherington III, *Acts of the Apostles*, 456.

353. Lake and Cadbury, *Acts of the Apostles*, 176.

354. Bauckham, "James and the Jerusalem Church," 453.

legal obligations on Gentile converts must be refused."[355] But James was not finished. For the sake of the harmony of Jewish and Gentile believers together in the same fellowship, he recommended that Gentile believers be instructed to follow four rules. Bruce explains,

> James gives it as his considered opinion that they should be asked to respect their Jewish brethren's scruples by avoiding meat which had idolatrous associations or from which blood had not been properly drained, and by conforming to the high Jewish code of relations between the sexes instead of remaining content with the lower pagan standards to which they had been accustomed. This would smooth the path of social and table fellowship between Christians of Jewish and Gentile birth.[356]

Whether this is an entirely correct assessment is certainly the cause of debate among writers on this subject. Surely, "abstain from fornication" must entail a great deal more than adopting the Jewish high code of sexual relations. Paul repeatedly addresses his converts on the matter of sexual purity quite separate from any cultural considerations. With respect to the other three rules, evidently Gentile Christians came to apply them all, regardless of cultural context. They were accepted as binding on Christians long after there were few or no Jewish people in their churches:

> That Christians abstain from eating blood is taken for granted by the Letter of the Churches of Vienne and Lyons (*ap.* Eusebius, *Hist. Eccl.* 5.1.26), Minucius Felix (*Oct.* 30.6–7), Tertullian (*Apol.* 9.13; *De Pud.* 12.4–5; *De Mon.* 5) and Clement of Alexandria (*Strom.* 4.15). Origen (*C. Cels.* 8.29–30) refers explicitly to the decree and clearly sees no problem in regarding all three of the first three prohibitions as binding on and actually observed by Christians in his time. None of these writers relate the decree to table-fellowship between Jewish and Gentile Christians, which would, in any case, hardly have been a matter of concern in their contexts.[357]

With this historical note in mind, it still needs to be said that the rules recommended by James must have been particularly relevant to the table-fellowship issue. If the assembly in Jerusalem wanted to deal with all the pressing ethical issues in the churches in Antioch, Syria, and Cilicia, they would have had to write quite a long list for their readers. It was the

355. Bruce, *Acts*, 311.

356. Ibid.

357. Bauckham, "James and the Jerusalem Church," 465.

table-fellowship problem that was causing conflict among the two groups of Christians.

The final decision of assembly, written by the elders and apostles, addresses six different matters:

1. They disavowed the actions of their own people who had troubled the believers in Antioch (v. 24).

2. They made explicit that the final decisions were arrived at through the guidance of the Holy Spirit (v. 28).

3. The assembly arrived at a unified decision (v. 25).

4. The assembly was sending their representatives, Judas and Silas, to Antioch (vv. 25, 27).

5. The church in Jerusalem and the apostles were fully in support of the mission work of Barnabas and Paul (vv. 25–26).

6. They listed four rules for ethical/cultural behavior to help alleviate the conflict (vv. 28–29).[358]

The second point assured the churches in Antioch, Syria, and Cilicia that the process and final decision had been carried out by God's direction. As Suggit explains, "The structures of the Christian community as depicted in Acts are the ways in which the Spirit of God is shown to be at work in the church."[359] The action of the assembly in Jerusalem was one instance of the Spirit of God at work. Thus the good relationship the two churches had enjoyed was restored (v. 24).

One more action by the group helps evaluate the corporate decision-making in play. The apostles, elders, and the whole church (σὺν ὅλῃ τῇ ἐκκλησίᾳ) determined to send representatives to make the decision known to the church in Antioch as well as to other churches (v. 22). The decision to send included the appointing of messengers and the writing of the letter to the Gentile believers; note that the main verb is ἔδοξε, "decided" (NRSV). It is followed by the infinitive πέμψαι, "to send." The infinitive is accompanied by two participles: ἐκλεξαμένους, "choosing," and γράψαντες, "writing" (both aorist, middle). The actual writing was in the name of the

358. Dunn, *Theology of Paul's Letter to the Galatians*, 27–28, says that the Jerusalem Council ended up concluding that there were two gospels. This of course would require a critical revision of the letter from the Jerusalem church to Antioch. It also flies in the face of Paul's statements in Gal 1:6–9. Dunn is answered by Wiarda, "The Jerusalem Council," 235–36.

359. Suggit, "The Holy Spirit and We Resolved," 46.

apostles and the elders. The reason for the naming of these two groups is that the church in Antioch had asked specifically for an answer from them (v.2). Nevertheless, Luke considers the total action as being on the part of the apostles, the elders, and the whole church together.

Following the pattern of the Greek assembly, the church made a public expression about its findings. Luke's wording of this phenomenon is identical to that used by Greek writers to denote the public decision of a Greek (political) assembly The reason one can conclude there was a public expression of a decision which mirrors the Greek assembly is the use of the phrase, τότε ἔδοξε τοῖς . . . The word ἔδοξε (aorist, singular) from δοκέω has three basic meanings, according to BDAG:[360]

1. "think, believe, suppose" (transitive idea)

2. "seem" (intransitive, either have the appearance or be influential)

3. "think, believe" (impersonal idea)

For the third definition, δοκέω with the infinitive means, "it seems best to me" or "I decide." This is the construction in Acts 15:22.[361] Furthermore, LSJ explains that this construction was frequently used in Greek literature to denote a public resolution, as do Brandis and Hornblower.[362] The standard expression is ἔδοξε τῇ βουλῇ καί τῷ δήμῳ: "It seemed good to the council and the people." Examples include *Herod.* 1.3—"the Greeks decided . . . to demand back"; Ar., *Th.*372—"It was decided by the council with the Demos"; *Thuc.* 4.118—"The Athenian people passed the following decree"; *J.Ant.* 16.166 (from Augustus Caesar)—"it seemed good to me and my counselors"; *OGIS*, 233.10—"it was decided by the assembly." So it appears that the apostles, the elders, and the whole church, following the historical pattern of Greek assemblies, made a public resolution to send messengers whom the body had chosen, who would carry a letter which the elders and the apostles had written.[363]

360. *BDAG*, 255a–b.

361. *BDAG*, 255b.

362. *LSJ*, 442 (II.4.b); Brandis, "ἐκκλησία," 5:2186. Hornblower, *A Commentary on Thucydides*, 2:368–69.

363. The Majority Text of v. 23 reads, Οἱ ἀπόστολοι καὶ οἱ πρεσβύτεροι καὶ οἱ ἀδελφοί ("the apostles and the elders and the brothers") whereas the *UBS* Text reads, Οἱ ἀπόστολοι καὶ οἱ πρεσβύτεροι ἀδελφοί. ("the apostles and the elders: your brothers"). The reading of the UBS Text is accepted for this study. Metzger, *Textual Commentary on the Greek New Testament*, 436, says that the Majority Text reading "appears to be an emendation made in order to avoid what in Greek is a somewhat harsh apposition of ἀδελφοὶ with both Οἱ ἀπόστολοι and πρεσβύτεροι.

Witherington's comments about the normal method of settling disputes in the Graeco-Roman world help one understand and summarize what was occurring in Acts 15. In order to settle the dispute, one sovereign body, the church in Antioch, sent representatives to the people most responsible to act: the apostles and the Jerusalem elders. In Jerusalem, all involved regarded the proper place of debate and decision-making to be the Christian ἐκκλησία (as would be expected in the Graeco-Roman culture). After the representatives from Antioch were received by the whole church in Jerusalem, the major debate (though not all the debate) took place in the ἐκκλησία, where all sides could be heard. The issue was ultimately answered by reciting before the assembly what God had already done about the admission of Gentiles without circumcision into the church and providing scriptural rationale for the conclusion on the matter. The assembly viewed the final result of the debate to have been brought about by the Holy Spirit. Finally, following the recommendation of James, the assembly sent messengers from their midst with a letter written by the apostles and elders, setting rules of Christian behavior which were pertinent to the issue at hand, commending the ministries of Paul and Barnabas, and disavowing the actions of some of their members who had caused unrest in the Antioch church. It is an impressive example of conflict resolution resulting in harmony on all sides, without either group having to surrender its own important principles.

DECISION BY A GROUP ACTING INDEPENDENTLY OF THE DIRECT AUTHORITY OF A CHURCH: ACTS 16:9–11

Acts 16:9–11 marks the beginning of the "we" passages in Acts, in which Luke writes as an eyewitness of the events that are recorded. The missionary group was initially two men: Paul and Silas (15:40). During their visit to Lystra, Paul chose Timothy to be a member of the church planting team as well (16:1–3). Evidently at Troas, Luke was also invited to join the group because in 16:10 he writes, "Immediately we sought to go on into Macedonia."

Paul and his co-workers, after leaving Galatia, moved north, then later in an easterly direction toward the coast.[364] The missionary party was

---

364. Schnabel, *Early Christian Mission*, 2:1139–48, argues that Paul entered the province of Asia at Apameia and traveled north, rather than south, as does Ramsay, *St. Paul*

prohibited twice by the Holy Spirit in their attempts at missionary work: first, in Asia (16:6) and then in Bithynia (16:7—here the expression is "the Spirit of Jesus"). As they traveled a long distance (over 300 km) northward through the eastern part of the province of Asia, they were all the while forbidden by the Holy Spirit to preach ("from which we may infer that their original plan had been to do this very thing").[365] The missionary party next decided to go to Bythinia, according to Longenecker, "to evangelize the strategic cities and important Black Sea ports there, all of which were interconnected by an elaborate Roman road system."[366] After being forbidden by the Holy Spirit to evangelize in Bythinia, they traveled westward, another 300 km toward the coast.

The statements about the Holy Spirit's prohibitions are significant, because they record a human effort which relies on the directions of the Spirit, even when those directions appear impractical. As Bruce states, "The missionary journeys of Paul exhibit an extraordinary combination of strategic planning and keen sensitiveness to the guidance of the Spirit of God."[367] Why the missionary party was hindered by the Holy Spirit from preaching in Asia is not stated. One suggestion is that it may have been because of hostility in Pisidian Antioch.[368] However, within several days, Paul was a good distance away from Antioch, and a few years later Paul would return to the west coast of Asia to do a lengthy mission work. There simply is no explanation for why the Holy Spirit said no. Nor is there an explanation as to how the group received the information from the Holy Spirit. For Luke, the fact that the prohibitions took place is adequate enough to explain the progress of the Christian mission.

Troas was a Roman colony, a port city, and a geographical point through which much land traffic passed on its way southward and westward.[369] It may have been the case that the group made its way to Troas, thinking that the next area of ministry might be on the other side of the Aegean.[370] Bowers suggests that Paul's only motive for going to Troas would

---

the Traveller, 195, and Bruce, Acts of the Apostles: Greek Text, 354–55, and Beitzel, Moody Atlas of Bible Lands, 178–79. For a different view of the direction Paul's party took, see Jewett, "Mapping the Route of Paul's Second Mission," 1–22.

365. Bruce, Acts, 326.
366. Longenecker, Acts, 457.
367. Ibid., 325.
368. Ibid., 1148.
369. Schnabel, Early Christian Mission, 2:1145.
370. Farrar, Life and Work of St. Paul, 1:477–48.

have been to find a ship across the Aegean.[371] Witherington counters that "Paul tended to head for colony cities such as Philippi or Corinth, and Troas was one such city." He just as likely intended to plant a church there as to travel across the Aegean.[372] On the other hand, Paul had been forbidden to preach the Word in Asia. At Troas, Paul was still in the province of Asia.

It was at Troas that Paul received his vision to go to Macedonia (16:9). The event of a vision, though not frequent in the experience of the early church, would not have been regarded as unusual by the believers. There are seven other instances in the book of Acts in which believers receive instruction from the Lord through visions: 9:10, 12; 10:1–6; 10:9–16; 12:5–10; 18:9; 23:11.

Though God spoke only to Paul in the vision (16:9), the missionary team concluded that God was calling all of them (συμβιβάζοντες ὅτι προσκέκληται ἡμᾶς ὁ Κύριος—v. 10). The response of the group was immediate, mutual obedience (εὐθέως ἐζητήσαμεν ἐξελθεῖν, "we sought passage to Macedonia at once"—v. 10, NASB). In all phases of his ministry following his departure from Antioch in Syria (Acts 15:40), Paul was the leader of his missionary team. Nevertheless, the Holy Spirit directed all (not just Paul). All the members of the team entered into the decisions of where to go. They did not go unwillingly or without the real, personal goal of fulfilling the next step directed by God. Paul called his missionary companions, "fellow workers" (συνεργοί, e.g., Rom 16:21; Phlm 24). Bard Pillette summarizes Paul's use of this term:

> Fellow worker was Paul's most widely used designation. It was used to describe his helpers and colleagues in missionary work. It stressed mutual commitment to the same work under the same "employer" without implying any differences of rank or office. The idea of equality was presumed in that all the workers functioned together without distinction of worth. Yet, that did not mean that Paul did not exercise authority over his co-workers.[373]

As the members of the missionary team would have had different functions, according to their talents, each would need adequate information to perform his tasks, upon which all the rest would also be dependent. The individual ministries in the group would have to be coordinated. Times

371. Bowers, "Paul's Route through Mysia," 507–11.
372. Witherington III, *Acts of the Apostles*, 479.
373. Pillette, "Paul and His Fellow Workers," 117.

of discussion, reporting, and sharing of ideas would have been necessary, regardless of how clearly Paul led the group.

Still another matter which needs mentioning to clarify this type of group decision-making is that the missionary team, as a unit, had to make its own decisions about where and how to conduct each successive phase of the ministry. The missionary team was not sent out by one church, but by different churches: Paul and Silas had been commissioned by the church in Antioch (Acts 15:40); Timothy was recommended by the church in Lystra and was commissioned through the laying on of the hands of the elders of that church (1 Tim 4:14). We do not know what Luke's previous church connection had been. Nevertheless, all were given a free hand in their actions by their sending churches (as would have been necessary). The Acts 15:40—16:11 passage is the clearest example of a commissioning with a free hand that is recorded in the New Testament. The reason for giving this authority is understandable, as Kevin Bauder notes:

> Antioch . . . was in no position to direct Paul and his companions during their missionary journeys. Communication was slow, and decisions had to be made quickly. Even if communication had been possible, people in Antioch could not be expected to know enough of Paul's circumstances to be able to direct him wisely. The bulk of the decisions had to be made by Paul's team as he traveled.[374]

Regarding Paul's missionary work a few years later, Bauder adds,

> Paul's team was composed of members of local churches. Presumably, each one was accountable to his own local congregation in the long run. In the short run, however, the team had considerable latitude to make its own decisions. It determined its own direction in ministry and managed its own personnel. Even Paul was not above submitting to direction, most likely from other team members, but certainly from a source other than his own local church (Acts 17:14–15).[375]

No doubt, in Paul's case, churches gave him a free hand because the churches involved trusted Paul to consequently follow the direction of the Holy Spirit. He had been called by the Lord to perform the task of evangelism, and previous to the time of being sent out, he had fulfilled his call with a selfless and intense passion.

---

374. Bauder, "Service Organizations."
375. Ibid.

In summary, Acts 16:6–11 describes a missionary team which was pursuing its objective of evangelizing in the Roman Empire. Although the team had a strategy, it was fully submissive to the leading of the Holy Spirit, to the point of canceling attempts at evangelism when the Lord clearly directed not to begin. They acted together, with Paul as the leader. The goals God gave to Paul became the personal goals of every member of the team. Human action, strategy, and discussion did not deter the voice and work of the Holy Spirit. All of these became his tools. Such a missionary team could be trusted to function independently and, at the same time, fulfill the mutual goals of both the Lord and the churches they represented.

CHAPTER SUMMARY

The book of Acts records history. If one accepts the historical record of Acts, one must conclude that the early church had a church order. In addition to the Seven (later deacons) and elders, the early church adopted methods of handling all-church issues by involving the entire church in corporate decision-making, or, in one instance, a missionary team in corporate decision-making. The early church understood that its authority came from three sources: Jesus the Messiah, the Scriptures, and the Holy Spirit. In the decisions made, on which Luke elaborates in detail, all three authorities are mentioned. The apostles learned their concepts of leadership from Christ, who taught them to be servants first and not to be lords over the other disciples. Furthermore, Christ emphasized that all Christians are brothers, putting them on the same plane. Finally, the Holy Spirit indwells each believer, giving each a significant ability to exercise spiritual discernment.

The early church and particularly the apostles learned their lessons from Jesus well, because they demonstrated significant sensitivity to other believers in the accounts about controversy in the book of Acts. They regarded the other Christians as capable in deciding several kinds of issues, including the choice of leaders or representatives, the exercise of church discipline, the determination of doctrine and practice, and choices in ministry. In eight instances, an entire church chose its leaders or representatives (Acts 1:15–26; 6:1–6; 11:19–22; 11:30; 15:2, 22, 36–41; 1 Cor 16:1–4 with 2 Cor 8:18–19). In another instance, Acts 8:14–17, the apostles chose representatives from their midst to ratify and further a new work. In yet another instance, Acts 13:1–3, the action of the entire church was very likely (in view of Acts 14:27 and 15:40). In one instance, only the action of Paul and

Barnabas is recorded; however, congregational involvement in the choice of elders was very likely on account of historical and biblical patterns of choosing leaders.

One instance of corporate decision-making deals at length with church discipline (1 Cor 5:1–13 with 2 Cor 2:5–11). The entire church was called upon to enact the discipline. This resulted in a decision in which the majority of the church body determined to put the offending brother out of their midst.

In Acts 15, Luke describes how the church in Antioch addressed the problem of the limits of the Law of Moses for Gentile Christians by sending messengers to seek an answer from the apostles and the elders of the Jerusalem church. The process of handling the controversy involved the entire church in Jerusalem. Though there was evidently one period in which just the apostles and the elders met together, the primary place of debate was in the assembly, in which Peter's speech essentially ended the debate about Gentiles being under the Law of Moses. The entire assembly then sent messengers from their own church back to Antioch. The apostles and the elders, who had been requested to render a decision, sent the churches in Antioch, Syria, and Cilicia their united view about the doctrine (they disavowed those who had taught the Gentiles to obey the Law of Moses) and what rules to follow to aid harmonious fellowship between Jewish and Gentile believers, particularly table-fellowship. As members from the Jerusalem church were responsible for the strife begun in Antioch and as the church in Jerusalem needed to unify its own position on Gentile Christians and the Law of Moses, corporate decision-making was the most effective way of settling the controversy.

Finally, a missionary team exercised independent authority in taking successive, strategic steps in mission work (Acts 16:6–11). The group followed Paul as the leader but accepted his goals as their own personal goals. Since Paul viewed his companions as "co-workers," there would have been interaction in the group which helped lead to decisions for the team. All planning, however, was subordinated to the directions and restrictions of the Holy Spirit. Representing at least two churches, the missionary team was entrusted with responsibility as a trusted company that could act independently and still fulfill the desires of the sending churches.

In addition to those things found in examining passages which describe corporate decision-making in the New Testament, it is also important to mention what was not revealed in the texts. Conspicuously absent in any of the accounts in Acts or 1 and 2 Corinthians is any action regulating how teaching or preaching was done. Instead, 1 Corinthians 14 and the pastoral epistles give indication that this is a matter for those given the task of preaching to regulate. Furthermore, there is no record of church action about personal choice of diet (with the exception of not eating blood or things sacrificed to idols), attire, attendance at or celebration of events. Romans 14, in fact, would militate against such action on the part of the New Testament church. There is no demonstration or instruction in the New Testament to carry out group discipline for these matters. Finally, there is no indication in the book of Acts of synodal or monarchial decisions that were binding on a part or the whole of the body of Christians then existent.

The apostles especially (including Paul) demonstrated again and again their sensitivity to both the concerns of their fellow-Christians and the enterprise of Christ. There is no question but that the authority of the apostles was highly regarded in the church, particularly by the time of the events of Acts 15. Yet the apostles repeatedly chose the path of corporate decision-making to address serious issues most effectively. When error demanded hard words from the apostles, they did not hesitate to apply them; however, correction and reproof were never done with the thought of removing the status given by Christ: "You are all brothers."

5

Reflection of the New Testament Pattern in Christian Documents from 95 CE to 350 CE

IF THERE IS A pattern of corporate decision-making in the church of the New Testament, one would certainly expect that pattern to carry over for a time, if not a long time, into the life of Christian churches. In fact, this precedent is easily demonstrated in the writings of church fathers. This chapter will trace the following: the role of the church in the election of church leaders, the role of the church in discipline, and the autonomy of the church in inter-church meetings.

THE ROLE OF THE CHURCH IN THE ELECTION OF CHURCH LEADERS

It is not difficult to demonstrate that, after the death of the apostles, from the earliest extant post-apostolic writings until about 350 CE, church leaders were elected by local congregations with the participation of the whole body. Ferguson says, "In regard to organizational matters, we should note that in the early history of Christianity there was a congregational selection and commissioning of ministers. Our earliest notices refer to election by local congregations."[1] For the entire timespan in question, Neumann claims that the bishops and presbyters were elected by all the people.[2] Hatch asserts

1. Ferguson, "'Congregationalism' of the Early Church," 134.
2. Neumann, "Bischof, I," 6:663.

that, "There was always, in the case at least of those which had been from the beginning the chief grades of ecclesiastical office, viz., bishop, presbyter, deacon, and reader, either the reality or the semblance of an election."[3] The appointment (κατάστασις) of officers was the responsibility of the apostles (or later, the bishops), but the choice of the officers was from the people.[4]

Clement of Rome

In his letter to the church of Corinth, Clement of Rome described the apostolic tradition for selecting presbyters. A great deal has been written about the letter of 1 *Clement*, mostly emphasizing his view of ecclesiastical office.[5] In particular, 1 *Clement* criticized the Corinthian church for its removal of some of its elders (3.3; 44.6; 47.6). Clement reminded the Corinthian church of how elders were originally chosen:

> Our apostles likewise knew, through our Lord Jesus Christ, that there would be strife over the bishop's office. . . . Those, therefore, who were appointed by them or, later on, by other reputable men with consent of the whole church, and who have ministered to the flock of Christ blamelessly, humbly, peaceably, and unselfishly, and for a long time have been well spoken of by all—these men we consider to be unjustly removed from their ministry. (44.1–3)

This statement is preceded by Clement's appeal to Moses and the establishment of the Aaronic priesthood. Clement's main emphasis in the passage is on the importance of God's order. Leitzmann's evaluation of this portion of the letter is the same as many make, in that he calls it "the hour of birth of Catholic ecclesiology." Above all, Clement argues for a chain of succession of the ἐπίσκοποι.[6] But Bowe, like Hatch, counters that this evaluation is a misinterpretation of what Clement said:

> Clement offers here not a paradigm but an *analogy*. . . . The function of the analogy, however, is to demonstrate not so much a priestly hierarchy to be replicated in the Christian offices (Clement

---

3. Hatch, "Ordination," 2:1504.
4. Haddan, "Bishop," 1:213.
5. Bowe, *Church in Crisis*, 144.
6. Leitzmann, *Geschichte der Alten Kirche*, 204.

> nowhere does this), but to illustrate the value of an ordered system and the necessity of faithfulness to "what God has appointed."[7]

Furthermore, there is no mention of succession. Clement does not refer to individual apostles or their connection to specific churches.[8] Koester remarks, "Clement is not interested in the doctrine of apostolic succession but wants to speak generally about the continuance and stability of offices in the Christian Churches."[9]

For the concerns of this study, the phrase, "with consent of the whole church" (συνευδοκησάσης τῆς ἐκκλησίας πάσης), is a significant point. Clement believed that the whole church needed to be involved in the certification of an overseer in his office, for his service to be legitimate. The overseers were appointed (κατασταθέντας) by the apostles. καθηίστημι plus the accusative means to authorize or appoint.[10] Interestingly, this is the same construction Paul uses to tell Titus to appoint elders in Crete. If Clement was actually citing the exact nature of apostolic practice, he is illuminating what is meant by the appointing of elders in Acts 14:23 and Titus 1:5. What this section of 1 Clement certainly teaches is that a part of determining who will be an overseer in the local church is the responsibility of the whole church. (Clement uses the terms ἐπίσκοποι and πρεσβύτεροι interchangeably, 44.4–5.)[11]

Another point which makes it clear that Clement believed that the church as a body rightly makes decisions about who serves in an office is his later statement that a church may legitimately dismiss an elder (πλῆθος here being understood in the sense of the congregation):

> Now, then, who among you is noble? Who is compassionate? Who is filled with love? Let him say, "If it is my fault that there are rebellion and strife and schisms, I retire; I will go wherever you wish, and will do whatever is ordered by the people (προτασσόμενα ὑπὸ τοῦ πλήθος). Only let the flock of Christ be at peace with its duly appointed presbyters." (1 Clem. 44.3)[12]

---

7. Bowe, *Church in Crisis*, 145–46. Hatch, *Organization of the Early Christian Churches*, 117.

8. Bowe, *Church in Crisis*, 147.

9. Koester, *Introduction to the New Testament*, 2:290.

10. *BDAG*, 390c.

11. Lightfoot and Harmer, *Apostolic Fathers*, 78.

12. Ibid., 77.

Bowe argues that the issue for Clement was not *that* elders were dismissed, but *how* they were dismissed:

> What is most striking in *1 Clement* 44 is the lengths to which Clement goes to insist that there was no "legitimate reason" for deposing the presbyters, since (as he states three times) their conduct in office was blameless (ἀμέμπτως, 44.3, 4, 6). The logical implication seems to be that if the office bearers do not fulfill their office faithfully, they may be removed (or at least disciplined) by the community.[13]

George Williams agrees, saying, "Clement . . . does not so much contest the right of the laity to eject their liturgical leaders as to chastise them for having presumed to do so when their leaders had in fact 'offered the sacrifices *with innocence and holiness.*'"[14] In a parallel event, sixty to seventy years later, Polycarp expressed that an elder, Valens, had been legitimately dismissed from his office by the action of the whole church. He urged the whole church to restore Valens and his wife to repentance (Pol., *Phil.* 11).[15] At least for Clement and Polycarp, then, removal of elders from office by the whole church is legitimate Christian polity.

Many writers view Clement's argument regarding the appointment of elders as unhistorical.[16] Campenhausen, however, disagrees:

> It is quite impossible to maintain that in saying this he is putting forward something completely unheard of. In his concern with the concrete situation of conflict Clement only works out more precisely and systematically something which must have been taken more or less for granted in every church where the system of elders had gained control.[17]

In fact, if the letter was written in 95 CE,[18] it is highly improbable that Clement could have successfully invented something new and attributed it to the apostles. Paul was in Corinth as the church founder and visited the church, at the latest, forty years earlier. He was in Rome at his death in 65 or 66 CE. People were undoubtedly still alive in both places who would either

---

13. Bowe, *Church in Crisis*, 150.
14. Williams, "The Role of the Layman," 291.
15. Lightfoot and Harmer, *Apostolic Fathers*, 216.
16. Williams, "The Role of the Layman," 148.
17. Campenhausen, *Ecclesiastical Authority*, 91.
18. Lightfoot and Harmer, *Apostolic Fathers*, 25.

confirm or dispute Clement's statements. From the evidence of *1 Clement*, the whole congregation was responsible at least to decide with other leaders who would serve as elder of the church. The church body was also responsible to dismiss elders, if a genuinely valid reason called for the action.

The Didache and the Letters of Ignatius

The *Didache*, dated about 100 CE, instructed churches to "elect (χειροτονήσατε) for yourselves bishops and deacons worthy of the Lord" (15.1).[19] As noted in chapter 4, χειροτονέω, when referring to a group, has the force of "elect" when the meaning can be determined. Ignatius told two churches (τὴν ἐκκλησίαν ὑμῶν) to appoint (χειροτονῆσαι) messengers to go to other churches (Ign., *Phil.* 10.1; Ign., *Smyr.* 11.2).[20] This action is reminiscent of the records in the book of Acts where churches sent messengers to other churches; this happened at least twice from Antioch to Jerusalem and twice from Jerusalem to Antioch (Acts 11:23, 30; 15:2, 22). These historical events from sixty years earlier would have created a tradition in Antioch. The tradition, in turn, could have prompted Ignatius of Antioch to recommend the same kind of action to the church in Philippi and in Smyrna (if it was not a regular occurrence in the sixty intervening years).

Eusebius, Origen, and Hippolytus

Eusebius is cited here, though he wrote after 300 CE, because he recorded the choice of elders (bishops) from the first and second century CE. Though one may question the historical accuracy of his records, he was working with earlier traditions which would have described the events in the way he relates. Eusebius said that the successor of James at the church in Jerusalem came about in the following way:

> After the martyrdom of James, and the capture of Jerusalem, which immediately followed, the report is, that those of the apostles and the disciples of the Lord, that were yet surviving, came together from all parts with those that were related to our Lord according to the flesh. For the greater part of them were yet living. These consulted together, to determine whom it was proper

19. *BDAG*, 1083c, translates χειροτονήσατε, in this instance, as "elect for yourselves." Lightfoot and Harmer, *Apostolic Fathers*, 267, translate it "appoint for yourselves."

20. Lightfoot and Harmer, *Apostolic Fathers*, 215, 192.

to pronounce worthy of being the successor of James. They unanimously declared Simeon the son of Cleophas, of whom mention is made in the sacred volume, as worthy of the episcopal seat there. (*Hist. eccl.* 3.11)[21]

Thus Eusebius describes the choice of James' successor as an action on the part of the whole church, in consultation with James' relatives.

Origen states that the head of the church must be ordained in the presence of all the people (*et praesentia populi ut scient omnes*), in order to avoid any doubt or change of mind (*Levit. hom.* 6.3).[22] Hippolytus instructs, "Let the bishop be ordained after he has been chosen by all the people. When he has been named and shall please all, let him, with the presbytery and such bishops as may be present, assemble with the people on a Sunday" (*Trad. ap.* 1.1–2).[23] Ferguson comments,

> This statement is typical of instructions in the church-order literature, both in the expectation of popular election and in the description of the public nature of the ordination. Not only the selection but also the appointment occurred in the gathering of the church in which one was called to serve.[24]

Although *The Apostolic Constitutions* originated in Rome, it was also translated into Arabic, Coptic, and Ethiopic; through these translations it was able to have extensive influence on church organization in the Christian communities of Egypt and Syria.[25]

Cyprian

By the time of Cyprian, bishops had become clergy with regional authority, not simply the authority in a local church. Cyprian stressed the participation of the laity in the choice of the bishop more than any other church father. In fact, Granfield says, "He stated emphatically that the entire community—clergy, laity, and neighboring bishops—should participate in the selection of Episcopal leaders."[26] Cyprian always viewed the election of

21. Cruse, *Ecclesiastical History of Eusebius Pamphilius*, 99.
22. Origen, *Homilies on Leviticus*, 1–16, 120–21.
23. Hippolytus, *The Apostolic Tradition*, 33.
24. Ferguson, "'Congregationalism' of the Early Church," 134.
25. Granfield, "Episcopal Elections in Cyprian," 99.
26. Ibid., 95.

bishops as an act of the clergy shared with the people.[27] This is particularly significant in view of the fact that he elevated the role of the bishop to a previously unknown level of authority. His clearest statement on the subject of lay participation in the election of bishops and presbyters (he calls them "priests") is the following:

> Which very thing, too, we observe to come from divine author-ity, that the priest should be chosen in the presence of the people under the eyes of all, and should be approved worthy and suitable by public judgment and testimony. . . . And the bishop should be chosen in the presence of the people, who have most fully known the life of each one, and have looked into the doings of each one as respects his habitual conduct. And this also, we see, was done by you in the ordination of our colleague Sabinus; so that, by the suf-frage of the whole brotherhood, and by the sentence of the bish-ops who had assembled in their presence, and who had written letters to you concerning him, the episcopate was conferred upon him, and hands were imposed on him in the place of Basilidies. (*Ep.* 67.4–5)[28]

Cyprian based his teaching on three passages: Numbers 16:26, the choosing of Aaron before all the people; Acts 1:15, the choice of Matthias by the entire church; and Acts 6:2, the choice of the first deacons. Granfield concludes, "There seems to be little doubt that Cyprian described an estab-lished legal custom when he discussed the election of bishops."[29]

There are three stages in Cyprian's view of the choice of bishops: 1) *testimonium*, in which both clergy and people publicly offered their views on the qualification of the candidates; 2) *suffragium*, in which the clergy and the people indicated whom they wished to be bishop (the method is not specified); and 3) *iudicium*, in which the entire electing body affirmed the result of the election.[30] The role of the people in the choice of bishops changed significantly in the century spanning between the early church fathers and Cyprian: once bishops were elected, the people no longer had a voice in removing them from office.[31] The right of the people to elect bish-ops was again asserted by the Council of Ancyra (canon 18, 314 CE). After

27. Funk, "Die Bischofswahl in Altertum," 27.

28. *ANF*, 5:370.

29. Granfield, "Episcopal Elections in Cyprian," 99.

30. Ibid., 102–3.

31. Campenhausen, *Ecclesiastical Authority*, 273.

this synod, the emphasis on the election of clergy by the people dwindled, until it finally came to an end.[32]

THE ROLE OF THE ENTIRE CHURCH IN CHURCH DISCIPLINE

Church discipline played a significant role in the life of Christian churches until the time of Constantine. In their practice of discipline, churches were as much motivated by survival as by the idea of obeying the Scriptures. "In the midst of 'a crooked and perverse nation' they could only hold their own by the extreme of circumspection. Moral purity was not so much a virtue at which they were bound to aim as the very condition of their existence."[33] Two instances of the affirmation of church authority in discipline (specifically the removal of elders from office), have already been mentioned: by Clement of Rome and by Polycarp. Tertullian's view of penance offers another instance and is quite severe.[34] His treatise reveals a spirit far removed from Polycarp, who like Paul, urged the acceptance of the disciplined members back into the fellowship of the church. Still, Tertullian retained the concept of discipline as the right of the whole church. As a part of the penitential process that Tertullian described, he explained confession (*exomologesis*) as taking place before the elders, "God's dear ones," and all the brethren (*Paen.* 9).[35] Tertullian also stated, "We meet together as an assembly and congregation. . . . In the same place also exhortations are made, rebukes and sacred censures are administered. For with a great gravity is the work of judging carried on among us" (*Apol.* 39).[36] Origen explains that "sinners, and especially those who lead dissolute lives," were excluded by the Christians from the community (*Cels.* 3.51).[37] This would indicate an act of the whole church.

32. Haddan, "Bishop," 1:214.

33. Hatch, *Organization of the Early Christian Churches*, 69.

34. Tertullian's prescription for penance includes, "With regard also to the very dress and food, it commands (the penitent) to lie in sackcloth and ashes, to cover his body in mourning, to lay his spirit low in sorrows, to exchange for severe treatment the sins which he has committed; moreover, to know no food and drink but such as plain. . . to feed prayers on fastings, to groan, to weep and to make outcries unto the Lord your God." (*Paen.* 9)

35. *ANF*, 3:694.

36. *ANF*, 3:46.

37. *ANF*, 4:484.

Writing somewhat later than Origen in the third century CE, Cyprian frequently addressed the subject of discipline. During Cyprian's ministry as bishop of Carthage, he was forced to flee the city on account of persecution. Of those who remained behind, some lapsed from the faith. When the persecution had passed, there was continuing controversy over the readmission of the *lapsi*. Cyprian does not instruct the presbyters but rather the church (whom he calls, "most brave and beloved brethren") to "anxiously and cautiously weigh the wishes of those who petition you, since, as friends of the Lord . . . you must inspect both the conduct and the doings and the deserts of each one" (*Ep.* 10.3).[38] Cyprian also mentioned that some of the lapsed who had repented were to receive help in their sickness, as decided by the council (*Ep.* 52.2).[39] Regarding those who had become schismatics, Cyprian says that the church should separate itself from them. In his argumentation he quotes Matthew 18:17: "If he shall neglect to hear the Church, let him be unto thee as a heathen man and a publican" (*Ep.* 54.14).[40] Cyprian also urges restraint on the part of the congregation as they judged the repentant *lapsi* (59.3–4).[41] In this case, according to one suggestion, there may have been "vindictive motivation of the laity in testing the penitent."[42] What is clear in Cyprian's writings is that he regarded the participation of the congregation in discipline as essential.

THE AUTONOMY OF THE LOCAL CHURCH IN INTER-CHURCH MEETINGS

In the second century CE, churches began representative meetings between churches.[43]

> At first these assemblies were more or less informal. Some prominent and influential bishop invited a few neighbouring communities to confer with his own: the result of the deliberations of such a conference was expressed sometimes in a resolution, sometimes in a letter addressed to other Churches. . . . But so far from such

38. *ANF*, 5:291.

39. *ANF*, 5:336.

40. *ANF*, 5:344.

41. *ANF*, 5:355–56.

42. Williams, "The Role of the Layman," 293.

43. Hatch, *Organization of the Early Christian Churches*, 166.

letters having any binding force on other Churches, not even the resolutions of the conference were binding on a dissident minority of its members.[44]

In 155 CE Polycarp traveled to Rome to consult with Bishop Anicetus in an attempt to resolve the conflict between the Roman church and the churches in Asia Minor and Syria over the observation of the Christian Passah (*Ecc. Hist.* 4.14.1).[45] Though neither side gave ground, there was no disruption of the relationship between the two churches, as Ferguson notes, "The failure of this meeting to reach agreement on a common observance of the Pasch resulted in the parties agreeing to disagree, both maintaining their own practice but preserving fellowship."[46]

Two events caused inter-church meetings to become more frequent and, ultimately, regular. First, Bishop Victor of Rome determined to force other churches to follow the Roman observance (i.e., the date) of the Christian Passah. He was later convinced to rescind his threat of excommunication (*Ecc. Hist.* 5.23.3–4).[47] The controversy of the Christian Passah continued until 325 CE when the Roman time of observation became the law of the church.[48] The fixing of a uniform date for the observance of the Christian Passah arose out of a determination to distance Christians from Jewish influence:

> In AD 325, Constantine wrote a letter to those bishops who had not been present at the Council of Nicea concerning the date of Easter. The following consideration contained in this letter, "We ought not, therefore, to have anything in common with the Jews," sums up one of the key ideas behind much subsequent legislation against the Jews. All things Jewish were understood to be totally incompatible with Christianity.[49]

A second impetus for regular regional meetings came from the rise and spread of Montanism. Church leaders in various regions gathered together to determine how to handle the "Phrygian Heresy."[50]

---

44. Ibid., 166–67.
45. Cruse, *Ecclesiastical History of Eusebius Pamphilius*, 141.
46. Ferguson, "'Congregationalism' of the Early Church," 130.
47. Cruse, *Ecclesiastical History of Eusebius Pamphilius*, 207.
48. Schaff, *History of the Christian Church*, 2:218.
49. Diprose, *Israel and the Church*, 93.
50. Ferguson, "'Congregationalism' of the Early Church," 130–31.

> From such ad hoc meetings developed the practice of regular, usually annual synods of bishops in a province or region. The correspondence of Bishop Cyprian of Carthage indicates that by the mid-third century synods of Bishops in North Africa were highly developed institutions.[51]

However, even the ecumenical councils of the fourth century were not looked upon as authoritative in advance. Instead, they represented the spirit of the churches.[52] "The ancient church developed no theory of reception in regard to conciliar authority; the consensus of the faithful in fact determined the acceptance of doctrines."[53]

The correspondence of the churches with one another in the second century was from church to church, as may be observed in the letters of Clement, Ignatius (who wrote as an individual to entire churches), and Polycarp. This demonstrates the autonomy of the individual churches. Again, the change is observed in the time of Cyprian. His letters, though often to the entire church, were also frequently from bishop to bishop, not from church to church.[54]

The End of the Role of the Laity in Elections and Discipline

It is legitimate to ask how this understanding and practice of corporate decision-making in the early church were abandoned. Several factors are cited by church historians:

1. Following the official recognition of the Christian faith by the Roman government in 325 CE, secular rulers began to interfere with the rule of the church, and the voice of the people in choosing bishops gradually diminished.[55]

2. From the middle of the third century CE, concurrent with the development of the Episcopacy, Christianity began to increase rapidly. The church became a "church of the masses,"[56] with infant baptism

---

51. Ibid., 131.
52. Florovsky, "Authority of the Ancient Councils," 179.
53. Ferguson, "'Congregationalism' of the Early Church," 132.
54. Ibid., 133.
55. Neumann, "Bischof, I," 6:666.
56. Harnack, *Die Mission und Ausbreitung des Christentums*, 1:243.

aiding this phenomenon.[57] The church soon ceased to be the Religion of Morality.[58] Thus the leadership of the church lost confidence in the ability of the laity to make right decisions.

3. Christianity began to see itself as the "new Israel" or the "true Israel." As a result, churches began to view their bishops and presbyters as a legitimate succession of the priests and Levites in the Old Testament.[59] The clergy then became a separate, higher order.

With the rise of monasticism in the fourth century CE, the distinction between the church and the world became the distinction between those who lived according to a higher morality and spirituality and those who did not, within the church. The clergy obtained an exceptional status, and the role of the clergy in determining church polity became dominant.[60]

SUMMARY

The writings of the church fathers in the second and third centuries CE demonstrate that corporate decision-making by the whole church in matters of electing church leaders as well as enacting church discipline was widespread. It therefore confirms the interpretation that the New Testament portrays the practice of corporate decision-making for normal church life, as well as the fact that churches functioned independently, rather than under the direction of a council or regional director over many churches.

---

57. Hatch, *Organization of the Early Christian Churches*, 136.

58. Harnack, *Die Mission und Ausbreitung des Christentums*, 236.

59. Diprose, *Israel and the Church*, 99–136.

60. Hatch, *Organization of the Early Christian Churches*, 155–56. Hatch does not draw this conclusion in this portion of his book. However, his chapter, "The Clergy as a Separate Class," from which this citation comes, is one of his explanations for why church order changed from its original, democratic form to an hierarchical one.

Conclusion

THERE IS NO QUESTION that the early church had its own polity. Though the organization of the church is not spelled out in detail, its broad structure is very apparent. The view that the churches Paul planted had no regular structure or officers, but rather were run through the operations of the exercise of charismatic gifts, is an unnecessary dichotomy, and requires the judgment of numerous passages of the book of Acts as non-historical. Studies of the historical style of writing in the time of Christ, as well as epigraphical and archeological findings, have repeatedly contradicted the assessment that Acts lacks historicity. Instead, Acts is judged by many historians as well as exegetes of various confessions to be very reliable. In addition, the notion that Christian groups should be created without organization flatly contradicts the Jewish world view in which Paul was trained. Thus, the interpretation that Paul's churches or the church in Jerusalem did not have an established polity simply does not hold.

This study has been concerned with one aspect of church order: namely, group decision-making in churches. The New Testament, especially the book of Acts, both presents accounts and briefly mentions corporate decision-making in numerous passages. Group decisions were made in the areas of leadership and representative selection, church discipline, establishment of doctrine and practice, conflict resolution, and missions work (independent of interaction with the whole church). Occasions which required group action included the naming of a twelfth apostle to replace Judas, the need of new ministries, the need to affirm and encourage new outposts of the Christian mission, the sending out of missionaries, the determination of new directions for the Christian mission, the requirement of new leaders for churches, the representation of one church to another, the carrying of collections from one city to another, the conflict of cultural differences within the body of Christ, doctrinal conflict, and the correction of immorality or unethical behavior in the church body.

The idea that churches as a body should gather to make decisions was not alien in either Jewish or non-Jewish cultures. In the Graeco-Roman world, the idea of the *polis* government was widely practiced and well-ingrained in people's minds. Likewise, voluntary associations, which normally functioned in a democratic fashion, were a normal part of society throughout the Roman Empire. Finally, in the history of Israel and in Jewish life during the Graeco-Roman period, corporate decision-making, though not universal, was identifiable in most places where Jewish people lived. This cultural background would have made corporate decision-making both understandable and normal for the churches of the New Testament.

Most, though not all, information about corporate decision-making in the church is contained in historical sections in the New Testament. There are few direct orders in the Bible instructing a church when to engage in group decision-making. Most of the teaching, instead, is by way of example. The historical examples, however, illustrate obedience to the instruction in the New Testament regarding Christian relationships and interactions. For instance, the church understood Jesus as Messiah and Lord. All its decisions would need to be in submission to his lordship. Jesus instructed his disciples that they were all brothers, all on an equal plane. No disciple is to call another "father" or "rabbi." Thus, no Christian, even an apostle, could rightfully claim a superior authority over the body of Christ. Another major determining factor for the necessity of group decision-making and its implementation is the truth that all Christians are indwelt and gifted by the Holy Spirit. They are capable of spiritual discernment. The corporate decisions of churches in the New Testament were viewed as the outworking of God's Spirit in the church. The nature of the church itself was also a crucial factor in determining the need and method for corporate decisions. The church is the ἐκκλησία, an assembly, a body which together lives, decides, and acts. The church is also the body of Christ. All corporate decisions made by a church had to be both honoring to its head and sensitive to all members of the body.

Not all group decisions of churches, however, involved the whole church. On at least one occasion, the apostles decided alone to send a representative to a new work. On another occasion, a missionary team decided, independent of its sending churches, what its strategy would be. On still another occasion, the apostles and elders together answered another church's question about the authority of the Law of Moses in their own church. It is important to note that the New Testament presents no corporate decision-making for the determination of the messages to be preached or the Scripture to be taught. That would have militated against the repeated truth in the Old and New Testament of how God chose to speak through his messengers. Instead, the believers in a church responsible for teaching the Word of God were accountable to one-another for what had been preached or taught. Likewise, corporate decision-making in the New Testament never involved what holidays were to be celebrated and when, or what, foods were to be eaten (with the exception of avoiding eating blood and meat offered to idols). These unmentioned matters are left to the believer's conscience. Finally, the New Testament does not evidence over-arching or regional structures that dictated decisions to churches. Major decisions were made corporately in the individual churches or issues were settled between churches.

In the corporate decision-making of the churches in the New Testament, the actions of the twelve apostles, James, Paul, and Barnabas are instructive. They show a marked sensitivity to the other members of the church, or to other churches, in controversial matters. The apostles did not use their authority to force their views upon churches, but in many instances allowed entire churches to voice their views and together resolve the problems. At the same time, the apostles and other leaders demonstrated initiative in how they went about settling serious matters. When believers went so far as to compromise with sin, the apostles did not hesitate to correct them. In all their decisions, both the apostles and the people of the churches demonstrated an attentiveness to the Holy Spirit and a submission to Christ and his Word. Instead of following their own best interests, they were driven by the command of Christ to take the gospel into all the world. This directive aided the New Testament believers significantly in deciding issues.

The cessation of corporate decision-making by churches took place gradually over the centuries following the death of the apostles. Some theologians of the late Middle Ages as well as the leaders of the Protestant Reformation (including the Radical Reformation) were convinced that the course for the church was a break with the centuries-old hierarchy of the Roman church. As the alternative, they pointed to the simplicity of the church structure of the New Testament. It is significant that as they made this evaluation, they recommended a type of church life which included corporate decision-making.

CONCLUSIONS FOR THE CHURCH TODAY

The Bible supplies more than sufficient instruction to churches on how to structure and conduct church order.[1] Churches today would be wise to follow the pattern of corporate decision-making described in the New Testament. Many leaders, including deacons and elders, are better chosen by the whole body than by the designation of one person or a select group in the church. When divisive issues arise in the church body, it is crucial that church leaders listen with sensitivity and seek a solution that will both honor Christ and respect all in the assembly. Christians today, as those in the New Testament, need to be viewed as Spirit-indwelt believers who can together arrive at a good solution. The church will need guidance from its leaders, including instruction in what steps are to be taken, how, and why. In particular, when a doctrinal problem arises, the leaders of a church must clearly instruct their people on right doctrine as the decision-making process proceeds.

The church leaders of the New Testament led their churches to handle controversial issues as they arose. They did not introduce controversial issues to the church for corporate decision-making (unless the choice of a replacement of Judas was controversial, of which there is no indication in Scripture). Church leaders today would do much better by letting inevitable controversies come to the church, rather than making the introductions themselves.

The size of a church apparently was not an issue in determining whether a church could make a corporate decision. As was noted, the Jerusalem church had five thousand men in its membership as it handled, corporately, the introduction of a new ministry and the election of new leaders. If a church today is too large to allow corporate decision-making, it should likely re-think either its size or its inner structures.

Like the churches in the New Testament, churches today will be effective and sound in their corporate decision-making if they are sensitive to the leading of the Holy Spirit and submissive to the teachings of the Bible. As then, so now there will be strong competitive concerns which would tempt a church or groups within it to neglect or re-interpret the Bible for their own interests. A healthy decision-making process, which results in a long-term profitable decision, will sacrifice special interest for the sake

---

1 Dever, *Nine Marks,* 221, says, "There is no ideal constitution for a church. But that doesn't mean that the Bible has nothing to say about how we are to organize ourselves."

of scriptural instruction. In addition, the churches of the New Testament were driven by the command of Christ to make disciples of all nations and animated by the promise of his presence. Today's churches which are highly motivated by the desire to fulfill the Great Commission will, by that desire, steer their way clear through many difficult issues to arrive at harmonious and fruitful corporate decisions.

Necessary Decision to Be Made
(Under the authority of Christ, the Word, and the Spirit)

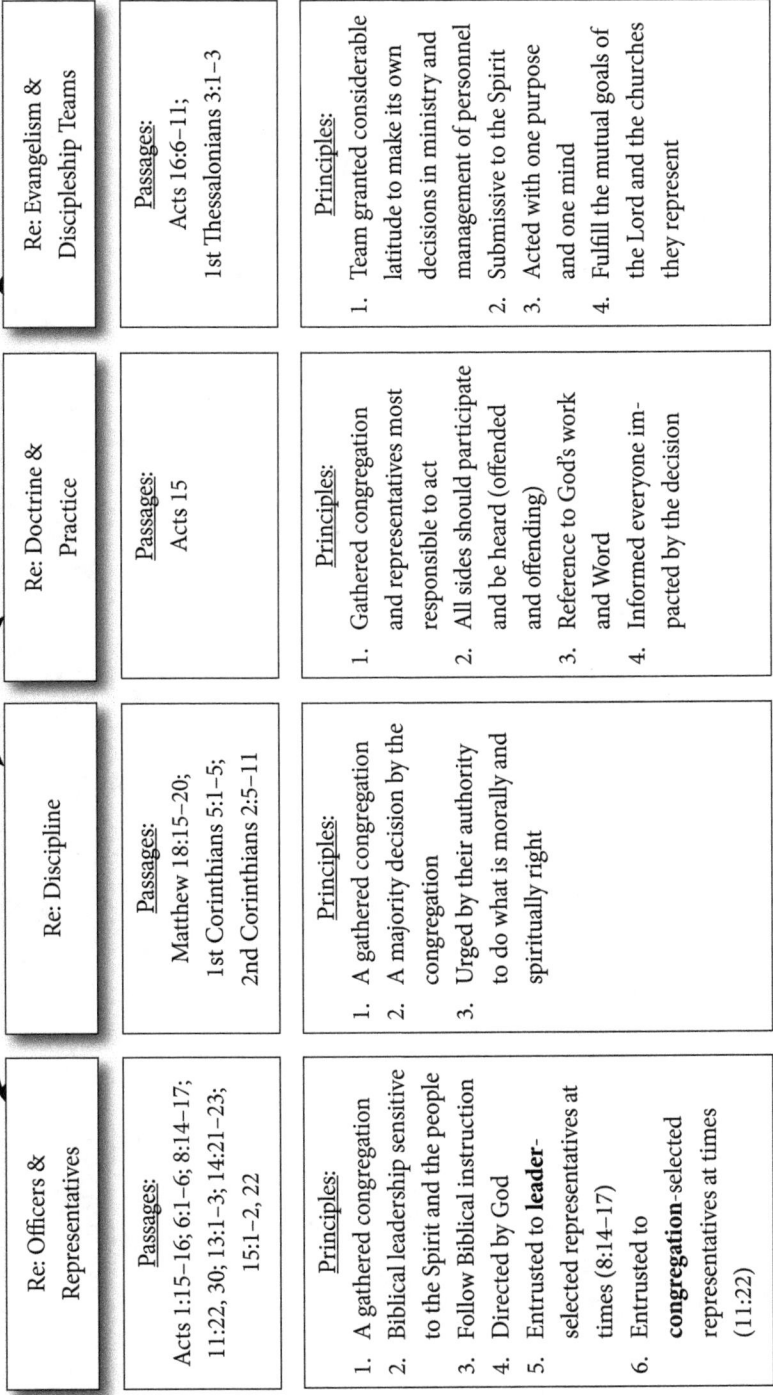

Re: Officers & Representatives

Passages:
Acts 1:15–16; 6:1–6; 8:14–17; 11:22, 30; 13:1–3; 14:21–23; 15:1–2, 22

Principles:
1. A gathered congregation
2. Biblical leadership sensitive to the Spirit and the people
3. Follow Biblical instruction
4. Directed by God
5. Entrusted to **leader**-selected representatives at times (8:14–17)
6. Entrusted to **congregation**-selected representatives at times (11:22)

Re: Discipline

Passages:
Matthew 18:15–20; 1st Corinthians 5:1–5; 2nd Corinthians 2:5–11

Principles:
1. A gathered congregation
2. A majority decision by the congregation
3. Urged by their authority to do what is morally and spiritually right

Re: Doctrine & Practice

Passages:
Acts 15

Principles:
1. Gathered congregation and representatives most responsible to act
2. All sides should participate and be heard (offended and offending)
3. Reference to God's work and Word
4. Informed everyone impacted by the decision

Re: Evangelism & Discipleship Teams

Passages:
Acts 16:6–11; 1st Thessalonians 3:1–3

Principles:
1. Team granted considerable latitude to make its own decisions in ministry and management of personnel
2. Submissive to the Spirit
3. Acted with one purpose and one mind
4. Fulfill the mutual goals of the Lord and the churches they represent

Bibliography

Adna, Jostein. "James' Position at the Summit Meeting of the Apostles and the Elders in Jerusalem." In *The Mission of the Early Church to Jews and Gentiles*, edited by Jostein Adna, 123–61. Tübingen: Mohr/Siebeck, 2000.

Akin, Daniel L. "The Single-Elder-Led Church." In *Perspectives on Church Government: Five Views of Church Polity*, edited by Chad Owen Brand and R. Stanton Norman, 25–86. Nashville: Broadman & Holman, 2004.

Alexander, Loveday C. A. *Acts in Its Ancient Literary Context*. JSOTSupp 289. Sheffield: University of Sheffield Press, 2004.

———. "Chronology of Paul." In *DPL*, 115–23.

———. "Fact, Fiction and the Genre of Acts." *NTS* 44 (1998) 380–99.

Alford, Henry. *The Greek New Testament*. 4 vols. 1884–94. Reprint, Chicago: Moody, 1958.

Alon, Gedaliah. *The Jews in Their Land in the Talmudic Age*. Translated by Gershon Levi. Jerusalem: Magnes, 1980.

Ambaum, Jan. "Die Identität des Priesters." *Comm* 10 (1981) 421–34.

Andrewartha, John M. "The New Testament Teaching of Church Elders." ThD diss., Southwestern Baptist Theological Seminary, 1989.

Ante-Nicene Fathers, The. Edited by Alexander Roberts and James Donaldson. 1885–87. 10 vols. Reprint, Peabody, MA: Hendrickson, 1994.

Applebaum, Shim'on. "The Organization of the Jewish Communities of the Diaspora." In *The Jewish People in the First Century*, edited by Samuel Safrai and Menahem Stern, 2:701–27. Philadelphia: Fortress, 1976.

Apuleius. *Metamorphoses*. Translated by J. Arthur Hanson. Cambridge, MA: Harvard University Press, 1989.

Arichea, Daniel C., Jr. "Who Was Phoebe? Translating *Diakonos* in Romans 16:1." *The Bible Translator* 39 (1988) 401–15.

Ascough, Richard S. "Greco-Roman Philosophic, Religious, and Voluntary Associations." In *Com-munity Formation in the Early Church and in the Church Today*, edited by Richard N. Longenecker, 3–19. Peabody, MA: Hendrickson, 2002.

———. "A Question of Death: Paul's Community-Building Language in 1 Thessalonians 4:13–18." *JBL* 123 (2004) 509–30.

———. "Roger W. Gehring. *House Church and Mission: The Importance of Household Structures in Early Christianity*, Review Article." *CBQ* 67 (2005) 528–30.

———. "The Thessalonian Christian Community as a Professional Voluntary Association." *JBL* 119 (2000) 311–28.

———. *What Are They Saying about the Formation of Pauline Churches?* New York: Paulist, 1998.

Ashcraft, Morris. "Paul Defends His Apostleship, Galatians 1 and 2." *RevExp* 49 (1972) 459–69.

Avis, Paul. *The Anglican Understanding of the Church.* London: SPCK, 2000.

Babcock, William S. "*In Memory of Her* from a Patristic Perspective: A Review Article." *SecCent* 4/3 (1984) 177–84.

Baker, Robert A. "An Introduction to the Development of the Study of Ecclesiology." ThD diss., Southwestern Baptist Theological Seminary, 1944.

Balch, David L., editor. *Social History of the Matthean Community.* Minneapolis: Fortress, 1991.

Banks, Robert. *Paul's Idea of Community.* 2nd ed. Peabody, MA: Hendrickson, 1994.

Baron, Salo Wittmayer. *A Social and Religious History of the Jews.* Vol. 2, *Ancient Times to the Beginning of the Christian Era.* New York: Columbia University Press, 1957.

Barr, James. *The Semantics of Biblical Language.* London: SCM, 1961.

Barrett, C. K. *Church, Ministry, and Sacraments in the New Testament.* Grand Rapids: Eerdmans, 1985.

——. *A Commentary on the First Epistle to the Corinthians.* New York: Harper & Row, 1968. Reprint, Peabody, MA: Henrickson, 1987.

——. *A Critical and Exegetical Commentary on the Acts of the Apostles.* 2 vols. International Critical Commentary. Edinburgh: T. & T. Clark, 1994.

——. "The Interpretation of the OT in the New." In *The Cambridge History of the Bible,* edited by Peter Ackroyd and C. F. Evans, 1:377–411. Cambridge: Cambridge University Press, 1970.

——. *Paul: An Introduction to His Thought.* Louisville: Westminster John Knox, 1994.

——. *The Second Epistle to the Corinthians.* Peabody, MA: Hendrickson, 1987.

Bartchy, Scott. "Divine Power, Community Formation, and Leadership in Acts." In *Community Formation in the Early Church and in the Church Today,* edited by Richard N. Longenecker, 89–104. Peabody, MA: Hendrickson, 2002.

Bartlett, David L. *Ministry in the New Testament.* Minneapolis: Fortress, 1993.

Bauckham, Richard. "James and the Jerusalem Church." In *The Book of Acts in Its First-Century Setting,* edited by Bruce W. Winter, 4:415–80. Grand Rapids: Eerdmans, 1995.

Bauder, Kevin. "The New Testament and Service Organizations." In the Nick of Time, Nov. 4, 2005. Online: http://seminary.wcts1030.com/publications/20051104.pdf.

Bauer, Walter. *A Greek-English Lexicon of the New Testament and Other Early Christian Literature.* 3rd ed. Edited by Frederick William Danker. Chicago: University of Chicago Press, 2001.

——. *Wörterbuch zum Neuen Testament.* 6th ed. Edited by Kurt and Barbara Aland. Berlin: de Gruyter, 1988.

Baur, Ferdinand Christian. Über den Ursprung des *Episcopats in der christlichen Kirche.* Tübingen: Fues, 1838.

Beardslee, W. A. "The Casting of Lots at Qumran and in the Book of Acts." *NovT* 4 (1960) 245–52.

Beckwith, Roger. *Elders in Every City: The Origin and Role of the Ordained Ministry.* Waynesboro, GA: Paternoster, 2003.

Beitzel, Barry. *The Moody Atlas of Bible Lands.* Chicago: Moody, 1985.

Benedict, James. "The Corinthian Problem of 1 Corinthians 5:1–8." *Brethren Life and Thought* 32 (1987) 70–73.

Ben-Sasson, Haim Hillel. "Community." In *EncJud.* 5:808–10.

Berger, Klaus. "Volksversammlung und Gemeinde Gottes." *ZTK* 73 (1976) 167–206.

Berkhof, Louis. *Systematic Theology*. Grand Rapids: Eerdmans, 1941.

Bernard, J. H. *The Second Epistle to the Corinthians*. 5 vols. Expositor's Greek Testament. 1897–1910. Reprint, Grand Rapids: Eerdmans, 1979.

Bernhardt, Rainer. *Polis und römische Herrschaft in der späten Republik (149–31 v.Chr.)*. Berlin: de Gruyter, 1985.

Best, E. "Bishops and Deacons: Philippians 1:1." In *Studia Evangelica*, edited by F. L. Cross, 4:371–76. Berlin: Akademie, 1968.

———. *Paul and His Converts*. Edinburgh: T. & T. Clark, 1988.

Bingham, D. Jeffrey. "Evangelicals, Irenaeus, and the Bible." In *The Free Church and the Early Church: Bridging the Historical and Theological Divide*, edited by D. H. Williams, 27–46. Grand Rapids: Eerdmans, 2002.

Blanton, Richard E. "Beyond Centralization: Steps toward a Theory of Egalitarian Behavior in Archaic States." In *Archaic Studies*, edited by Gary M. Feinman and Joyce Marcus, 135–72. Santa Fe: School of American Research, 1998.

Blue, Bradley. "Acts and the House Church." In *The Book of Acts in Its First Century Setting*, edited by David W. J. Gill and Conrad Gempf, 2:119–222. Grand Rapids: Eerdmans, 1994.

Bobertz, Charles A. "The Development of Episcopal Order." In *Eusebius, Christianity, and Judaism*, edited by Harold W. Attridge and Gohei Hata, 183–211. Leiden: Brill, 1992.

Bock, Darrell L. *Acts: Baker Exegetical Commentary on the New Testament*. Grand Rapids: Baker, 2007.

Botermann, Helga. "Paulus und das Urchristentum in der antiken Welt." *TRu* 56 (1991) 296–305.

Bowe, Barbara Ellen. *A Church in Crisis: Ecclesiology and Paraenesis in Clement of Rome*. Harvard Dissertations in Religion 23. Minneapolis: Fortress, 1988.

Bowers, W. P. "Paul's Route through Mysia: A Note on Acts XVI.8." *JTS* 30 (1979) 507–11.

Brand, Chad Owen, and R. Stanton Norman. *Perspectives on Church Government: Five Views of Church Polity*. Nashville: Broadman & Holman, 2004.

Brandis, G. C. "ἐκκλησία." In *Paulys Real-Encyclopädie der classischen Altertumswissenschaft*, edited by August Pauly, 5:2163–99. Stuttgart: Metzler, 1905.

Branick, Vincent P. *The House Church in the Writings of Paul*. Wilmington, DE: Glazier, 1989.

Brown, David. *The Acts of the Apostles*. Jamieson-Fausset-Brown Commentary 3/2. 1871. Reprint, Grand Rapids: Eerdmans, 1973.

Brown, Francis, S. R. Driver, and Charles A. Briggs, editors. *A Hebrew and English Lexicon of the Old Testament*. Oxford: Clarendon, 1907.

Brown, Raymond E. *An Introduction to the New Testament*. Anchor Bible Reference Library. New York: Doubleday, 1997.

Bruce, A. B. *The Training of the Twelve*. Grand Rapids: Kregel, 1971.

Bruce, Frederick Fyvie. *The Acts of the Apostles: Greek Text with Introduction and Commentary*. Grand Rapids: Eerdmans, 1990.

———. "The Acts of the Apostles: Historical Record or Theological Reconstruction?" In *Aufstieg und Niedergang der römischen Welt: Geschichte und Kultur Roms im Spiegel der neueren Forschung*, edited by H. Temporini and W. Haase, 25/3.2:2569–2603. Berlin: de Gruyter, 1972.

———. *The Book of Acts*. New International Commentary on the New Testament. Grand Rapids: Eerdmans, 1977.

———. *1 and 2 Corinthians*. New Century Bible. Grand Rapids: Eerdmans, 1996.

Bultmann, Rudolf. *Theologie des Neuen Testaments*. 2nd ed. Tübingen: Mohr, 1954.

Burer, Michael H., and Daniel B. Wallace. "Was Junia Really an Apostle? A Re-examination of Rom 16.7." *NTS* 47 (2001)76–91.

Burtchaell, James Tunstead. *From Synagogue to Church: Public Services and Offices in the Earliest Christian Communities*. Cambridge: Cambridge University Press, 1994.

Cadbury, H. J. "The Hellenists." In *The Beginnings of Christianity*, edited by. F. J. Foakes Jackson and J. Kirsopp Lake, 1:59–74. 1920–1922. Reprint, Grand Rapids: Baker, 1979.

———. *The Making of Luke-Acts*. 1958. Reprint of 2nd ed., Peabody, MA: Hendrickson, 1999.

Callam, Daniel. "Bishops and Presbyters in the Apostolic Fathers." *Studia Patristica* 31 (1997) 107–11.

Callan, Terrance. "The Background of the Apostolic Decree." *CBQ* 55 (1993) 284–97.

Calvin, John. *Commentary on the Acts of the Apostles*. Translated by Henry Beveridge. 2 vols. Grand Rapids: Baker, 1989.

———. *Commentary on the Epistles of Paul the Apostle to the Corinthians*. Translated by John Pringle. 2 vols. 1898–99. Reprint, Grand Rapids: Baker, 1989.

———. *Institutes of the Christian Religion*. Edited by John T. McNeill. Translated by Ford Lewis Battles. 2 vols. Philadelphia: Westminster, 1967.

Campbell, J. Y. "The Origin and Meaning of the Christian Use of the Word EKKLHSIA." *JTS* 49 (1948) 130–42.

Campbell, R. Alastair. "The Elders of the Jerusalem Church." *JTS* 44 (1993) 511–39.

———. *The Elders: Seniority within Earliest Christianity*. Edinburgh: T. & T. Clark, 1994.

Campenhausen, Hans von. *Ecclesiastical Authority and Spiritual Power in the Church of the First Three Centuries*. Translated by J. A. Baker. London: Black, 1969. Reprint, Peabody, MA: Hendrickson, 1997.

———. *Kirchliches Amt und geistliche Vollmacht*. Tübingen: Mohr, 1969.

Carlson, Leland H., editor. *The Writings of Henry Barrow*. Vol. 3 of *Elizabethan Nonconformist Texts*. London: Allen & Unwin, 1962.

Carson, Donald A. "Matthew." In *The Expositor's Bible Commentary*, edited by Frank E. Gaebelein, 8:3–602. Grand Rapids: Zondervan, 1984.

———, editor. *The Church in the Bible and in the World*. Grand Rapids: Baker, 1987.

Carson, Donald A., Douglas J. Moo, and Leon Morris. *An Introduction to the New Testament*. Grand Rapids: Zondervan, 1992.

Catechism of the Catholic Church. New York: Doubleday, 1995.

Chadwick, Henry. *The Early Church*. Rev. ed. Penguin History of the Church. London: Penguin, 1993.

Chan, Simon. *Spiritual Theology: A Systematic Study of the Christian Life*. Downers Grove, IL: InterVarsity, 1998.

Chaney, Charles. "The Pastoral Epistles on Care Giving." In *Caring for the Harvest Force*, edited by Tom A. Steffen and F. Douglas Pennoyer, 29–42. Pasadena, CA: William Carey Library, 2001.

Chisholm, Robert B. "δω" In *NIDOTTE*, 3:335–40.

Chrysostom, John. "On the Priesthood." In *Nicene and Post Nicene Fathers*, vol. 9, 33–83. New York: Christian Literature, 1887. Reprint, Peabody, MA: Hendrickson, 1994.

Cicero. *De Officiis*. Translated by Walter Miller. Cambridge, MA: Harvard University Press, 1961.

———. *De Republica*. Translated by Clinton Walker Keyes. Cambridge, MA: Harvard University Press, 1928.

Clarke, Andrew D. *Secular and Christian Leadership at Corinth*. Leiden: Brill, 1993.

———. *Serve the Community of the Church: Christians as Leaders and Ministers*. First-Century Christians in the Graeco-Roman World. Grand Rapids: Eerdmans, 2000.

Clearwaters, Richard C. *The Local Church of the New Testament*. Minneapolis: Central C. B. Press, 1954.

Clowney, Edmund P. *The Church*. Downer's Grove, IL: InterVarsity, 1995.

Cohen, Shaye J. D. *From the Maccabees to the Mishnah*. Library of Early Christianity. Philadelphia: Westminster, 1987.

Cohnen, L. "Bishop, Presbyter, Elder." In *NIDNTT*, 1:188–201.

Collins, John N. *Diakonia: Re-interpreting the Ancient Sources*. Oxford: Oxford University Press, 1990.

Conzelmann, Hans. *Die Apostelgeschichte*. Handbuch zum Neuen Testament 7. Tübingen: Mohr, 1961.

Couch, Mal, et al. *A Biblical Theology of the Church*. Grand Rapids: Kregel, 1999.

Coulter, Roger Clayton. "The Distinction between the Spiritual Gift of Pastor-Teacher and the Office of Elder in the New Testament." ThM thesis, Dallas Theological Seminary, 1979.

Cowen, Gerald P. *Who Rules the Church?: Examining Congregational Leadership and Church Government*. Nashville: Broadman & Holman, 2003.

Cox, Geoffrey S. R. "The Emerging Organization of the Church in the New Testament, and the Limitations Imposed Thereon." *Evangelical Quarterly* 38 (1966) 22–39.

Cranfield, C. E. B. "Diakonia in the New Testament." In *The Bible and Christian Life*, edited by C. E. B. Cranfield, 69–93. Edinburgh: T. & T. Clark, 1985.

Cruse, Christian Frederick. *The Ecclesiastical History of Eusebius Pamphilius*. Grand Rapids: Baker, 1955.

Cullmann, Oscar. *Christ and Time*. Translated by F. V. Filson. London: SCM, 1962.

Culver, R. D. "Apostles and Apostolate in the New Testament." *BSac* 134 (1977)131–43.

Dassman, Ernst. *Ämter und Dienste in der frühchristlichen Gemeinden*. Bonn: Borengässer, 1994.

Daube, David. *The New Testament and Rabbinic Judaism*. Jordan Lectures in Comparative Religion 2. London: School of Oriental and African Studies, 1956. Reprint, Peabody, MA: Hendrickson, n.d.

Davies, J. G. "Deacons, Deaconesses, and the Minor Orders in the Patristic Period." *JEH* 14 (1963) 1–16.

Deissmann, Adolf. *Bible Studies*. Translated by Alexander Grieve. Edinburgh: T. & T. Clark, 1901.

Denzinger, Heinrich J. D. *The Sources of Catholic Dogma*. Translated by Roy J. Deferrari. St. Louis: Herder, 1957.

Dever, Mark. *Nine Marks of a Healthy Church*. Rev. ed. Wheaton, IL: Crossway, 2004.

Dexter, Henry. *Congregationalism*. Boston: Congregational, 1865.

Dibelius, Martin. "Stilkritisches zur Apostelgeschichte." In *Eucharistērion: Studien zur Religion und Literatur des Alten und Neuen Testaments: Hermann Gunkel zum 60*, 2:27–49. Göttingen: Vandenhoeck & Ruprecht, 1923.

———. *Studies in the Acts of the Apostles*. Edited by Heinrich Greeven. London: SCM, 1951.

Dickinson, Royce, Jr. "The Theology of the Jerusalem Conference—Acts 15:1–35." *ResQ* 32 (1990) 65–86.

Diprose, Ronald E. *Israel and the Church: The Origin and Effects of Replacement Theology.* Waynesboro, GA: Authentic Media, 2004.

Dixon, Suzanne. *The Roman Family.* Baltimore: Johns Hopkins University Press, 1992.

Dockery, David S. "Acts 6—12: The Christian Mission Beyond Jerusalem." In *RevExp* 87 (1990) 423–37.

Doellinger, Ignaz. *Beitraege zur Sektengeschichte des Mittelalters.* 2 vols. 1890. Reprint, Darmstadt: Wissenschaftliche Buchgesellschaft, 1968.

Drews, Robert. *Basileus: The Evidence for Kingship in Geometric Greece.* New Haven: Yale University Press, 1983.

Duke, William Cecil, Jr. "Apostolic Authority in the Primitive Church." Ph.D. diss., Southern Baptist Theological Seminary, 1982.

Dulles, Avery. *Models of the Church.* Rev. ed. New York: Doubleday, 2002.

Dunn, James D. G. *Baptism in the Holy Spirit: A Re-Examination of the New Testament Teaching on the Gift of the Spirit in Relation to Pentecostalism Today.* Philadelphia: Westminster Press, 1970.

———. *The Epistles to the Colossians and to Philemon.* New International Greek Testament Commentary. Grand Rapids: Eerdmans, 1996.

———. *The Partings of the Ways.* London: SCM, 1991.

———. *Unity and Diversity in the New Testament.* London: SCM, 1984.

Dupont, J. *The Sources of Acts: The Present Position.* London: Darton & Longman, 1964.

Eastwood, Martin. "Church, God, and Martyrdom, in Ignatius of Antioch and Justin Martyr." EarlyChurch.org.uk. Online: http://www.earlychurch.org.uk/article_ignatius_eastwood.html.

Ehrman, Bart D. *Lost Christianities.* Oxford: Oxford University Press, 2003.

Ellis, E. Earl. "Paul and His Co-workers." *NTS* 17 (1971) 437–52.

———. *Pauline Theology: Ministry and Society.* Eugene, OR: Wipf & Stock, 1997.

———. "Pastoral Letters." In *DPL* 658–66.

Engle, Paul E., and Steven B. Cowan, editors. *Who Runs The Church?: Four Views on Church Government.* Grand Rapids: Zondervan, 2004.

Epictetus. *Discourses.* Vols. 3 and 4. Translated by W. A. Oldfather. Cambridge, MA: Harvard University Press, 1952.

———. *The Enchiridion.* Translated by W. A. Oldfather. Cambridge, MA: Harvard University Press, 1952.

Erickson, Millard. *Christian Theology.* Grand Rapids: Baker, 1985.

Esler, Philip F. *Community and Gospel in Luke-Acts: The Social and Political Motivations of Lucan Theology.* Society for New Testament Studies Monograph Series 57. Cambridge: Cambridge University Press, 1987.

———. *The First Christians in Their Social Worlds.* London: Routledge, 1994.

Estep, William R. *The Anabaptist Story.* Grand Rapids: Eerdmans, 1975.

Farrar, Frederic W. *The Life and Work of St. Paul.* 2 vols. New York: E. P. Dutton, 1902. Reprint, Minneapolis: Klock & Klock, 1981.

Fee, Gordon. *1 and 2 Timothy, Titus.* New International Biblical Commentary. Peabody, MA: Hendrickson, 1988.

———. *The First Epistle to the Corinthians.* New International Commentary on the New Testament. Grand Rapids: Eerdmans, 1987.

Ferguson, Everett. *Backgrounds of Early Christianity*. 2nd ed. Grand Rapids: Eerdmans, 1993.

————. *The Church of Christ: A Biblical Ecclesiology for Today*. Grand Rapids: Eerdmans, 1996.

————. "The 'Congregationalism' of the Early Church." In *The Free Church and the Early Church: Bridging the Historical and Theological Divide*, edited by D. H. Williams, 129–40. Grand Rapids: Eerdmans, 2002.

————. "Ordination in the Ancient Church." *ResQ* 5 (1961) 67–82.

Filson, Floyd. "The Significance of the Early House Churches." *JBL* 58 (1939) 105–12.

Findlay, G. G. *St. Paul's First Epistle to the Corinthians*. Expositors Greek Testament. 1897–1910. Reprint, Grand Rapids: Eerdmans, 1979.

Fitzmyer, Joseph A. *The Acts of the Apostles*. Anchor Bible 31. New York: Doubleday, 1998.

Fleming, Daniel E. *Democracy's Ancient Ancestors: Mari and Early Collective Governance*. Cambridge: Cambridge University Press, 2004.

Florovsky, Georges. "The Authority of the Ancient Councils and the Tradition of the Fathers: An Introduction." In *Glaube, Geist, Geschichte: Festschrift für Ernst Benz*, edited by G. Müller and W. Zeller, 177–88. Leiden: Brill, 1967.

Frame, John M. "Dealing with Differences in Government." In *Evangelical Reunion: Denominations and the Body of Christ*, 108–13. Grand Rapids: Baker, 1991. Republished in *IIIM Magazine Online* 3/11, March 12–18, 2001. Online: http://thirdmill.org/newfiles/joh_frame/PT.Frame.EVR.11.html.

————. *Evangelical Reunion*. Grand Rapids: Baker, 1991.

Franklin, Lloyd David. Review of *From Synagogue to Church: Public Services and Offices in the Earliest Christian Communities* by James Tunstead Burtchaell. *JECS* 3 (1995) 499–500.

Fraser, Richard. "Office of Deacon." In *Presb* 11/1 (1985) 13–19.

Freyne, Sean. *Galilee from Alexander the Great to Hadrian: 323 B.C.E. to 135 C.E.* Wilmington, DE: Glazier, 1980.

Friend, W. C. H. *The Rise of Christianity*. Philadelphia: Fortress, 1984.

Fuglseth, Kare Sigvald. *Johannine Sectarianism in Perspective: A Sociological, Historical, and Comparative Analysis of the Temple and Social Relationships in the Gospel of John, Philo, and Qumran*. Novum Testamentum Supplements 119. Leiden: Brill, 2005.

Fung, Ronald Y. K. "Ministry in the New Testament. " In *The Church in the Bible and the World*, edited by D. A. Carson, 154–212. Grand Rapids: Baker, 1987.

————. "Ministry, Community and Spiritual Gifts." *Evangelical Quarterly* 56 (1984) 3–20.

Funk, F. X. "Die Bischofswahl in christlichen Altertum und im Anfang des Mittelalters." In *Kirchengeschichliche Abhandlungen und Untersuchungen*, edited by F. X. Funk, 23–39. Paderborn: Schöningh, 1897.

Furnish, Victor Paul. *2 Corinthians*. Anchor Bible 32A. New York: Doubleday, 1998.

Gaechter, P. *Petrus und seine Zeit: Neutestamentliche Studien*. Innsbruck: Tyrolia, 1958.

Garner, G. G. "Travel in Biblical Times." In *NBD*, 1212–14

Garrett, James Leo, Jr. "The Congregation-Led Church." In *Perspectives on Church Government*, edited by Chad Owen Brand and R. Stanton Norman, 157–208. Nashville: Broadman & Holman, 2004.

————. "The Pre-Cyprianic Doctrine of the Priesthood of All Christians." In *Church, Ministry, and Organization in the Early Church Era*, edited by Everett Ferguson. Studies in the Early Church, 13:253–69. New York: Garland, 1993.

Gasque, W. Ward. *A History of the Interpretation of the Acts of the Apostles.* Peabody, MA: Hendrickson, 1989.

Getz, Gene A. *Elders and Leaders.* Chicago: Moody, 2003.

Getz, Gene A., and Larry Richards. "A Biblical Style of Leadership: Gene Getz Debates Larry Richards." *Leadership* (1981) 68–78.

Gibbon, Edward. *The Decline and Fall of the Roman Empire.* Vol. 1. New York: Random House, n.d.

Giles, Kevin. "Is Luke an Exponent of Early Protestantism? (part 2)." *EvQ* 55 (1983) 3–20.

———. *What on Earth Is the Church?* London: SPCK, 1995.

Gill, David W. J. "Acts and the Urban Elites." In *The Book of Acts in Its First-Century Setting,* edited by David W. J. Gill and Conrad Gempf, 2:105–17. Grand Rapids: Eerdmans, 1994.

Gizewski, Christian. "Duoviri, Duumviri." In *Brill's New Pauly: Encyclopaedia of the Ancient World,* edited by Hubert Cancik and Helmuth Schneider, 4:739. Leiden: Brill, 2004.

Glasscock, Ed. "The Biblical Concept of Elder." *BSac* 144 (1987) 244–57.

———. *Moody Gospel Commentary: Matthew.* Chicago: Moody, 1997.

Global Anabaptist Mennonite Encyclopedia Online. Online: http://www.gameo.org/encyclopedia.

Goetz, Karl Gerold. *Petrus als Grunder und Oberhaupt der Kirche und Schauer von Geschichten nach den altchristlichen Berichten und Legenden.* Vol. 13 of *Untersuchungen zum Neuen Testament* Leipzig: Hinrichs, 1927.

Gooding, David. *True to the Faith: A Fresh Approach to the Acts of the Apostles.* London: Hodder & Stoughton, 1990.

Gore, Charles. *The Church and the Ministry.* Rev. ed. Edited by C.H. Turner. London: Longmans, Green, 1886. Reprint, London: SPCK, 1936.

Granfield, Patrick. "Episcopal Elections in Cyprian: Clerical and Lay Participation." In *Church, Ministry, and Organization in the Early Church Era,* edited by Everett Ferguson. Studies in the Early Church, 13:95–106. New York: Garland, 1993.

Grant, Robert M. *Early Christianity and Society.* London: Collins, 1978.

Green, Joel B., and Michael C. McKeever. *Luke-Acts and New Testament Historiography.* Grand Rapids: Baker, 1994.

Greenwood, John. *A Handbook of the Catholic Faith.* New York: Doubleday, 1956.

Grenz, Stanley J. *Revisioning Evangelical Theology.* Downer's Grove, IL: InterVarsity, 1993.

Grundmann, Walter. "δόκιμος, κ.τ.λ.." In *TDNT,* 2:255.

Gundry, Robert H. *Matthew: A Commentary on His Literary and Theological Art.* Grand Rapids: Eerdmans, 1982.

Gutbrod, Walter. "Ἰουδαῖος, κ.τ.λ. in the New Testament." In *TDNT,* 3:375–391.

Guthrie, Donald. *New Testament Introduction.* 4th ed. Downers Grove, IL: InterVarsity, 1990.

Guy, Laurie. *Introducing Early Christianity.* Downer's Grove, IL: InterVarsity, 2004.

Haddan, Arthur West. "Bishop." In *A Dictionary of Christian Antiquities,* edited by William Smith and Samuel Cheetham, 1: 209–49. London: Murray, 1875.

Haenchen, Ernst. *Die Apostelgeschichte.* 14th ed. Das Neue Testament Deutsch 5. Göttingen: Vandenhoecht & Ruprecht, 1965.

Hagner, Donald A. *Matthew 14—28.* Word Bible Commentary 33b. Dallas: Word, 1995.

Hammett, John S. *Biblical Foundations for Baptist Churches: A Contemporary Ecclesiology.* Grand Rapids: Kregel, 2005.

Hanson, Morgens Herman. "Democracy, Athenian." In *OCD*, 451–53.

Hanson, Richard C. *Studies in Christian Antiquity.* Edinburgh: T. & T. Clark, 1985.

Harland, Philip A. *Associations, Synagogues, and Congregations.* Minneapolis: Fortress, 2003.

Harnack, Adolf von. *Kirchenverfassung und Kirchenrecht.* Leipzig: Hinrichs, 1910.

———. *Lukas der Arzt: Der Verfasser des dritten Evangeliums und der Apostelgeschichte.* Leipzig: Heinrichs,1906.

———. *Die Mission und Ausbreitung des Christentums.* 2. vols. Leipzig: Hinrichs, 1924.

———. *Neue Untersuchung zur Apostgelgeschichte und zur Abfassungszeit der Synoptischen Evangelien.* Beiträge zur Einleitung in das Neue Testament 4. Leipzig: Hinrichs,1911.

Harris, Horton. *The Tübingen School.* Grand Rapids: Baker, 1990.

Harris, Murray J. *2 Corinthians.* Expositors Bible Commentary. Grand Rapids: Zondervan, 1976.

Hatch, Edwin. "Ordination." In *A Dictionary of Christian Antiquities* 2:1501–2. London: Murray, 1875.

———. *The Organization of the Early Christian Churches.* London: Rivingtons, 1881.

Hatch, Edwin, and Henry A. Redpath. *A Concordance to the Septuagint.* 2nd ed. Oxford: Clarendon, 1897–1906. Reprint, Grand Rapids: Baker, 1997.

Hatch, Nathan O. *The Democratization of American Christianity.* New Haven: Yale University Press, 1989.

Hayes, John H., and Sara R. Mandell. *The Jewish People in Classical Antiquity.* Louisville: Westminster John Knox, 1998.

Heimert, Alan. *Religion and the American Mind.* Cambridge, MA: Harvard University Press, 1966.

Hemer, C. J. *The Book of Acts in the Setting of Hellenistic History.* Edited by Conrad H. Gempf. Wissenschaftliche Untersuchungen zum Neuen Testament 49. Tübingen: Mohr, 1989.

———. "Luke the Historian." *Bulletin of the John Rylands University Library* 60 (1977) 28–51.

Hengel, Martin. *Acts and the History of Earliest Christianity.* Translated by John Bowden. London: SCM, 1979.

———. *Judaism and Hellenism: Studies in Their Encounter in Palestine during the Early Hellenistic Period.* Translated by John Bowden. Philadelphia: Fortress, 1974.

———. *Judentum und Hellenismus.* 3rd ed. Wissenschaftliche Untersuchung zum Neuen Testament 10. Tübingen: Mohr, 1988.

Heppe, Heinrich. *Reformed Dogmatics.* Translated by G. T. Thomson. London: Wakeman Trust, 1950.

Hicks, E. L. "On Some Political Terms Employed in the New Testament." *The Classical Review* 1 (1887) 4–8.

Hillstrom, Leonard. "The New Testament Teaching on the Office, Qualifications, Appointment, and Work of the Elders." ThD diss., Grace Theological Seminary, 1980.

Hindmarsh, Bruce. "Is Evangelical Ecclesiology an Oxymoron?" In *Evangelical Ecclesiology: Reality or Illusion?* edited by John G. Stackhouse, Jr., 15–37. Grand Rapids: Baker, 2003.

Hinson, E. Glenn. "Review Article: From Synagogue to Church: Public Services and Offices in the Earliest Christian Communities." *CH* 64 (1995) 335–36.

Hippolytus. *The Apostolic Tradition.* Translated by Burton Scott Easton. Cambridge: Cambridge University Press, 1934.

Bibliography

Holmberg, Bengt. *Paul and Power*. Philadelphia: Fortress, 1978. Reprint, Eugene, OR: Wipf & Stock, 2004.

Holtzmann, Heinrich. *Lehrbuch der neutestamentlichen Theologie*. Tübingen: J. C. B. Mohr, 1897.

Hornblower, Simon. *A Commentary on Thucydides*. 3 vols. Oxford: Clarendon, 1996.

———. "Greece: The History of the Classical Period." In *The Oxford History of Greece*, edited by John Boardman, Jasper Griffin, and Oswin Murray, 142–76. Oxford: Oxford University Press, 1986.

Horrell, J. Scott. *From the Ground Up: New Testament Foundations for the 21st Century*. Grand Rapids: Kregel, 2004.

Hort, Fenton John Anthony. *The Christian Ecclesia*. London: Macmillan, 1900.

Horton, Michael Scott. *Made in America: The Shaping of Modern American Evangelicalism*. Grand Rapids: Baker, 1991.

Houghton, Myron J. "Congregational Rule versus Elder Rule." *Faith Pulpit* (1986) n.p.

Hughes, Philip Edgcumbe. *Paul's Second Epistle to the Corinthians*. New International Commentary on the New Testament. Grand Rapids: Eerdmans, 1962.

Huther, Jacob. *The Epistles of James, Peter, John, and Jude*. Translated by Timothy Dwight. A Critical and Exegetical Commentary of the New Testament. New York: Funk & Wagnalls, 1884.

Irenaeus. *Against Heresies*. In *Ante Nicene Fathers*, edited by Alexander Roberts, James Donaldson, and A. Cleveland Coxe, 1:308–578. Peabody, MA: Hendrickson, 1994.

Jackson, F. J. Foakes, and Kirsopp Lake. *The Beginnings of Christianity*. 5 vols. 1920–1933. Reprint, Grand Rapids: Baker, 1965.

Jay, Eric G. "From Presbyter-Bishops to Bishops and Presbyters." *SecCent* 1.3 (1981) 125–62.

Jefford, Clayton N. "Presbyters in the Community of the Didache." *StPatr* 21 (1989) 124–28.

Jeremias, J. *Jerusalem in the Times of Jesus*. Translated by F. H. and C. H. Cave. Philadelphia: Fortress, 1969. First published as *Jerusalem zur Zeit Jesu* (Göttingen: Vandenhoeck & Ruprecht, 1962).

———. "πολλοί." In *TDNT*, 6:536–45.

Jeska, Joachim. "Stephanus—Zentrale Gestalt oder Randfigur der Apostelgeschichte?" *BK* 55 (2000) 68–73.

Jewett, Robert. "Mapping the Route of Paul's Second Missionary Journey from Dorylaeum to Troas." *TynBul* 48 (1997) 1–22.

———. "Tenement Churches and Communal Meals in the Early Church: The Implications of a Form-Critical Analysis of 2 Thessalonians 3:10." *BR* 38 (1993) 23–43.

Jinkins, Michael. "The 'Gift' of the Church: *Ecclesia Curcis, Peccatrix Maxima,* and the *Missio Dei*." In *Evangelical Ecclesiology: Reality or Illusion?* edited by John G. Stackhouse, Jr., 179–209. Grand Rapids: Baker, 2003.

Johnson, Luke Timothy. *The Acts of the Apostles*. Sacra Pagina 5. Collegeville: Liturgical, 1992.

———. "Reading Romans: Book Review of *Romans: A Commentary*, by Robert Jewett." *Christian Century* (2008) 36. Online: http://www.religion-online.org/showarticle.asp?title=3512.

Johnston, George. *The Doctrine of the Church in the New Testament*. Cambridge: Cambridge University Press, 1943.

Jones, A. H. M., et al. "Antioch." In *OCD*, 107.

————. *The Cities of the Eastern Roman Empire.* 2nd ed. Oxford: Clarendon, 1971.

————. *The Greek City: From Alexander to Justinian.* Oxford: Clarendon, 1979.

Judge, E. A. "The Social Identity of the First Christians." In *Social Distinctives of the Christians in the First Century: Pivotal Essays by E. A. Judge,* edited by David M. Scholer, 117–36. Peabody, MA: Hendrickson, 2008.

————. "The Social Pattern of Christian Groups in the First Century." In *Social Distinctives of the Christians in the First Century: Pivotal Essays by E. A. Judge,* edited by David M. Scholer, 1–56. Peabody, MA: Hendrickson, 2008.

Katz, Lisa. "Israel: Democratic and Jewish? The Democratic Jewish State of Israel." About. com. Online: http://judaism.about.com/od/politics/a/democracy.htm.

Katz, Steven T. "Issues in the Separation of Judaism and Christianity after 70 C.E.: A Reconsideration." *JBL* 103 (1984) 43–76.

Kee, Howard Clark. "The Transformation of the Synagogue after 70 C.E.: Its Import for Early Christianity." *NTS* 36 (1990) 1–24.

Keener, Craig S. *Paul, Women, and Wives.* Peabody, MA: Hendrickson, 1992.

Kelly, William. *Lectures on the Church of God.* Sound Teaching on Electronic Media. Online: http://www.stempublishing.com/authors/kelly/7subjcts/Church.html.

Kereszty, Roch. "The Unity of the Church in the Theology of Irenaeus." *SecCen* 4.4 (1984) 202–18.

Kirby, Gilbert. "Congregationalism." In *NIDCC,* 251–53

Kirk, J. Andrew. "Apostleship Since Rengstorf: Towards a Synthesis." *NTS* 21 (1975) 249–64.

————. "Did Officials in the New Testament Church Receive a Salary?" *ExTim* 84 (1973) 105–8.

Kirk, Kenneth E., editor. *The Apostolic Ministry: Essays on the History and the Doctrine of Episcopacy.* London: Hodder & Stoughton, 1946.

Kistemaker, Simon. *Acts.* New Testament Commentary. Grand Rapids: Baker, 1990.

Kittel G., and G. Friedrich, editors. *Theological Dictionary of the New Testament.* Translated by G. W. Bromiley. 10 vols. Grand Rapids: Eerdmans, 1964–1976.

Klassen, Walter. *Anabaptism in Outline: Selected Primary Sources.* Scottdale, PA: Herald, 1981.

Klauck, Hans-Josef. *Hausgemeinde und Hauskirche im frühen Christentum.* Stuttgart: Katholisches Bibelwerk, 1979.

————. *1 Korintherbrief.* Würzburg: Echter, 1986.

————. *2 Corinthians.* Echter Kommentar. Würzburg: Echter, 1986.

Kloppenborg, John S. "*Collegia* and *Thiasoi*: Issues in Function, Taxonomy and Membership." In *Voluntary Associations in the Graeco-Roman World,* edited by John S. Kloppenborg and Stephen G. Wilson, 16–30. London: Routledge, 1996.

————. "Edwin Hatch: Churches and Collegia." In *Origins and Method: Towards a New Understanding of Judaism and Christianity: Essays in Honour of John C. Hurd,* edited by Bradley H. McLean, 212–38. JSNTSupp 86. Sheffield: JSOT Press, 1993.

Knight, George W., III. *The Pastoral Epistles.* New International Greek Testament Commentary. Grand Rapids: Eerdmans, 1992.

Knowling, R. J. *The Acts of the Apostles.* Expositors Greek Testament. Reprint, Grand Rapids: Eerdmans, 1979.

Koester, H. *Introduction to the New Testament.* 2 vols. Philadelphia: Fortress, 1982.

Bibliography

Kolb, Frank. "Antiochia in der früheren Kaiserzeit." In *Geschichte, Tradition, Reflexion,* edited by F. S. Martin Hengel, 2:97–118. Griechische und Römische Religion. Tübingen: Mohr/Siebeck, 1996.

Koumoulides, John A., editor. *The Good Idea: Democracy and Ancient Greece.* New Rochelle: Caratzas, 1995.

Kruse, C. G. "Apostle, Apostleship." In *DLNT,* 76–82.

Kuen, Alfred. *Gemeinde nach Gottes Bauplan.* Wuppertal: Brockhaus, 1975.

Küng, Hans. *Christianity.* Translated by John Bowden. New York: Continuum, 2002.

———. *The Church.* Translated by Ray and Rosaleen Ockenden. London: Search, 1968. Originally published as *Die Kirche* (Freiburg: Herder, 1967).

Lahey, Stephen E. *Philosophy and Politics in the Thought of John Wyclif.* Cambridge: Cambridge University Press, 2003.

Lake, Kirsopp, and Henry J. Cadbury. *Part I, The Acts of the Apostles.* Vol. 4 of *The Beginnings of Christianity,* edited F. J. Foakes Jackson and Kirsopp Lake. 1932. Reprint, Grand Rapids: Baker, 1965.

Lampe, G. W. H. *A Patristic Greek Lexicon.* Oxford: Clarendon, 1961.

Lane, William L. "Social Perspectives on Roman Christianity during the Formative Years from Nero to Nerva: Romans, Hebrews, 1 *Clement.*" In *Judaism and Christianity in First-Century Rome,* edited by Karl P. Donfried and Peter Richardson, 196–244. Grand Rapids: Eerdmans, 1998.

Laney, J. Carl. *A Guide to Church Discipline.* Minneapolis: Bethany, 1985.

Latourette, Kenneth Scott. *A History of the Expansion of Christianity.* Vol. 1. New York: Harper & Brothers, 1937.

Lechler, Gotthardus Victor, editor. *Johannes de Wiclif Tractatus de Officio Pastorali.* Leipzig: Edelmann, 1863.

Le Cornu, H., and J. Shulam. *A Commentary on the Jewish Roots of Acts.* Jerusalem: Academon, 2010.

Leitzmann, Hany. *Geschichte der Alten Kirche.* 5th ed. Berlin: de Gruyter, 1975.

Lenski, R. C. H. *The Interpretation of 1 and 2 Corinthians.* Minneapolis: Augsburg, 1963.

Levine, Amy-Jill. *The Social and Ethnic Dimensions of Matthean Social History.* Lewiston, NY: Mellen, 1988.

Levine, Lee. *The Ancient Synagogue: The First Thousand Years.* 2nd ed. New Haven: Yale University Press, 2005.

Levinskaya, Irina. *The Book of Acts in Its Diaspora Setting.* Vol. 5 of *The Book of Acts in Its First-Century Setting,* edited by Bruce W. Winter. Grand Rapids: Eerdmans, 1996.

Lewis, David M. "The First Greek Jew." *JSS* 2 (1957) 264–66.

Lewis, Jack P. "The Jewish Background of the Church." *ResQ* 2 (1958) 154–63.

Liddell, H. G., R. Scott, and H. S. Jones. *A Greek-English Lexicon.* 9th ed. Oxford: Oxford University Press, 1968.

Lienhard, Joseph T. "Acts 6:1–6: A Redactional View." *CBQ* 37 (1975) 228–36.

Lightfoot, Joseph B., and J. R. Harmer. *The Apostolic Fathers: Greek Texts and English Translations of Their Writings.* 2nd ed. Edited by Michael W. Holmes. Grand Rapids: Baker, 1992.

Lightfoot, Joseph B. *The Epistle of St. Paul to the Galatians.* 1865. Reprint, Grand Rapids: Zondervan, 1957.

———. *St. Paul's Epistles to the Colossians and to Philemon.* London: Macmillan, 1879.

———. *St. Paul's Epistle to the Philippians,* 12th ed. London: Macmillan, 1888. Reprint, Grand Rapids: Zondervan, 1976.

Linton, Olaf. *Das Problem der Urkirche in der neuern Forschung.* Uppsala: Minerva, 1932.

Lohse, Eduard. "χειροτονέω." In *TDNT*, 437.

———. *Die Ordination im Spätjudentum und im Neuen Testament.* Berlin: Evangelische Verlagsanstalt, 1951.

Longenecker, Richard N. *The Acts of the Apostles.* Expositor's Bible Commentary 9. Grand Rapids: Zondervan, 1981.

———. *Biblical Exegesis in the Apostolic Period.* Grand Rapids: Eerdmans, 1975. Reprint, Carlisle: Paternoster, 1995.

———. *Paul: Apostle of Liberty.* Grand Rapids: Baker, 1964.

———. "Paul's Vision of the Church and Community Formation." In *Community Formation in the Early Church and the Church Today*, edited by Richard Longenecker, 73–88. Peabody, MA: Hendrickson, 2002.

———, editor. *Community Formation in the Early Church and in the Church Today.* Peabody, MA: Hendrickson, 2002.

Löning, Karl. "Der Stephanuskreis und seine Mission." In *Die Anfänge des Christentums*, edited by J. Becker et al., 82–101. Stuttgart: Kohlhammer, 1987.

Lowndes, Arthur. "Bishop: Anglican View." In *ISBE*, 479–81.

Lucian. *The Passing of Peregrinus.* Translated by A.M. Harmon. Cambridge, MA: Harvard University Press, 1936.

Lüdemann, Gerd. *Early Christianity according to the Traditions in Acts: A Commentary.* Minneapolis: Fortress, 1989.

Lumpkin, William R. *Baptist Confessions of Faith.* Rev. ed. Valley Forge: Judson, 1969.

Luscombe, David. "Wyclif and Hierarchy." In *From Ockham to Wyclif*, edited by Anne Hudson and Michael Wilks, 233–44. Studies in Church History Subsidia 5. Oxford: Blackwell, 1987.

Luther, Martin. *Luther Deutsch: Die Werke Luthers in Auswahl.* Edited by Kurt Aland. 10 vols. Göttingen: Vandenhoeck & Ruprecht, 1983.

Lynch, John E. "Church, Church Polity." In *Encyclopaedia of Religion*, 3:473–85. New York: MacMillan, 1987.

MacArthur, John, Jr. *Acts 1–12.* The MacArthur New Testament Commentary. Chicago: Moody, 1994.

———. *The Master's Plan for the Church.* Chicago: Moody, 1991.

MacGorman, J. W. "The Discipline of the Church." In *The People of God: Essays on the Believers' Church*, 74–95. Nashville: Broadman, 1991.

MacKinnon, James. *Calvin and the Reformation.* New York: Russell & Russell, 1962.

MacLeod, Donald. "Church Government." In *New Dictionary of Theology*, edited by Sinclair B. Ferguson and David F. Wright, 143–46. Downers Grove, IL: Invervarsity, 1988.

———. "Deacons and Elders." *Scottish Bulletin of Evangelical Theology* 13 (1991) 26–50.

Magie, David. *Roman Rule in Asia Minor: To the End of the Third Century after Christ.* Vol. 1. Princeton: Princeton University Press, 1950.

Malherbe, Abraham J. *Social Aspects of Early Christianity.* 2nd ed. Wilmington, DE: Glazer, 1983.

Mappes, David A. "Expositional Problems Related to the Eldership in 1 Timothy 5:17–25." PhD diss., Dallas Theological Seminary, 1997.

March, Jennifer R. "Elections and Voting." In *OCD*, 516.

Marquardt, Joachim. *Römische Staatsverwaltung.* 3rd ed. Vol. 1. 1884. Reprint, Darmstadt: Wissenschaftliche Buchgesellschaft, 1957.

Marshall, I. Howard. *Commentary on Luke.* New International Greek Testament Commentary. Grand Rapids: Eerdmans, 1978.

———. "Congregation and Ministry in the Pastoral Epistles." In *Community Formation in the Early Church and the Church Today,* edited by Richard Longenecker, 105–25. Peabody, MA: Hendrickson, 2002.

Marsilius of Padua. *Defensor Pacis.* Translated by Alan Gerwirth. New York: Columbia University Press, 2001.

Martin Luthers Ausgewählte Werke. Vol. 3. Munich: Raiser, 1938.

Mason, Steve N. "*Philosophiai*: Graeco-Roman, Judean and Christian." In *Voluntary Associations in the Graeco-Roman World,* edited by John S. Kloppenborg and Stephen G. Wilson, 31–58. London: Routledge, 1996.

Maynard-Reid, P. U. "Samaria." In *DLNT,* 1075–77.

McCready, Wayne O. "*Ekklesia* and Voluntary Associations." In *Voluntary Associations in the Graeco-Roman World,* edited by John S. Kloppenborg and Stephen G. Wilson, 59–73. London: Routledge, 1996.

McKenzie, John L. *Authority in the Church.* London: Chapman, 1966.

McLachlan, Douglas. "Who Makes the Decisions at Your Church?" *Baptist Bulletin* (1998) 12–15.

McLoughlin, William G. *New England Dissent:* 1630–1833. 2 vols. Cambridge, MA: Harvard University Press, 1971.

McRay, John. *Paul: His Life and Teaching.* Grand Rapids: Baker, 2003.

Meeks, Wayne. *The First Urban Christians.* New Haven: Yale University Press, 1983.

———. *The Moral World of the First Christians.* Philadelphia: Westminster, 1986.

Meier, John P. "The Jerusalem Council: Gal 2:1–10; Acts 15:1–29." *Mid-Stream* 35 (1996) 465–75.

Merkle, Benjamin L. *The Elder and Overseer: One Office in the Early Church.* New York: Lang, 2003.

———. "Hierarchy in the Church? Instruction from the Pastoral Epistles Concerning Elders and Overseers." *The Southern Baptist Journal of Theology* 7/3 (2003) 32–43.

Metzger, Bruce M. "Paul's Vision of the Church: A Study of the Ephesian Letters." *ThTo* 6 (1949) 49–63.

———. *A Textual Commentary on the Greek New Testament.* New York: United Bible Societies, 1975.

Meyer, Ben F. *The Early Christians: Their World Mission and Self-Discovery.* Wilmington, DE: Glazier, 1986.

Meyer, Eduard. *Ursprüng und Anfänge des Christentums.* Vol. 3. Stuttgart: Cotta'sche Buchhandlung, 1923.

Meyer, Heinrich A. W. *Critical and Exegetical Handbook of the Acts of the Apostles.* Translated by Paton J. Golag. Edinburgh: T. & T. Clark, 1883. Reprint, Winona Lake: Alpha, 1979. Originally published as *Kritisch exegetisches Handbuch über die Apostelgeschichte.* 4th ed. (Göttingen: Vandenhoeck & Ruprecht,1870).

———. *Critical and Exegetical Handbook of the Gospel of Matthew.* Translated by Peter Christie. New York: Funk & Wagnalls, 1884.

Minear, Paul S. "Christ and the Congregation, 1 Corinthians 5–6." *RevExp* 80 (1983) 341–50.

———. *Images of the Church in the New Testament.* 1960. Reprint, Louisville: Westminster John Knox, 2002.

Minton, Ronald. "Biblical Perspectives on Elders." ThD diss., Central Baptist Seminary, 1990.

Mommsen, Theodor. *Römisches Staatsrecht*. Vol. 1. Leipzig: Hirzel, 1887.

Moo, Douglas J. *The Epistle to the Romans*. New International Commentary on the New Testament. Grand Rapids: Eerdmans, 1996.

Moodie, Dunbar. "A Response to Richard Norris." *AThR*, Supplementary Series 9 (1993) 33–35.

Moore, Robert Ian. "Petrus von Bruis." In *TRE*, 26:286.

Morris, Ian. "The Strong Principle of Equality and the Archaic Origins of Greek Democracy." In *Demokratia: A Conversation on Democracies, Ancient and Modern*, edited by Josiah Ober and Charles Hedrick, 17–56. Princeton: Princeton University Press, 1996.

Morris, Leon. "Church Government." In *Evangelical Dictionary of Theology*, edited by Walter A. Elwell, 238–41. Grand Rapids: Baker, 1984.

Mosbech, Holger. "*Apostolos* in the New Testament." *Studia Theologica* 2 (1948) 186.

Moulton, James Hope, and George Milligan. *The Vocabulary of the Greek Testament, Illustrated from the Papyri and Other Non-Literary Sources*. 1930. Reprint, Grand Rapids: Eerdmans, 1976.

Müller, Ludwig. *Katholische Dogmatik*. Freiburg: Herder, 2004.

Munck, Johannes. "Paul, the Apostles, and the Twelve." *Studia Theologica* 3 (1950) 96–110.

Murray, Oswyn. "Liberty and the Ancient Greeks." In *The Good Idea: Democracy in Ancient Greece*, edited by John A. Koumoulides, 33–56. New Rochelle: Caratzas, 1995.

Murray, Oswyn, and Simon Price. *The Greek City: From Homer to Alexander*. Oxford: Clarendon, 1990.

Nagel, Norman. "The Twelve and the Seven in Acts 6 and the Needy." *Concordia Journal* 31 (2005) 113–25.

Nassif, Bradley. Review of *From Synagogue to Church: Public Services and Offices in the Earliest Christian Communities* by James Tunstead Burtchaell. *CH* 64 (1995) 335–36.

Neander, August. *Geschichte der Pflanzung und Leitung der christlichen Kirche durch die Apostel*. 5th ed. 3 vols. Gotha: Perthes, 1890.

Neumann, Johannes. "Bischof, I." In *TRE*, 6:663–82.

Nicene and Post-Nicene Fathers, The. Series 1. Edited by Philip Schaff. 14 vols. 1886–1889. Reprint, Peabody, Mass.: Hendrickson, 1994.

Nideng, Norman. "Stop the Voting: You're Wrecking My Church." *Moody Monthly* (1982) 7–9.

Norris, Richard A., Jr. "The Beginnings of Christian Priesthood." *AThR*, Supplementary Series 9 (1984) 18–32.

Nuttall, Clay. *The Weeping Church: Confronting the Crisis of Church Polity*. Schaumburg, IL: Regular Baptist, 1985.

O'Brien, P. T. "Church." In *DPL*, 123–31.

———. "The Church as a Heavenly and Eschatological Entity." In *The Church in the Bible and in the World*, edited by D. A. Carson, 88–119. Grand Rapids: Eerdmans, 1987.

Obrist, Willy. "A Consecrated Hierarchy: An Obstacle to a Democratizing of the Catholic Church." In *The Tabu of Democracy within the Church*, edited by James Provost and Knut Walf, 27–37. London: SCM, 1992.

O'Connor, J. Murphy. *St Paul's Corinth: Text and Archaeology*. Wilmington, DE: Glazier, 1983.

Ogden, Roger. *The New Reformation: Returning the Ministry to the People of God.* Grand Rapids: Zondervan, 1990.

Ollrog, Wolf-Henning. *Paulus und seine Mitarbeiter: Untersuchung zu theorie und Praxis der paulinischen Mission.* Neukirchen-Vluyn: neukirchener, 1979.

Olson, Jeannine E. *Deacons and Deaconesses through the Centuries.* Saint Louis: Concordia, 2005.

Olson, Roger E. "Free Church Ecclesiology and Evangelical Spirituality: A Unique Compatibility." In *Evangelical Ecclesiology: Reality or Illusion?* edited by John G. Stackhouse, Jr., 161–78. Grand Rapids: Baker, 2003.

Origen. *Homilies on Leviticus, 1–16.* Translated by Gary Wayne Barkley. The Fathers of the Church 83. Washington: Catholic University of America Press, 1990.

Orr, William F., and James Arthur Walther. *1 Corinthians.* Anchor Bible 32. New York: Doubleday, 1976.

Osborne, G. R. "Elder." In *DJG*, 201–3.

Osborne, Robin. "The Demos and Its Divisions in Classical Athens." In *The Greek City: From Homer to Alexander*, edited by Oswyn Murray and Simon Price, 265–93. Oxford: Clarendon, 1990.

Osiek, Carolyn, and Margaret Y. Macdonald. *A Woman's Place: House Churches in Earliest Christianity.* Minneapolis: Fortress, 2006.

Overman, J. Andrew. *Matthew's Gospel and Formative Judaism: The Social World of the Matthean Community.* Minneapolis: Fortress, 1990.

Oxford Classical Dictionary, The. 3rd ed. Edited by Simon Hornblower and Anthony Spawforth. Oxford: Oxford University Press, 1996.

Oxford Dictionary of the Christian Church, The. 2nd ed. Edited by F. L. Cross and E. A. Livingstone. Oxford: Oxford University Press, 1983.

Oz-Salzberger, Fania. Interviewed by Kristin Eliasberg. "An Ancient Consitution," *Tablet*, December 3, 2003. Online: http://www.tabletmag.com/jewish-news-and-politics/1435/an-ancient-constitution.

Panning, Armin J. "Acts 6: The Ministry of the Seven." *Wisconsin Lutheran Quarterly* 93/1 (1966) 11–17.

Parrott, William F. "The Role of the Congregation in the Government of the Church." ThM thesis, Dallas Theological Seminary, 1984.

Patterson, Paige. "Single-elder Congregrationalism." In *Who Runs the Church: Four Views on Church Government*, edited by Paul E. Engle and Steven B. Cowan, 131–52. Grand Rapids: Zondervan, 2004.

Payne, J. Barton. "1, 2 Chronicles." In *The Expositor's Bible Commentary*, edited by Frank E. Gaebelein, 4:303–564. Grand Rapids: Zondervan, 1988.

Pelikan, Jaroslav. *Acts.* Brazos Theological Commentary. Grand Rapids: Brazos, 2005.

———. *The Emergence of the Catholic Tradition (100–600).* Chicago: University of Chicago Press, 1971.

Pervo, R. I. *Profit with Delight: The Literary Genre of the Acts of the Apostles.* Philadelphia: Fortress, 1987.

Pesch, R. *Die Apostelgeschichte.* Evangelisch-katholischer Kommentar zum Neuen Testament 5/1. 2 vols. Neukirchen-Vluyn: Neukirchener, 1986.

Peterson, David. "The 'Locus' of the Church–Heaven or Earth?" *Chm* 112/3 (1998). Online: http://www.biblicalstudies.org.uk/pdf/churchman/112-03_199.pdf.

Philo. *Works.* Translated by F. H. Colson. 10 vols. Loeb Classical Library. Cambridge, MA: Cambridge University Press, 1937.

Pillette, Bard M. "Paul and His Fellow Workers: A Study of the Use of Authority." ThD diss., Dallas Theological Seminary, 1992.

Piper, John, and Wayne Grudem, editors. *Recovering Biblical Manhood and Womanhood: A Response to Evangelical Feminism*. Wheaton, IL: Crossway, 1993.

Pliny the Younger. *Letters and Panergyricus*. Vol. 2. Translated by Betty Radice. Cambridge, MA: Harvard University Press, 1969.

Plümacher, Eckard. "Die Apostelgeschichte als historische Monographie." In *Les Actes des Apotres*, edited by J. Kremer, 457–66. Leuven: University Press, 1976.

———. *Lukas als hellenistischer Schrifsteller: Studien zur Apostelgeschichte*. Studien zur Umwelt des Neuen Testaments 9. Göttingen: Vandenhoeck & Ruprecht, 1972.

Plummer, Alfred. *The Second Epistle of Paul to the Corinthians*. 1915. Reprint, Edinburgh: T. & T. Clark, 1975.

Plutarch. *De Iside et Osiride*. Translated by J. Gwyn Griffiths. Cardiff: University of Wales, 1970.

Poland, Franz. *Geschichte des griechischen Vereinswesens*. Leipzig: Teubner, 1909.

Polhill, J. B. *Acts*. New American Commentary 26. Nashville: Broadman, 1992.

Polybius. *The Histories*. Translated by W. R. Paton. Vol. 3. Cambridge, MA: Harvard University Press, 1960.

Porter, Stanley E. "Did Jesus Ever Teach in Greek?" *TynBul* 44 (1993) 199–235.

Powell, Mark Allen. "Reading Acts as History." *AsTJ* 46 (1991) 49–62.

Prior, Michael. *Paul the Letter-Writer and the Second Letter to Timothy*. JSNTSupp 23. Sheffield: Sheffield Academic, 1989.

Proctor, John. "Proselytes and Pressure Cookers: The Meaning and Application of Acts 15:20." *International Review of Missions* 85 (2006) 469–83.

Pryor, J. W. *John: Evangelist of the Covenant People*. Downer's Grove, IL: InterVarsity, 1992.

Purcell, Nicholas. "Travel." In *OCD*, 1547–48.

Quinn, Jerome D. "Die Ordination in den Pastorbriefen." *Comm* 10 (1981) 410–20.

Rabello, A. M. "The Legal Condition of the Jews in the Roman Empire." *ANRW* 2/13 (1980) 662–762.

Radmacher, Earl. *The Nature of the Church*. Hayesville, NC: Schoettle, 1996.

———. *The Question of Elders*. Portland: Western Conservative Baptist Theological Seminary, 1977.

Ramsay, William M. "Roads and Travel in the New Testament." In *Hastings Dictionary of the Bible*, 5:368–402. London: T. & T. Clark, 1898. Reprint, Peabody, MA: Hendrickson, 1988.

———. *St. Paul the Traveller and the Roman Citizen*. London: Hodder & Stoughton, 1897.

Ratzinger, Joseph. *Called to Communion*. San Francisco: Ignatius, 1996.

———. "Die kirchliche Lehre vom sacramentum ordinis." *Comm* 10 (1981) 434–45.

Ratzinger, Joseph, and Hans Maier. *Demokratie in der Kirche*. Limburg: Lahn, 2000.

Reallexikon für Antike und Christentum. Edited by Theodor Klauser, et al. 22 vols. Stuttgart: Hiersemann, 1950–.

Reicke, Bo. "The Constitution of the Primitive Church." In *The Scrolls and the New Testament*, edited by Krister Stehdahl, 143–156. London: SCM, 1958.

Rengstorf, Karl Heinrich. "ἀποστέλλω, κ.τ.λ." In *TDNT*, 397–447.

———. "Die Zuwahl des Matthias." *Studia Theologica* 15 (1961) 35–67.

Reviv, Hanoch. *The Elders in Ancient Israel*. Jerusalem: Magnes, 1989.

Reymond, Robert L. *Paul, Missionary Theologian: A Survey of His Missionary Labours and Theology*. Rearn, Ross-shire, UK: Mentor, 2000.

Bibliography

———. "The Presbytery-Led Church." In *Perspectives on Church Government*, edited by Chad Owen Brand and R. Stanton Norman, 87–156. Nashville: Broadman & Holman, 2004.

Richardson, Peter. "Building 'an Association (*Synodos*) . . . and a Place of their Own.'" In *Community Formation in the Early Church and in the Church Today*, edited by Richard N. Longenecker, 36–56. Peabody, MA: Hendrickson, 2002.

———. "Early Synagogues as Collegia in the Diaspora and Palestine." In *Voluntary Associations in the Graeco-Roman World*, edited by John S. Kloppenborg and Stephen G. Wilson, 90–109. London: Routledge, 1996.

Ridderbos, Herman. *Paul: An Outline of His Theology*. Translated by John Richard De Witt. Grand Rapids: Eerdmans, 1975.

Ritschl, Johann Albrecht. *Die Entstehung der altkatholischen Kirche*. Bonn: Marcus, 1857.

Roberts, C. H., T. C. Skeat, and A. D. Nock. "The Guild of Zeus Hypsistos." *HTR* 29 (1936) 39–88.

Robertson, C. K. "The Limits of Theological Leadership: Challenges to Apostolic Homeostasis in Luke-Acts." *AThR* 87 (2005) 273–90.

Roloff, Jürgen. *Die Apostelgeschichte: Übersetzt und Erklärt*. Vol. 5 of *Das Neue Testament Deutsch*. Göttingen: Vandenhoeck & Ruprecht, 1981.

———. *Die Kirche im Neuen Testament*. Göttingen: Vandenhoeck & Ruprecht, 1993.

———. "Konflikte und Konfliktlösungen in der Apostelgeschichte." In *Themen der paulinischen Missionspredigt auf dem Hintergrund der spätjudisch-hellenistischen Missionsliteratur*, edited by Claus Bussmann and Walter Radl, 23/3:111–26. Frankfurt: Lang, 1991.

Rost, Christian F., et al. *Handwörterbuch der Griechischen Sprache*. 4 vols. Leipzig: Vogel, 1857.

Rothe, Richard. *Der Anfänge der Christlichen Kirche und Ihre Verfassung: Ein geschichtler Versuch*. Wittenberg: Zimmerman, 1837.

Safrai, S., and M. Stern. *The Jewish People in the First Century*. Vols. 1 and 2. Amsterdam: Van Gorcum, 1976.

Safrai, Samuel. "Jewish Self-Government." In *The Jewish People in the First Century*, edited by Samuel Safrai and Menahem Stern, 1:377–419. Assen: Van Gorcum, 1974.

———. "The Synagogue." In *The Jewish People in the First Century*, edited by Samuel Safrai and Menahem Stern, 2:908–40. Philadelphia: Fortress, 1976.

Saldarini, Anthony. *Matthew's Christian-Jewish Community*. Chicago: University of Chicago Press, 1994.

Sandmel, Samuel. *The First Christian Century in Judaism and Christianity: Certainties and Uncertainties*. New York: Oxford University Press, 1969.

Saucy, Robert. "Authority in the Church." In *Walvoord: A Tribute*, edited by Donald K. Campbell, 219–38. Chicago: Moody, 1982.

———. *The Church in God's Program*. Chicago: Moody, 1972.

Schaff, Philip, editor. *The Creeds of Christendom*. 3 vols. New York: Harper & Row, 1931. Reprint, Grand Rapids: Baker, 1990.

———. *History of the Christian Church*. 8 vols. New York: Scribners, 1910.

Schatz, Klaus. *Der Päpstliche Primat*. Würzburg: Echter, 1990. Translated by John A. Otto and Linda A. Maloney as *Papal Primacy: From Its Origins to the Present* (Collegeville, MN: Liturgical, 1996).

Schemeil, Yves. "Democracy before Democracy?" *International Political Science Review* 21.2 (2000) 99–120.

Schenke, Ludger. *Die Urgemeinde: Geschichte und Theologische Entwicklung.* Stuttgart: Kohlhammer, 1990.

Schillebeeckx, Edward. *Church: The Human Story of God.* Translated by John Bowden. London: SCM, 1990.

Schirrmacher, Thomas. *Ethik.* Vol. 1. Neuhausen: Hännsler, 1994.

Schmid, Heinrich. *Doctrinal Theology of the Evangelical Lutheran Church.* Translated by Henry E. Jacobs and Charles E. Hay. Minneapolis: Augsburg, 1899.

Schmidt, K. L. "ἐκκλησία." In *TDNT*, 501–36.

Schmidt, T. E. "Discipline." In *DPL*, 214–18.

Schmithals, Walter. *The Office of Apostle in the Early Church.* Translated by J. E. Steely. Nashville: Abingdon, 1969.

Schnabel, Eckhard J. *Early Christian Mission.* 2 vols. Downer's Grove, IL: InterVarsity, 2004.

Schnackenburg, Rudolf. "Apostles before and during Paul's Time." Translated by M. Kwiran and W. W. Gasque. In *Apostolic History and the Gospel,* edited by W. W. Gasque and R. P. Martin, 287–303. Grand Rapids: Eerdmans, 1970.

Schoedel, William R. *Ignatius of Antioch: A Commentary on the Letters of Ignatius of Antioch.* Philadelphia: Fortress, 1985.

Schöllgen, Georg. "Monepiskopat und monarchischer Episkopat: Eine Bemerkung zur Terminologie." *ZNW* 77 (1986) 146–51.

Schrage, Wolfgang. *Der erste Brief an die Korinther.* Evangelisch-katholischer Kommentar zum Neuen Testament. Neukirchen-Vluyn: Neukirchener, 1991.

Schuler, Christof. *Ländliche Siedlungen und Gemeinden im hellenistischen und römischen Kleinasien.* Munich: Beck, 1998.

Schulz, Ray. "Junia or Junias." *ExpTim* 98 (1987) 108–10.

Schürer, Emil. *The History of the Jewish People in the Age of Jesus Christ.* Vol. 2. Rev. ed. Edited by Geza Vermes, Fergus Millar and Matthew Black. Edinburgh: T. & T. Clark, 1979.

Schüssler Fiorenza, Elisabeth. *In Memory of Her: A Feminist Reconstruction of Christian Origins.* New York: Crossroads, 1985.

———. "Missionaries, Apostles, Coworkers: Romans 16 and the Reconstruction of Women's Early Christian History." *Word and World* 6 (1986) 420–33.

Schweizer, Eduard. *Church Order in the New Testament.* Translated by Frank Clarke. London: SCM, 1961.

———. *Gemeinde und Gemeindeordnung im Neuen Testament.* Zürich: Zwingli, 1959.

Scott, J. Julius, Jr. "The Church's Progress to the Council of Jerusalem according to the Book of Acts." *BBR* 7 (1997) 205–224.

Shepherd, Massey Hamilton, Jr. "The Development of the Early Ministry." *AThR* 26 (1944) 135–50.

Shilo, Shmuel. "Majority Rule." In *EncJud* 804–06.

Shipley, Graham. *The Greek World after Alexander: 323–30 B.C.* Routledge History of the Ancient World. London: Routledge, 2000.

Slee, Michelle. *The Church in Antioch in the First Century C.E.* JSNTSupp 244. Sheffield: Sheffield Academic, 2003.

Smeaton, George. *The Doctrine of the Holy Spirit.* 1889. Reprint, Edinburgh: Banner of Truth, 1988.

Snow, Charles M. *Religious Liberty in America.* Washington, DC: Review & Herald, 1914.

Bibliography

Sobosan, Jeffrey G. "The Role of the Presbyter: An Investigation into the *Adversus Haereses* of Saint Irenaeus." *SJT* 27 (1974) 129–47.

Sohm, Rudolf. *Kirchenrecht.* Vol. 1. Leipzig: Duncker & Humbolt, 1892.

South, James T. *Disciplinary Practices in Pauline Texts.* Lewiston, NY: Mellen Biblical, 1992.

Spencer, F. Scott. "Neglected Widows in Acts 6:1–7." *CBQ* 56 (1994) 715–33.

———. *The Portrait of Philip in Acts: A Study of Roles and Relations.* JSNTSupp 67. Sheffield: University of Sheffield, 1992.

Stamps, Dennis. "The Use of the Old Testament in the New Testament as a Rhetorical Device: A Methodological Proposal." In *Hearing the Old Testament in the New,* edited by Stanley Porter, 9–37. Grand Rapids: Eerdmans, 2006.

Staveley, E. S. *Greek and Roman Voting and Elections.* London: Thames & Hudson, 1972.

Stegemann, Ekkehard, and Wolfgang Stegemann. *The Jesus Movement: A Social History of Its First Century.* Translated by O. C. Dean, Jr. Minneapolis: Fortress, 1999.

Steger, Carlos Alfredo. *Apostolic Succession in the Writings of Yves Congar and Oscar Cullmann.* Andrews University Seminary Doctoral Dissertation Series 20. Berrien Springs: Andrews University, 1995.

Steinhauser, Kenneth B. "Authority in the Primitive Church." *Patristic and Byzantine Review* 3 (1984) 89–100.

Stephanus, H. *Thesaurus Graecae Linguae.* Vol. 9. Graz: Akademische Druck, 1954.

Stockton, David. "The Founding of the Empire." In *The Oxford History of the Roman World,* edited by John Boardman, Jasper Griffin, and Oswyn Murray, 146–79. Oxford: Oxford University Press, 1988.

Strack, Hermann L., and Paul Billerbeck. *Kommentar zum Neuen Testament aus Talmud und Midrasch.* 5 vols. Munich: C. H. Beck, 1922–61.

Strathmann, H. "λειτουργέω, λειτουργία." In *TDNT,* 215–31.

Strauch, Alexander. *Biblical Eldership: An Urgent Call to Restore Biblical Church Leadership.* Littleton: Lewis and Roth, 1986. Rev. ed. Littleton, CO: Lewis & Roth, 1995.

———. *Minister of Mercy: The New Testament Deacon.* Littleton, CO: Lewis & Roth, 1992.

Streeter, Burnett H. *The Primitive Church.* New York: Macmillan, 1929.

Suetonius. *The Twelve Caesars.* Rev ed. Trans. Robert Graves. London: Penguin, 1979.

Suggit, John N. "The Holy Spirit and We Resolved . . . (Acts 15:28)." *JTSA* 79/1 (2006) 38–48.

Suhl, Alfred. "Ein Konfliktlösungsmodel der Urkirche und seine Geschichte." *BK* 45 (1990) 81–87.

Swete, H. B., editor. *Essays on the Early History of the Church and the Ministry.* London: Macmillan, 1918.

Taylor, L. Roy. "Presbyterianism." In *Who Runs the Church: Four Views of Church Government,* edited by Paul E. Engle and Steven B. Cowan, 71–98. Grand Rapids: Zondervan, 2004.

———. "A Presbyterian's Response to Single-elder Congregationalism." In *Who Runs the Church: Four Views of Church Government,* edited by Paul E. Engle and Steven B. Cowan, 161–67. Grand Rapids: Zondervan, 2004.

Taylor, Nicholas. *Paul, Antioch and Jerusalem: A Study in Relationships and Authority in Earliest Christianity.* JSNTSupp 66. Sheffield: University of Sheffield, 1989.

Tcherikover, Victor. *Hellenistic Civilization and the Jews.* Translated by S. Applebaum. Philadelphia: Atheneum, 1977.

Theissen, Gerd. *Social Reality and the Early Christians*. Translated by Margaret Kohl. Edinburgh: T. & T. Clark, 1992.

———. *The Social Setting of Christianity*. Translated by John H. Schütz. Philadelphia: Fortress, 1982.

———. "Soziale Schichtung in der korinthischen Gemeinde." In *Studien zur Soziologie des Urchristentums*, edited by Gerd Theissen, 231–71. Tübingen: Mohr, 1979.

———. "Die Starken und die Schwachen in Korinth." In *Studien zur Soziologie des Urchristentume*, edited by Gerd Theissen, 272–89. Tübingen: Mohr, 1979.

———. *Studien zur Soziologie des Urchristentums*. Tübingen: Mohr/Siebeck, 1979.

Thiselton, Anthony T. *The First Epistle to the Corinthians*. New International Greek Testament Commentary. Grand Rapids: Eerdmans, 2000.

Thrall, Margaret E. *A Critical And Exegetical Commentary on the Second Epistle to the Corinthians*. International Critical Commentary. Edinburgh: T. & T. Clark, 1994.

Toon, Peter. "Episcopalianism. " In *Who Runs the Church: Four Views of Church Government*, edited by Paul E. Engle and Steven B. Cowan, 19–48. Grand Rapids: Zondervan, 2004.

Towner, Philip H. "Households and Household Codes." In *Dictionary of Paul and His Letters*, edited by Gerald F. Hawthorne, Ralph P. Martin, and Daniel G. Reid, 416–19 Downer's Grove, IL: InterVarsity, 1993.

Trebilco, Paul R. *Jewish Communities in Asia Minor*. Cambridge: Cambridge University Press, 2006.

Turretin, Francois. *Institutes of Elenctic Theology*. Translated by George Musgrave Giger. Edited by James Dennison, Jr. 3 vols. Phillipsburg, NJ: Presbyterian & Reformed, 1997.

Unnik, W. C. van. "Luke's Second Book and the Rules of Hellenistic Historiography." In *Les Actes des Apotres*, edited by J. Kremer, 37–60. Leuven: University Press, 1976.

Vaughan, Robert, editor. *Tracts and Treatises of John de Wycliffe, D. D. with Selections and Translations from His Manuscripts, and Latin Works*. London: Blackburn & Pardon, 1845.

Ven, Johannes A. van der. *Ecclesiology in Context*. Grand Rapids: Eerdmans, 1996.

Verduin, Leonard. *The Reformers and Their Stepchildren*. Paris: Arkansas, 2001.

Vermes, Geza. *The Dead Sea Scrolls in English*. 3rd ed. London: Penguin, 1987.

Viola, Frank. *Reimagining the Church*. Colorado Springs: Cook, 2008.

Volz, Carl A. "The Pastoral Office in the Early Church." *Word and World* 9 (1989) 359–66.

Vos, Craig Steven de. "Stepmothers, Concubines and the Case of Porneia in 1 Corinthians 5." *NTS* 80 (1998) 104–14.

Waldron, Samuel E. "Plural-elder Congregationalism." In *Who Runs the Church?: Four Views on Church Government*, edited by Paul E. Engle and Steven B. Cowan, 185–221. Grand Rapids: Zondervan, 2004.

Wallace, Daniel B. *Greek Grammar beyond the Basics: An Exegetical Syntax of the New Testament*. Grand Rapids: Zondervan, 1996.

———. "Who Should Run the Church? A Case for the Plurality of Elders." Bible.org. Online: http://www.bible.org/page.php?page_id=414.

Walton, Steve. "Acts: Many Questions, Many Answers." In *The Face of New Testament Studies*, edited by Scot McKnight and Grant R. Osborne, 229–50. Grand Rapids: Baker, 2004.

Ward, Roy Bowen. "*Ekklesia*: A Word Study." *ResQ* 2 (1958) 164–79.

Warren, Charles. "House." In *A Dictionary of the Bible*, edited by James Hastings, 2:433. Edinburgh: T. & T. Clark, 1898.

Bibliography

Weber, Max. *Wirtschaft und Gesellschaft*. Tübingen: Mohr/Siebeck, 1922. Reprint, Paderborn: Voltmedia, n.d.

Weinfeld, Moshe. "Congregation." In *EncJud* 5:893–96

Weizsäcker, Karl von. *Das apostolische Zeitalter der christlichen Kirche*. Freiburg im Freiburg: Mohr, 1886.

Wette, Wilhelm M. L. de. *Lehrbuch der historisch-kritischen Einleitung in die Bibel Alten und Neuen Testaments. Zweyter Teil: Die Einleitung in das Neue Testament enthaltend*. 5th ed. Berlin: Reimer, 1848.

White, A. N. Sherwin. *Roman Society and Roman Law in the New Testament*. Oxford: Oxford University Press, 1963.

White, L. Michael. "Synagogue and Society in Imperial Ostia." In *Judaism and Christianity in First-Century Rome*, edited by Karl P. Donfried and Peter Richardson, 30–68. Grand Rapids: Eerdmans, 1998.

Wiarda, Timothy. "The Jerusalem Council and the Theological Task." *JETS* 46 (2003) 234–248.

Wikenhauser, Alfred. *Die Apostelgeschichte: Übersetzt und erklärt*. Regensburger Neues Testament. Regensburg: Pustet, 1961.

Wiles, G. P. *Paul's Intercessory Prayers*. Cambridge: Cambridge University Press, 1974.

Wilken, Robert L. "Collegia, Philosophical Schools, and Theology." In *The Catacombs and the Coliseum*, edited by Stephen Benko and John J. O'Rourke, 268–91. Valley Forge: Judson, 1971.

Williams, D. H., editor. *The Free Church and the Early Church: Bridging the Historical and Theological Divide*. Grand Rapids: Eerdmans, 2002.

Williams, George Huntston. "The Role of the Layman in the Ancient Church." In *Church, Ministry, and Organization in the Early Church Era*, edited by Everett Ferguson. Studies in the Early Church, 13:271–303. New York: Garland, 1993.

Wilson, Stephen. G. *The Gentiles and the Gentile Mission in Luke-Acts*. Monograph Series, Society for New Testament Studies 23. Cambridge: Cambridge University Press, 1973.

———. "Voluntary Associations: An Overview." In *Voluntary Associations in the Graeco-Roman World*, edited by John S. Kloppenborg and Stephen G. Wilson, 1–15. London: Routledge, 1996.

Windisch, Hans. "Ελλην, κ.τ.λ." In *TDNT*, 2:504–16.

Winter, Bruce W. *After Paul Left Corinth: The Influence of Secular Ethics and Social Change*. Grand Rapids: Eerdmans, 2001.

———. "If a Man Does Not Wish to Work. . . ." *TynBul* 40 (1989) 303–15.

Witherington, Ben III. *The Acts of the Apostles: A Socio-Rhetorical Commentary*. Grand Rapids: Eerdmans, 1998.

———. Review of *Reimagining Church: Pursuing the Dream of Organic Christianity*, by Frank Viola. The Ben Witherington Blog, September 6, 2008. Online: http://benwitherington.blogspot.com/2008/09/frank-violas-reimagining-church-part_06.html.

Wolf, C. Umhau. "Traces of Primitive Democracy in Ancient Israel." *JNES* 6/2 (1947) 98–108.

Wolff, Christian. *Der erste Brief des Paulus an die Korinther*. Theologischer Handkommentar zum Neuen Testament. Leipzig: Evangelische, 2000.

Works of Philo, The. Translated by E. D. Yonge. Peabody, MA: Hendrickson, 1993.

Young, Frances M. "On EPISKOPOS and PRESBUTEROS." *JTS* 45 (1994) 142–48.

Zaas, Peter S. "Cast out the Evil Man from Your Midst." *JBL* 103 (1984) 259–61.

Zwiep, Arie W. *Judas and the Choice of Matthias.* Wissenschaftliche Untersuchungen zum Neuen Testament 2/187. Tübingen: Mohr/Siebeck, 2004.

Scripture Index

~

NEW TESTAMENT

www.ingramcontent.com/pod-product-compliance
Lightning Source LLC
Chambersburg PA
CBHW060334100426
42812CB00003B/991